The Backyard Horseman
SECOND EDITION

RON RUDE

Mountain Press Publishing Company

Missoula, Montana

2008

Second edition published 2008
First edition published 1987

Library of Congress Cataloging-in-Publication Data

Rude, Ron, 1943–
    The backyard horseman / Ron Rude. — 2nd ed.
        p. cm.
      ISBN 978-0-87842-548-8 (pbk. : alk. paper)
      1. Horses. 2. Horsemanship. I. Title.
      SF285.R68 2008
636.1—dc22
                                                2008014049

PRINTED IN THE UNITED STATES OF AMERICA

Mountain Press Publishing Company
P.O. Box 2399
Missoula, Montana 59806
(406) 728-1900
www.mountain-press.com

To my dad and his dad . . . horsemen both

Contents

Foreword

The title of this book is somewhat misleading because, although aimed at the casual recreational rider, any and all horsemen will profit by the information contained herein. Not only does this book cover all aspects of horsemanship and horse husbandry, but it does so with reasonable comprehensiveness. I do not hesitate to say that even world-class competitive riders cannot read the following pages without frequently saying, "Right on! I agree completely!" and sometimes, "Why, I didn't know that!"

Horse people, because of their passion for the animal and its many uses, tend to read a lot. They buy books and subscribe to journals about horses and horsemanship. Consequently, there is a thriving industry in equine publications, with many new titles appearing each year. Additionally, horse people spend millions buying informative videos, taking courses, and attending training clinics and seminars.

Unfortunately, most of this information is either breed oriented or aimed at specific disciplines such as jumping, cutting, reining, dressage, driving, or roping. Or they are devoted to starting colts—something no novice, in my opinion, should do except under strict and expert supervision. It is too easy to get seriously injured and even easier to make mistakes that will create a poor attitude and improper responses on the part of the colt.

There is a paucity of material aimed specifically at the pleasure rider. Yet, a majority of the horses in the United States are not performance horses. They are not racehorses, or broodmares, or competitive English or Western horses. They are backyard companion animals, ridden for pleasure, rarely shown, and never used in endurance races, cattle work, or fox hunts.

In the past decade the horse population of the United States increased by two million. A majority of those horses are used mainly on weekends. Even those that are used competitively still primarily occupy a role as a companion animal.

This increasing popularity brings with it the need for the casual horse owner (or "backyard horseman") to be knowledgeable and diligent. Neglect a motorcycle or car and it doesn't suffer. But a horse is a living creature, capable of feeling hunger, thirst, and pain, and even loneliness. Conversely, it is capable of emotional attachment, of feeling playful, of joy and satisfaction. Moreover, a horse is a large and physically powerful animal, which, in the wild, must protect itself from predation by flight. This flightiness makes the horse dangerous to itself and to those handling it. Most accidents that injure or kill horses or the people who work with them are *preventable*. It is imperative that those of us who handle horses be well informed, no matter how casually we use them. That is the purpose of this book.

Ron Rude advises even the most casual rider to learn true riding skills. After all, a person who drives a car only once a month still needs to learn good driving skills. The reader is also advised to become aware of the revolution in horsemanship ("natural horsemanship") that began in the last quarter of the twentieth century. As an experienced equine veterinarian, I emphatically concur with Ron Rude's advice on purchasing horses and avoiding the common pitfalls that occur when inexperienced people buy horses.

This book provides important information on saddle fit, tack care, nutrition, equine behavior, fencing, pasture management—especially on small acreages—and the most common mistakes made by long-term experienced horse owners.

Especially important is the author's advice on safer horsemanship. Of the seven horse videos I've made in the past three decades, the poorest seller by far is titled *Safer Horsemanship*. Why is it not more popular considering it is the most important video I have made? For two reasons:

1. Too many people think they already know it all. Funny! I am in my eighties and *I'm* still learning.

2. Denial! People don't want to recognize that this creature they love is capable of killing them, or itself, when it is frightened.

The Backyard Horseman emphasizes safer horsemanship, and for this fact alone it is a valuable source of information for *all* horsemen, not just backyarders.

I especially concur with the author's controversial opinions on three subjects.

1. Competitive Western pleasure class horse shows are grotesque, and the carriage of both horses and riders in these shows is incompatible with the principles of good horsemanship.

2. Competitive reining classes for horses under five years of age (immature horses) are extremely destructive to those horses orthopedically. A majority suffer shortened useful lives.

3. The rewards of true horsemanship include fun, emotional attachment, personal growth, and improved quality of life. For children, it teaches compassion, responsibility, and self-reliance.

Do I disagree with Ron Rude on any point? Yes! Now in his sixties, he suggests having to give up horses in his late seventies.

No way! I'm not ready to give it up! I may ride differently than I did decades ago, but I still ride, and I believe that the benefits the author cites continue into old age.

Robert M. Miller, DVM

Preface

It's only fair that you ask what kind of horseman is talking to you in these pages, and whether that person can be trusted. After all, you never have and never will see this author appear as a clinician of national stature. Perhaps a bit about my experience and my intentions in writing this book might reassure you.

I'm not a show competitor, though I do seek (not necessarily successfully) the level of training some show people attain. I'm not a cowboy, but I do get called to help with cattle work. I'm not an outfitter, but I spend considerable time riding in mountainous backcountry, often alone, out exploring with a couple of spare horses trailing behind me. I'm not a professional trainer, but do I start young horses.

I grew up in the dairy environment of Minnesota, and by age ten I couldn't wait for Christmas vacations, because the best present I could get was a ride on old Molly as she and Barney, a draft-horse team driven by my uncle, pulled the day's cow manure to the frozen fields. By age eleven I had my first pony, and there was no looking back. When I was eighteen, and again at twenty-one, I worked as a wrangler for the Lazy K Bar guest ranch in the Crazy Mountains near Big Timber, Montana. I got the job by exaggerating how much I knew about horses. We handled upwards of seventy-five horses a day there, riding everything from fine old foolproof kids' horses to some pretty skittish range colts. I got lots of experience and lots of bruises. I came away a little arrogant about my "cowboying" time (wrangling guests is actually a long way from real cowboying), but beneath that arrogance was the fear that somebody would see how little I actually knew.

By that time I knew vaguely that I would have to do something with horses for the rest of my life, but I headed into a conventional career in public education, working twenty-five years as an English teacher and nine more as a school superintendent. Instead of becoming a particular kind of horseman, I became a serious, self-critical student of horsemanship in general. I consider myself a blue-collar fellow with a master's degree and a few publishing credentials who likes poetry and wise books, yet who thinks a day spent ahorseback has as much value as any academic endeavor.

In the late 1980s I wrote the first edition of this book, combining what I had learned about backyard horse keeping with a desire to teach others about it—particularly those whom I saw having too much trouble and not enough fun with their horses. I was gratified to learn from many contacts that the first edition struck home with its intended audience.

Since then there's been a major improvement in both quantity and quality of information about horses. Yet at the far end of human frailty, animal neglect and abuse continue. People still get hurt by horses. People still purchase horses thoughtlessly, still handle horses clumsily, still ignore the array of easily obtainable information. Thus, I'm happy to get this second opportunity to deliver the main message of this book, which is, in short, this:

Folks, it isn't just about *owning* horses. If you want any satisfaction out of the deal, you've got to *live* them.

Note regarding gender:

In referring to a horse that could be either male or female, I use the pronoun *he*. That's a matter of personal preference, and an old habit. I hope my comments about mares dispel any idea that I'm a chauvinist about equine gender. In referring to an owner or rider, I use *he* or *she* whenever necessary. Regardless of how I use pronouns, I long ago gave up any illusions about men being more capable "horse-men" than women. Horsemanship isn't confined to either gender, but I find *equestrian*, *horsewoman*, and *horsewomanship* to be clumsy words. If better nouns and pronouns that included both genders were available, I'd use them, especially in the book's title. I tip my hat to the horseman, regardless of his or her gender.

Acknowledgments

My ideas about horsemanship have been profoundly influenced by a handful of world-class professional horsemen, including Buck Braunaman, Richard Shrake, Ray Hunt, Dr. Robert M. Miller, Pat Parelli, and John Lyons, as well as by others whom these professionals acknowledge as their own masters.

Other than a brief correspondence with Dr. Miller, I've had no personal contact with any of these professionals, but they have formed me into the kind of horseman I am, which means, by my own analysis, the amateur product of what they have sought to accomplish. This book is in part an effort to translate the knowledge of these experts into the needs of the backyard horseman, and it is also a call for horse owners to study their work.

Prior to the work of these master horsemen, there was plenty of practical advice regarding horse handling, but even the best of it generally lacked the scientific and philosophical foundations that these mentors have made available to horse owners everywhere, and that make us not only better horsemen but also better humans.

Introduction

In some ways it's easy to make distinctions between the backyard horse owners for whom this book is written and the professionals who don't need this kind of information.

Backyard horsemen operate with limited space for facilities, some with as little as a single acre. Backyard horsemen are likely to own just a few horses, often only one. Backyarders typically spend most of their time at vocations that have little or nothing to do with horses. They are in the horse game for recreational purposes and usually have only limited funds to spend on horses. Backyard horsemen come in a wide range of levels of experi-ence and competence, from those who have almost none to those who compete with professionals.

Professional horsemen, on the other hand, are those who are attempting to reach or have reached the heights of specific skills in horsemanship. Professionals typically spend most of their time with horses, and they own or have available all the necessary facilities. Their personal finances and/or vocations allow significant ongoing expenditures on horse-related activities.

As a result of the obvious differences in skill and success levels, a somewhat stereotyped class distinction has developed over the years between

Horsemanship is a lifelong journey.

backyard horsemen and professionals. Some pros may be disdainful of us backyard owners.

But it isn't only talent or money that separate "us" from "them." It can also be a matter of attitudes, and that's harder to define. Unlike professionals, sometimes we backyarders don't objectively evaluate our situation. We may not set goals or wisely use the resources we do have. Sometimes we get defensive about our limited skills, and we may be stuck in our ways.

These are weaknesses that can be addressed. In many areas of horsemanship, as this book explains, a backyarder with some humility, initiative, persistence, and hard work can become as skillful as a professional.

In fact, breaking down those distinctions is one of the purposes of this book. In many areas—horse health, for instance—there is no excuse whatsoever for the class distinctions between backyarders and professionals.

Throughout *The Backyard Horseman*, two related terms are used repeatedly. *Horse ownership* refers to the concrete tasks of handling, using, and caring for one's own horses. *Horsemanship* refers more to the abstract relationship between humans and horses. While *The Backyard Horseman* speaks to the concrete, practical side of small-scale horse ownership, the book's main task is to help raise some consciousness of what horsemanship really means.

It's critical to understand that owning horses isn't quite like other kinds of ownership. In fact, it isn't really a matter of *possession* at all; horse ownership is actually a matter of *being*, or at least *becoming* something—in this case a human being connected to an animal. That relationship is on the one hand abstract and emotional, yet on the other hand concrete, rational, and down-to-earth.

Horsemanship is the goal of this relationship. This goal cannot be reached by tying oneself to the extreme of either an idealized emotional attachment to the horse or the concrete practicalities of ownership. The intrinsic rewards of horsemanship come from the former, and the necessary know-how comes from the latter. A horseman needs to develop in both directions. Failing to do that leaves a horse owner either drifting through his or her own touchy-feely world, or just a possessor of another meaningless material object.

CHAPTER 1

Myths about Horse Ownership

I suppose that at the beginning of mankind's connection to horses, the relationship was pretty practical. Horses were just another source of meat—an easier source than some others. Some time later, horses became a source of transportation, and after that, an easier way of killing one's enemies. These uses also were strictly practical. But I have a notion that there came to be an emotional relationship almost as early as the practical relationship. And the truth is that, ever since it began, the emotional attachment has been just as important.

I'll confess it right up front: I get so emotionally attached to some horses that I can get all choked-up talking about them. But throughout this book, I'll be trying repeatedly to balance practical information against the emotional attractions of horses. That effort grows out of my observation that we horse owners sometimes let emotional considerations crowd the rational ones right out of the picture. We carry the misperception that the emotional is all that really matters. We fall victim to the "follow your dream" cliché.

Our misperceptions may begin in the naivete of childhood, which is understandable—and curable with time. But our misperceptions can also be based on the romantic images that movies and novels portray. That's not as easily cured. A classic example of this type of romanticized misperception came in the 1990s with the book and movie *The Horse Whisperer*, wherein an East Coast horse becomes vicious and unmanageable after being mutilated in a collision with a truck. The owners trailer the horse to a Montana ranch, where he is rehabilitated by Robert Redford in a cowboy hat. As only movies can do, the story brought "horse whispering," also known as "soft" or "natural" horsemanship, more publicity in a few months than some of its proponents had generated in whole lifetimes.

Idealism certainly has its place, but for horse owning we need to be realists first. If you see yourself in any of the following delusions, perhaps you need a long, cold shower before you go any further with horses.

DELUSION #1

"My horse will love me because I'll be kind to him. I won't have any trouble and all our moments together will be intimate and exciting."

This is the kind of notion generated from books, movies, and advertising. And there *will* be such moments, more with some horses than with others, far more at feeding time than at any other time. Even though some horses seek human company more than others do, and some bend to human controls far more readily than others, any horse keeps his own agenda: food, water, the security of the herd, reproductive urges, some familiar room to roam, shelter from the worst weather and insects, and relief from the stress of demands outside this agenda. You'll notice the absence of "building a meaningful relationship with demanding bipeds who create fences and saddles."

If you doubt me here, turn your horse out in a thousand acres of good grass with a few other horses. Leave him for a few weeks, and then check whether he prefers your company or that of his herd. I think you'll learn that what a horse wants more than anything else is just to be a horse.

And maybe that's part of the attraction of horses: they don't give up their essential "horseness." That's admirable; it shows a certain kind of dignity. Horses don't whine for special treatment. Unabashed opportunists, they improvise and adapt. Thrown into the wild, a domestic horse will go contentedly feral in a few months, though when the weather is cold he might, without any feeling of guilt, raid a rancher's haystacks. Recaptured, he would soon re-adapt to his cramped surroundings.

We need to remember that humans will never fully be allowed into the horse's world. We can glimpse it, manipulate it to some extent, and the horse in turn will adapt to us and do some of what we ask. But he'll always retain something of himself for himself, and humans need to be realistic about what that might mean in terms of a horse's personality and performance.

DELUSION #2

"One horse is enough, and he won't cost much to keep."

If you consider only the cost of the cheapest possible horse and one winter's hay, this idea might be accurate. But if you're a bit more realistic, tallying up the cost of land or stall rent, fences, feed, tack, transportation, vet care, shoeing, and another horse (just like you, no horse wants to be alone for long), the idea that horses don't cost much is way off base.

DELUSION #3

"I'll get a couple of horses to keep the weeds down." A variation of this is "Horses are harmless and don't need much room."

Horses certainly will take care of weeds, but not in the way you might be thinking. At least in the arid and semiarid West, one horse can eat a couple of acres of grass to dusty death in a few weeks. Most noxious weeds are inedible and will survive this grazing, and quite a few will flourish as competition from grass diminishes while strong fertilizers are manufactured and delivered on-site. I'll say more on this in chapter 2.

It is possible, and sometimes practical, to keep horses in a severely limited space for a limited time, but on a permanent basis a horse needs much more room than humans do. The more a horse is confined, the more problems he'll have with manners and health.

DELUSION #4

"I plan to raise and sell horses for a profit."

There's an old saying that you can make a small fortune raising horses if you start with a large fortune.

The few people who do profit financially raising horses do so in a couple of ways. One, they use a horse operation that loses money as a tax write-off for other investments. The IRS lets this practice go unpunished only briefly.

Two, some people invest a major share of their energy and earnings in a particular bloodline or a particular competitive event. Along with a bit of luck, this intensive investment can bring a high-quality stallion, or enough cash winnings in high-stake events to create a professional reputation and, possibly, a devoted clientele. It's a cutthroat market, and success does not come simply by spouting names from familiar bloodlines, or by taking any old papered mare to any old papered stud and expecting clients to line up with their checkbooks open.

This second group seldom includes the small-scale owner, who generally does not have the time, space, facility, or spare capital to invest in such an operation, which can be a commitment of twenty or more years—if nothing goes wrong.

This is not to say that the dream is impossible to achieve. But the competition to reach a level of profitability is fierce. The number of breeders cranking out weanlings for sale annually is already higher than the market can absorb, which means that well-bred horses at that age are a dime a dozen. Keep those young horses longer and the investment increases daily, while chances of selling may not increase at all.

Realtors, by the way, love to sell "horse farms." This usually refers to a place where one can pour a lot of money into horses, but not a place where one can expect that horse breeding will make the payments.

DELUSION #5

"I'll enjoy horses because I need something to do with my spare time."

Seriously, how much time are you talking about? A couple of hours per week? Sunday afternoons?

Two or three evenings that aren't yet booked solid? That's not enough time to do horses justice.

If you cross off all those days when the weather is bad or you have the flu or friends are invited for dinner, all those evenings when the sun drops at five o'clock and the kids need transportation and you're working overtime, you may not have time for horses at all. Horses demand a host of chores large and small almost every day—and that's in addition to time for riding.

♘ DELUSION #6

"We had horses when I was a child, so I'll train my own."

Anyone with a bit of guts can climb on the average colt a few times, yank his head this way and that, and declare him broke to ride. But he isn't "broke" at all. He's just tolerating humans until their demands become too much. Even if he hasn't hurt anyone yet, he's likely to do so in the future.

In order to successfully start (break) and school (train) horses, you need to have ridden enough "finished" (well-broke) horses to know what kinds of things they do and don't do. You also need to know the progression of methods that skilled trainers use in bringing a horse from the unstarted to the finished state. None of this comes from childhood experiences with horses.

For instance, when I was seventeen I just knew I could break anything with four legs, so I climbed on Flip, a two-year-old, out in a swamp where he couldn't buck too hard. I'd read about that method in a story somewhere.

It worked. Whatever goofiness he tried, the muck kept him docile. It also caused him to strain some hip muscles, so he was stiff and weak for a long time. Eventually I was back at him, galloping madly about the pastures, convinced that the curb bit I put in his mouth would teach him to stop, and that when it did he'd be "broke." Flip finally did stop. He smacked into a tree and knocked himself to his knees. I blamed his lack of brains, but of course I should have blamed my own.

♘ DELUSION #7

"I'll buy a baby horse (or a young horse) and raise him. That's cheaper, and we'll be such good friends that training him will be easy."

No it isn't; no it won't.

Fences, storms, cars, dogs, freak accidents, and diseases all can kill or cripple a young horse long before he is rideable. "He got into the barbed wire

Horse to human communication: "Here's the hay. What's the delay?"

Young horses are high-risk ventures.

when he was young" is a universal lament. "An older horse kicked him, and now he has a permanent (fill in the blank with 'atrophied hole in his neck muscle' or 'stiff knee' or 'scar across his forehead')." Young horses are particularly prone to injury because their instantaneous response to any emergency, surprise, or change in environment is to flee, regardless of fences or other dangers.

A friend of mine noticed oats dribbling out the bottom of his yearling's jaw, right along the bone where the tongue is attached. Some unknown object had sliced clear through the jaw, and the grain just kept falling out. Fortunately, this particular injury was reparable, but it did leave a permanent lump on the jawbone.

In addition to considering the risks, you need to remember that a horse can only tolerate a little light work at age two, and really isn't ready for hard work until age five. Through all those years you feed, clean, worm, worry, and wait. And at the end, there's no guarantee that a hand-raised youngster will be easy to start and train. In fact, these pets are often difficult to work with just because they have no respect for their owner.

Sometimes this disrespect comes from owner mistakes, but other times it's because the colt didn't learn herd manners while growing up with other horses. Here's an example of what can happen. I once started a horse for a gentleman who had raised his papered pride and joy alone in a barn and small pen, fed him the best of feed, tolerated his hijinks, and generally treated him like the king of the castle. When the horse came to me he was an unruly, striking, biting, spoiled brat. Some of this was attributable to his high-powered diet, and some to typical undisciplined young-stallion behavior. But a good share of it, in my opinion, was the result of never having been subjected to the wrath of older horses in a herd. He simply did not know that life has rules.

In the several weeks I rode this young horse, I found him resentful of any attempts to change his long list of nasty habits. But instead of being dangerous, as I had initially feared, he was sullen and lazy. He never did "come my way" mentally—something most young horses begin within the first few days of training. The last I heard of this horse, he had carried his owner through a barbwire fence in a mad attack on two geldings in a neighboring pasture.

DELUSION #8

"I don't need to learn all that fancy stuff like 'leads' and 'collection.' I'll be happy if I just get a horse and ride him."

I spent the first ten adult years of my horse-owning career in this delusion. Then one afternoon a show-experienced young lady, trying out a horse I was selling, told me I was asking too much money for an "essentially green-broke" horse. I'd been riding the horse for two years and had put everything I knew into her training. The young lady bought the horse, and a year later I visited them. The horse's manners and training under that girl's knowledgeable care were so far above anything I had ever done that it darn near destroyed my ego.

The point is that what we might think of as the "fancy stuff" is true riding skill. Without study, practice, and progress, we aren't "horsemen," we're just passengers.

True, just plain riding may be enough for a time, and I'm not arguing that rapid advancement needs to become an obsession. And, particularly if you are a beginning horse owner or are returning to horse owning at a later age, you may get along fine with a safe horse that knows little except how to walk quietly on trail rides. There's nothing wrong with that. But anyone who intends to spend significant time with horses won't be satisfied with "just riding." Without learning or breaking some barriers or overcoming some fears, the whole experience is likely to go flat.

DELUSION #9

"Kids and horses just naturally go together."

This myth is reinforced by those family photos in which Mom, Dad, and all the kids are ahorseback, or Sis is waving her first pleasure class ribbon and wearing the world's biggest tinsel smile. But for such a photo to be taken requires a tremendous investment in time, work, and money. Add to this the fact that the day of the photograph was the only time all year when jobs, school, dental appointments, sports, relatives, and the weather cooper-

ated simultaneously, and you can understand why the event was worth a picture.

This delusion needs considerably more examination than the rest. You might begin by asking, deep down: Really now, why am I getting a horse for my child? One reason might be that Mom or Dad wants a horse but feels a little silly saying so. This scenario reminds me of when I was ten and bought my mother a three-pound replica of a Colt .45 for her birthday. It wasn't exactly what she had in mind for her charm bracelet, I guess, so she let me keep it for her in the leather holster I just happened to own.

Another possible reason, one I've had to squelch in myself, is the temptation for a horse-loving parent or grandparent to force the kids into horse activities. This might net a whole houseful of expert young riders, but it has the potential to backfire. It might generate a lifelong dislike of horses, and perhaps a resentment of the adults involved.

However, the fact that a child might say "I'm not interested" should not necessarily be the end of the conversation. While it is accurate to say that we inherit *talents*, or lack thereof, *interests* are not genetic. Rather, interests are something we pick up from experience. Thus, when a child (or adult) says "I'm just not interested," what he or she may be saying is "I'm ignorant on the subject, and I prefer to stay that way." Almost anything can be interesting once we learn something about it. The corollary is: if we refuse to learn, almost everything is uninteresting.

Consequently, parents who leave their children to randomly stumble into their own interests, rather than nudging those children toward a variety of possibilities, risk raising kids who have no serious interests at all. That seems to me a shirking of parental duty. If nothing else, the child who is always allowed the "not interested" escape becomes difficult for teachers who are left desperately trying to outwit the list of things the child refuses. And, much more seriously, this parental mistake can make life unhappy (if not clinically depressing) for the child who is ignorant of how many exciting things life offers.

Still another misguided reason for buying a horse for the children might be something much more casual: simply the idea that having a horse might be a nice thing. And owning a horse can be "nice," but it is much more complex than owning,

When considering horses for children, it might be helpful to think in terms of three age groups.

AGES SEVEN AND YOUNGER

Before age seven or so, kids can easily be frightened or hurt by horses and ponies. Children at this age cannot be left unsupervised, since they can't handle the animals, equipment, and countless tiny emergencies that can crop up. Young children generally think of horses as an extension of the fun and affection they expect from parents, rather than as the massive animals they are. Kids are often safer and happier riding behind a parent's saddle than having their own horse.

Some parents hurry the introduction to horses while the children are still in this youngest age group, allowing them to ride independently on old, slow horses. (A quiet pony is ideal for teaching this group some independence, but good ponies are hard to find.) However, there are real risks. Being able to say that your six-year-old child is "riding all over the place by herself" might be good for a parent's ego, but a child's broken bones or lingering fears after a trauma can quickly make this a hollow boast.

AGES EIGHT TO TWELVE

From roughly ages eight to twelve the situation changes. Some kids in this age group are mature enough to progress quickly, and many are ready for handling horses or ponies independently in some situations. Some are ready to compete in shows or other events. My own sons, mounted on reliable small horses, were durable and handy cow-herders by the time they were ten or eleven. However, few kids in this age group can grasp the concepts that are the foundation of horsemanship. Most become bored with repetition or routine. None can be left solely responsible for horse care. Parents must provide continuous supervision, assistance, and some form of professional instruction.

For some adults, kids' competitions are an extension of parental ego, and every mistake a kid makes is a chunk torn from the parent's identity. As pressure builds, it's common for semiskilled children and semihysterical parents to needlessly jerk, whack, and spur horses, which may be only semiprepared for the event.

On the upside, kids in this age group who learn to compete can also learn to focus their attention, win humbly, lose gracefully, and appreciate others' accomplishments as well as their own. They can gain valuable social and personal skills and begin to develop confidence.

AGES THIRTEEN TO EIGHTEEN

From ages thirteen to eighteen, some kids become skilled enough to compete against adults. Some might become the accomplished horsemen their parents only dreamed of becoming. But these teens are the mature and dedicated few. The rest are the normal majority for whom puberty and algebra provide continuous confusion, who prop up wobbly self-confidence with deeds of meaningless risk, who cannot yet control their emotions, who are further confused by destructive pop-culture messages that emphasize mindless image over thoughtful accomplishment, and who still need prompting with almost every aspect of daily life, including horse care. For this majority, parents need to walk a tightrope between too much pressure and not enough, and between parents' own interests and adolescents' still unformed ones.

Dad, child, and horse in a low-stress introduction, perhaps the start of a beautiful relationship

for example, a motorcycle. In short, horse ownership should not begin with a decision this casual.

It is quite possible that a child will develop a serious interest in horses, just as parents might be hoping. If that does happen, many benefits can come to the child—responsibility, accomplishment, compassion, companionship, maturity, competitiveness, and a healthy self-image, to name just a few.

But there are a few universals that parents should keep in mind:

• Only a small percentage of kids who like horses will actually use those horses over a long period of time.

• Even in the most horse-oriented families, not every child will be interested in horses, and every child's pursuits need equal support.

• A child who pursues his or her interests without parental encouragement is rare.

• Even the rare self-motivated child will require significant support from parents.

• No matter how carefully a horse project proceeds, it does carry significant risks.

Assuming that you have dispelled any myths about owning horses and you are still set on having a horse project in your future, I'll close this chapter with a few tips on getting started or restarted:

• If the project is for a child, find a way to get the child frequent lessons for a couple of years before actually investing in horses.

• If the project is for you, and if you're a novice adult, a regimen of lessons before buying is still wise.

• Assess resources objectively before buying. (That means not only money, but time, space, location, patience, courage, persistence, health, energy, and knowledge.)

• Set realistic, attainable, incremental goals, whether for yourself or your child, and keep working toward them. The first goals may not include ownership at all.

You want a horse? Start with a long period of self-examination. If you pass the exam, you might just be off to a good start.

When it works, it doesn't get any better than this.

CHAPTER 2
Stewardship

Since at least the 1960s, futurists have been predicting that rising populations and shrinking farmland will inevitably collide to produce food shortages. While the efficiency of modern farming methods has prevented this collision for Americans, neither efficiency nor technology can forestall the problem forever.

We backyard horsemen who enjoy the blessings of semirural living are contributors to the problem, taking up land that might otherwise produce food directly or indirectly. Many of us own small acreages that once were farmlands, rangelands, or wildlife wintering grounds. And we are dependent upon urban sprawl for goods, services, and employment. The breaking up of large farmable tracts into small ranchettes isn't likely to stop. Small-scale country life remains part of the American Dream, symbolizing independence, privacy, and self-sufficiency.

However, using land for horses isn't nearly as harmful as many other uses. Horses don't contribute to air and noise pollution as do snowmobiles, dirt bikes, or ATVs. Horses don't burn fossil fuels (although it does take petroleum to raise hay, lest we start feeling smug). Furthermore, pastures kept in reasonable condition could produce food for humans should the need arise. Horses and their waste are biodegradable. Horse pastures haven't been stripped of topsoil and covered with asphalt, nor are they toxic-waste dumps that will ooze poisons into our grandchildren's lives.

But our land can only be put back into food production if we treat it well. For the sake of our consciences and for the use of later generations, we have a duty to take care of it, and there are steps we can take to do so.

Living Lightly on the Land

The Back Country Horsemen of America organization is dedicated to maintaining backcountry trails, ensuring access to those trails, and educating the public about low-impact camping and livestock use in the backcountry. If there is any organization that deserves support from horse owners, it's the BCHA. Their guiding principle of treading lightly on the land should apply equally to our properties and facilities, and to horse owning in general.

A first simple rule is that we shouldn't keep more horses than we have a real purpose for. Several horses for each family member might be fun, but if only two of the horses are being used for anything other than hay consumption, common sense says two is the limit. That's easy to say, but it's hard to carry out. I have three horses for my own uses as I write this, and while I can occasionally justify that number, most days one would suffice.

I have at least been able to avoid the example of my growing-up years, when my family lived on a forty-acre farmstead, half meadow and half woodlot, adjoined by considerably more leased pasture. Our initial horse herd consisted of three saddle mares. Within a few years we had twelve horses of various ages, most receiving marginal training and limited use. They ate twenty or more tons of hay each winter and kept our pastures chewed flat from April through October. Only good soil and tough sod kept us from ruining that place. True, it was fun to watch a dozen horses race across the meadows, especially with babies flitting in and out of the herd. But a herd that size wasn't good for our limited acreage. That wasn't good stewardship.

Semirural living with room for horses

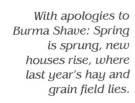

With apologies to Burma Shave: Spring is sprung, new houses rise, where last year's hay and grain field lies.

Sooner or later most owners end up with extras in the form of a retired horse, an injured one, a rescue case, or a "renter" who somehow never goes home. These and other situations are justifiable. But it's a real mistake to let yourself believe that "just one more won't matter."

I encountered a situation even worse during this writing. Two scruffy stallions, aged three and five, were living in a filthy pen with a scrawny pregnant mare and her four-month-old foal. In the next pen were another mare and her two-year-old stud colt. Whether this colt had yet bred his dam was anyone's guess. All of these horses were in poor flesh (though they weren't starving), all exhibited signs of serious parasite infestation, none had had any hoof care or training of any kind, and all were mixed-breed with no purpose for the mixing. The owner seemed oblivious to their physical condition, their lack of market value, their hopeless futures, the absence of shelter, and the mess on the property.

Within just a few human generations after the time of their introduction to America in the early 1500s, horses numbered in the tens of thousands—enough for both natives and whites to use and discard at will for the next three hundred years. Horses only drop one offspring a year, but under human care their survival rate is very high. Excess numbers of horses that we somewhat thoughtlessly produce or collect become burdens on soil and grasses, burdens on our pocketbooks and our time, and—as I mentioned in the first chapter—burdens on the market for quality horses. We need to fight the temptation to keep more horses than we need.

Pasture Management

Horses on unlimited range may not cover the same spot of grass more than a couple of times a season. In that almost extinct setting, they do far less damage than when we confine them. But in a confined domestic setting, their destructive capabilities gallop into view. They crop grass so close that they have to move their lips aside to get their teeth onto the tiny blades. They will jerk out roots and cheerfully munch these along with the grass itself. Shod hooves cut into the first inch of soil, crushing plants and turning up fragile roots. The weight of horses over a long period of time compacts the soil and makes life difficult for new plants. Horse urine is so strong it can kill back grass for weeks. When vegetation is ruined, erosion can set in. Only the toughest weeds survive—those so noxious horses won't touch them—and these spread quickly into neighboring lands. This is our fault, and therefore our problem.

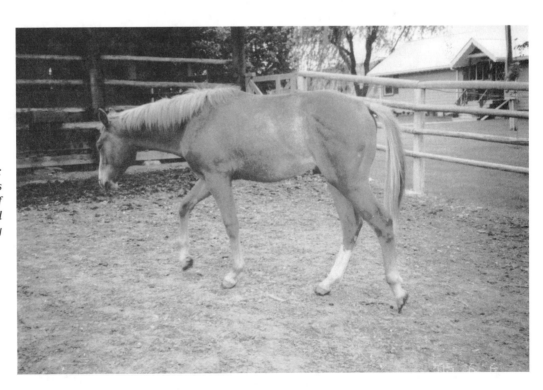

A simple equation: confined horses = destruction of grasses and soil quality

13

When space is limited to an acre or two, it's nearly impossible to manage it well enough to keep a healthy pasture. But on five or ten acres, there are ways to keep the land healthy. The first part of this discussion assumes sufficient acreage with good soil and sod.

One principle of good pasture management is to keep the herd small, as already discussed. Another important principle is pasture rotation. Horses are picky eaters, chewing some patches to the dirt and leaving some untouched. Cross-fencing even small acreages will force your horses to utilize all the grass. And, of course, while one plot is being hammered for a few weeks, another is resting and growing.

On fifteen or twenty acres, cross-fencing can provide three or more plots. Each plot in turn gets no grazing some years, partial grazing other years, and full-time grazing still other years. This cycle will be even more effective than simply rotating through all pastures every year.

A third practice for good pasture management is to limit daily pasturing hours. Equine digestive systems are built for small meals on sparse, dry grass, and horses very efficiently convert that diet to stored energy (fat). On heavy green grass, they convert much more than necessary, often to the point of illness. From a health standpoint, a growling tummy is far less harmful than are heart attacks or laminitis (a painful, often chronic hoof inflammation). From a pasture management standpoint, the real gain is that pasture will last a lot longer if it is subjected to less pounding as well as less grazing.

Keeping horses off the pasture for part of the day has an advantage for the horse as well as the land, so that you will want to do it even with an abundance of pasture. It helps keep a horse from becoming overweight.

While these practices work well on farmable land, different problems arise on steep hillsides, forest lands, and desert acreages. There is generally less topsoil, so the owner must take whatever erosion-control measures he or she can. This may mean serious guarding of existing sod conditions, or it may mean keeping horses confined even more than would occur on more productive plots.

The results of poor management on these sites aren't pretty. I've never understood people who build a beautiful new home on their 10-acre hillside site, then let their horses eat and stomp 9.5 acres of it into a bare-dirt eyesore.

In forested sites, horses destroy trees by stamping out roots in a few favorite spots. They chew bark, and these trees, too, die. In thick woodlands, some trees need to be removed because horses need sunlight. Heavy forests grow little grass, so what is available can quickly be overgrazed. Weeds and inedible brush flourish. This type of acreage, too, may require more confinement than free pasturing.

On hillside property above other homes or above watercourses, the horse owner is obligated to keep facilities particularly sanitary so urine and manure don't leach downhill. In some places it's more than neighborliness; zoning laws demand it.

It goes without saying that, where they can be used, irrigation systems vastly improve the chances of managing pastures successfully even on marginal soil. But irrigation can speed depletion of soil conditions, too, since close grazing and constant watering remove nutrients both above and below the surface.

Commercial fertilizers are the usual solution to deteriorating nutrient content, though they are expensive and do not add to the organic matter needed for soil health. A county extension agent can assist in finding the right fertilizer mix for local soils. An alternative in some situations is to allow grass to grow early in the summer, mow it with a "brush-hog" or chopper of some kind, and allow it to regenerate several inches of new growth before allowing any grazing. This makes a natural mulch, but it does limit grazing time.

Whatever the size of their operation, horse owners encounter pasture management decisions and the costs that result from these decisions. Perhaps the best time to analyze potential land-use problems is before starting a horse project.

Weed Control

I frequently drive by two pastures that leave me muttering curses upon their owner. They're on flat, damp ground where grass grows tenaciously from early spring through late fall. But these two pastures are covered with bull thistle, the taller and coarser cousin of Canadian thistle. Cattle wander in beaten trails between thickets of this nasty scourge. Bull thistle is kind of pretty when the big, purple blossoms sprout, and when the puffy white seed heads appear. But it's a kind of beauty we can do without. What bothers me about these two pastures is that the weed problem they pass on to other landowners is so unnecessary. The land is easily accessible by machinery. Chemical sprays could easily control this mess. If there is an aversion to chemicals, mowing just before blossoms form stresses thistles and could control them to a significant extent.

This is an extreme example set by a farmer rather than by backyard horse people. However, it's no secret that conscientious farmers grumble about "five-acre weed farms" when formerly productive farmland is subdivided. Those subdivisions attract a lot of horse owners, and our reputation for weed control isn't the best. The hay we buy brings in some weed seeds. Others are already in the soil, waiting for conditions to favor them; when horses chew and grind away the competition, up come the weeds.

In western Montana and surrounding areas, we struggle with various kinds of knapweed (inedible, non-native, and extremely aggressive), leafy spurge, tansy, yellow star thistle, Canadian thistle, bull thistle, rush skeletonweed, Dalmation toadflax, yellow toadflax, chickweed, and a host of others, some tall, some low and creepy. Almost none of these can be eaten by horses. Some are toxic, and almost all will crowd out grasses and otherwise diminish the value and productivity of property.

Whatever weeds are in your area, you can fight back, and a good place to start is with your county extension agent or county weed office. They'll tell you there are three strategies: prevention, eradication, and control. My own county weed office (Sanders County Weed Control) distributes a pamphlet called "How to Kill 'em" with information useful for a wide area of Montana, Idaho, Washington, and British Columbia, and I borrow from that pamphlet here.

Prevention, of course, is the best method of weed control, but it may not be possible. Eradication is an ideal goal, but probably not realistic; even if one species can be eradicated, its absence may simply create the environment for another noxious problem.

Consequently, control is the realist's goal. Weed control methods can be mechanical, such as summer fallowing followed by planting of competitive, useful crops, or simply mowing weeds before they can form seeds. Mulching and burning are also considered mechanical methods.

Some locations and species may respond to biological controls, such as the introduction of diseases or parasites that operate specifically against a particular weed, or the use of grazing animals such as goats or sheep for short periods at certain times of the year. Biological controls are ideal from an environmental perspective and are growing in importance, but in many situations they aren't adequate by themselves.

Chemical controls are the least desirable environmentally and are sometimes the most expensive, but they are generally the most effective when you're dealing with several acres or more. For most broadleaf weeds, a form of the herbicide 2,4-D works wonders, killing weeds but leaving the grass. You don't need a license to purchase and apply this product, but it does have restricted uses and, like all chemicals, does require careful handling. Picloram (Tordon is a brand name) works similarly but has residual effects lasting two or more years, and it does require licensed application.

Glyphosate (Roundup is one common brand name) kills both grasses and broadleaf plants. It's very effective, it doesn't require a license, and I've read that it breaks down rapidly without entering the food chain. (I personally don't trust any chemicals on this last count.) However, I don't like glyphosate for the simple reason that its "scorched earth" capability doesn't affect any seeds residing below the surface, and guess what? When the competition is gone, up come nastier things than what you were originally trying to control.

On my own small acreage, I have not won the war, but I haven't lost it either. I use a gallon or two of 2,4-D annually, most of it applied with a backpack sprayer on specific spots. At least every other year, I rent a larger sprayer and do a wider application. I manage upward of fifteen acres with this method.

Neighborliness

Good stewardship starts with care of our land, but it doesn't end there. It carries through as an attitude that influences whatever we do with our horses, including actions that affect our neighbors.

For instance, good stewardship might mean finding an acceptable way to dispose of horse manure. This could mean finding someone who wants the manure as fertilizer, or it could mean investing in a small manure spreader for your own use, or purchasing a permit to haul it to the local landfill.

Some kind of good-neighbor plan for manure is definitely needed, because, as my granddaughter announced solemnly one day when she was three, "Whenever you have horses, you have lots and lots of horse poop."

Stewardship might mean maintaining horse-proof fences so that neighbors don't need to live in fear and loathing of our large, garden-eating pets. Good stewardship includes showing respect for the property of others by asking permission to cross their land (even a corner of their land) and offering an occasional thank-you.

Self-respect and pride are also important. We need to look at our neighborhood to see whether our home and facility are up to local standards and expectations. When we keep our horses amidst defunct cars, rusted machinery, sagging barbed wire, decrepit shelters, broken gates, moldy hay, ratty tarps, and scattered piles of plastic twine, we create a poor impression of ourselves and of horse owners in general. We also may be decreasing the value and saleability of our property.

We must also be aware of the impact we have on our temporary neighbors when we leave home. On backcountry public lands, careless horse owners leave dirty campsites, battered vegetation, exposed tree roots, and eroded trails. When these things happen, we horse owners have no one but ourselves to blame if backpackers, ecological purists, and government officials conspire to ban horses from public lands. Leaving dirty stalls at a show facility, letting unruly dogs wander at a horse gathering, bringing a stallion when we've been asked not to, and galloping a horse in violation of trail-riding etiquette and safety are all examples of poor stewardship and indications that an attitude adjustment is necessary.

Resource Conservation

Stewardship also involves thinking carefully about the kind and quantity of natural resources used in horse activities. I won't tell you that junk gear is adequate, but you don't need the world's fanciest trailers or the skin of an endangered species on your boots. It won't tarnish your image to coordinate full trailers heading to events instead of everyone showing up with one horse banging around in a four-horse trailer. Of all the things I could be right or wrong about, there is one thing I know for sure: material possessions don't translate to true horsemanship.

I'm not advocating that Americans live under a cloud of guilt about our collective wealth. We have much comfort, convenience, and opportunity—enough to be the envy of the world. We can be proud of having built such an economic paradise and proud of our ability to maintain it. However, in some parts of the world the price of this book would feed a family for a week, and what some Americans spend to feed horses and other pets would be enough to buy food or health care for other Americans. When it comes to our relatively abundant resources, there are inequities and injustices as well as responsibilities that we should never take lightly.

Having the wherewithal to realize the dream of owning horses doesn't give us the right to waste resources and leave a mess for future generations. The earth is our life, and good stewardship means making sure that the land can continue to sustain those who come after us. What we do with our land—whether as a nation or on our own little plot—is one criterion by which future generations will judge us. Horsemen have as much responsibility as anyone else because we engage in an activity that is so inextricably tied to the earth.

CHAPTER 3
Tack and Tack Maintenance

As you page through tack catalogues or browse the aisles in a tack store, there appears to be no end to the equipment you need. But the truth is, while there are plenty of frills available, you can do nicely with a relatively few basic items.

Those basics should be of good quality, and quality is expensive. It may be tempting to pick up a set of screwdrivers from the three-for-a-dollar bin at the hardware store, but you know from experience that when the tool is really needed it will fail. The same is true of horse gear. Good equipment is seldom cheap, and cheap equipment is seldom good.

High-quality equipment that is properly maintained will provide many years of safe and efficient use. Regular maintenance saves money, but it is more than simple economics. It is also a matter of safety and stewardship.

This chapter discusses primarily Western gear, but the concepts also apply to English gear. The cost of Western and English gear is usually similar.

For training, trail riding, and other non-competitive activities, or for small, local shows, you might be able to get by with the basics. (See sidebar on page 18. But to show at a serious level, you need real show gear, including a second saddle, usually with some silver trimming if Western. Whether showing English or Western, you need the correct clothing—at minimum another $500 on boots, pants, shirts, vests, chaps, etc. That's not to mention entry fees, truck fuel, lodging, and meals.

This is not a cheap hobby.

Saddles

Saddles are a major purchase and a critical element of horse gear. You can get a basic idea of construction quality just by looking at the price tag. Saddle construction takes two sides of quality leather (upwards of $200 per side wholesale), a tree (close to $100 for synthetic, $200+ for wood and rawhide), plus hardware, stirrups, woolskin, and many hours of skilled craftsmanship. No saddle maker can bypass these basic requirements, though commercial saddle-makers do have mass-purchasing and assembly-line advantages. Even at that, when you see a new Western saddle priced anywhere under $1,000, you have to ask: What corners were cut to

Custom-built gear is expensive, but it's also a worthwhile use of your money.

The following items are, in my experience, sufficient for horse owners planning to ride in arenas or open country and do some light training, in addition to the feeding, grooming, and transporting of horses. Prices are approximate as of 2007.

One saddle; common choices are:	
New light-duty Western saddle, all leather	$700–$1,100
New heavy-duty Western saddle	$1,200–$2,000
New custom-made Western saddle	$2,500–$5,000
Good used heavy Western saddle	$500–$800
Saddle pad(s)	$50–$100 each
Headstalls (at least two) with reins, all leather	$50–$70 each
Bits (at least one snaffle, one curb-type)	$50 each
Halter and lead-rope	$30
Hobbles	$40
Cotton foot rope, 1 inch by 25 feet	$30
Foul-weather gear for you	$100–$200
Horse blanket	$100–$200
Feed tubs, hay bunks, etc.	$50+ each horse
Grooming equipment	$30
Shoeing every six to eight weeks	$60+ each shoeing
Parasite control four times a year	$10–$15 each dose
Grain (light ration)	$100+ annually
Hay (2 or 3 tons annually per horse)	$100+ per ton
Horse trailer or stock/utility trailer, such as:	
New entry-level two-horse trailer	$6,000+
New three-horse gooseneck with tack and dressing rooms	$15,000+
Good used two-horse trailer	$3,500+
New stripped stock trailer, bumper pull	$5,000+
New stripped 16-foot stock trailer, goose-neck hitch	$7,500+
Towing vehicle. If you don't already have a vehicle suitable for towing a trailer, you'll have to get one.	Costs vary widely

make this bargain possible? Sadly, there are people who know how to—and deliberately set out to—make a low-quality, unsafe saddle look attractive.

New or used, a reliable tree is the foundation of a saddle. The tree can be seen by lifting up the seat jockey (the loosely curved piece that lies under the rider's thigh). Traditional heavy-duty wood trees are covered with smooth, somewhat translucent rawhide. Cheaper, light-duty wood trees are covered with a fiberglass cloth or plain canvas, or are not covered at all. But that's not the whole story. A few high-end builders use synthetic resins to seal and strengthen the finest custom wood trees. On the low end of the quality scale, some builders do cover weak trees with a hasty rawhide wrap. Either method can confuse a buyer who may not have available both high- and low-end samples for comparison.

More confusion occurs because there are many good saddles built on trees made of injection-molded poly products. Some traditionalists still dislike these synthetics, but other builders (even some custom builders) argue that time and technology have proven these to be perfectly acceptable for many uses, at least if produced by a reputable firm. "Ralide" is one trusted brand name.

For reasons of safety, longevity, appearance, and the comfort of horse and rider, a cheap tree should be a red flag. No saddle maker would use top-quality leather on a low-quality tree, which leaves you with a cheap tree–cheap leather combo and little chance for quality repairs.

Used Western saddles should be checked for broken trees before any further consideration. Pick up the saddle and hold it with the seat toward your chest. Give it a series of bear hugs and releases, alternating with strong pulls outwards at the bottom edge of the skirts, as if you were trying to split the saddle in half lengthwise. If you feel weakness here, as if the tree were slightly hinged lengthwise, the tree may be broken. The only reason to consider a saddle with a broken tree would be if the leather were all good quality and the price very low; you could have a saddle maker put in a new, high-quality tree. Also try doing some violence to the horn, since it could be loose or broken.

The leather should be top quality. Good leather feels smooth, firm, and almost alive, though not oily. It should be heavy and uniform in thickness—approximately $3/16$ to $1/4$ inch. Poor leather is coarse, particularly on the underside; it also feels dry, hard,

A close-up of saddle tree construction shows the texture and almost translucent quality of good rawhide shrunk tight around wood.

and papery. Some cheap saddles are made of belly leather, the lower quality bottom edge of a cowhide. Belly leather is weak and raggy. It does not hold its shape with use.

A critical check is the rigging—the connection between cinches and tree, visible under the seat cover. There are several styles, but common to all good ones is heavy leather, and heavy screws rather than staples. The rigging should be checked periodically; loose screws should be tightened and worn leather replaced.

The placement of rigging in the saddle varies. With a full-double (also called full) rig, the pull of the front cinch follows a straight line down from the center of the horn over the cantle swells. A ⅞ rig is set 1½ inches behind this line, and a ¾ rig is set 3 inches behind it.

The full-double rigging is intended for roping, and it should always be used with a tightened rear cinch. If the rear cinch is left slack, this rigging tends to pull the front of the saddle down tight and leave the rear portion loose and moving around. (Any time a rear cinch is used it should be pulled snug. Left loose, it has no function except to tickle a jumpy horse or snag a branch in the woods.)

For general riding, a rigging set at the ⅞ or ¾ position is better, because these (1) keep the front cinch out of the horse's armpit better than a full rig does, helping to prevent cinch sores, and (2) pull the rear portion of the saddle down snug, even without the use of a rear cinch. Professional leather craftsman Dave Fish from Missoula, Montana, says he rerigs numerous saddles annually to ¾ or ⅞ position for riders who have sored their horses with a full double rig. The photos on this and the facing page show different styles of riggings, each of which can be either adjusted or constructed to settings from full to ¾.

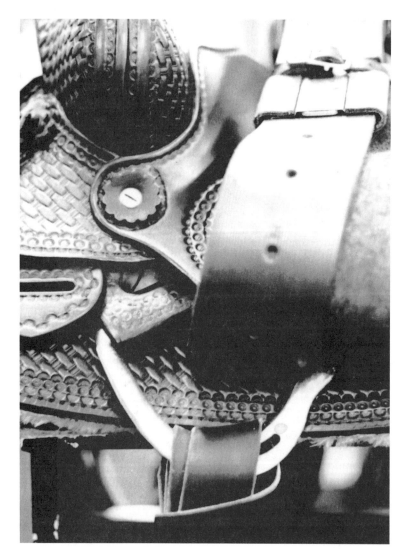

A heavy duty ¾ rig. The cinch pulls down from just behind the fork (the raised front portion of the saddle, also called "pommel" or "swells").

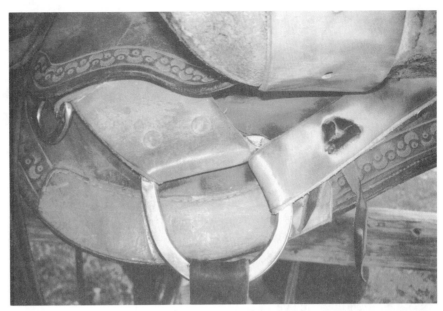

Conventional D-ring rigging. The main attachment pulls down directly under the saddle swells, and the secondary attachment pulls the rear portion of the saddle. The secondary piece can stretch and loosen, rendering it useless. When this happens, the D-ring rig is best used with a rear cinch regardless of position setting.

Flat-plate rigging works according to the same principle as the D-ring rigging, but the secondary pull cannot stretch because the entire system is one piece rather than two. Set at ⅞ or ¾, the flat plate works well without a rear cinch.

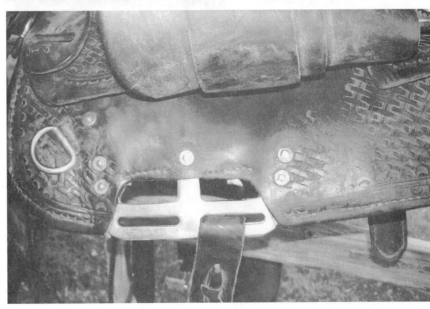

In-skirt three-way adjustable rigging has the advantage of the flat plate, plus it can be adjusted to full, ⅞, or ¾ by moving the cinch latigos. The disadvantage is that, under continued severe strain, this construction may not hold up as well as a flat-plate or conventional rig.

Stirrup leathers should be 2½ or 3 inches wide (3 inches is standard for full-sized saddles) and close to ¼-inch thick, with brand-name adjustment devices. (Blevins is a trustworthy brand.) Cheaper saddles have narrower leathers and tongue-style buckles, which may be adequate for children but are not strong enough for adults. An excellent safety option is the "breakaway" stirrup (www.breakawaystirrups.com), which releases from the stirrup leathers if the rider falls off, thus decreasing the chances of being dragged by the horse.

Saddle comfort for the rider depends on two factors. The first is reasonable physical condition of the rider, which comes from frequent riding and other kinds of exercise. The second is quality construction of the saddle seat. True craftsmen take a lot of care building the seat, yet no matter what the sales pitches are, any saddle maker works within the limits of bar design and seat style. Even padded seats or the most expensive custom construction can't guarantee all-day comfort. Common sense needs to counter hype on this subject.

Saddle seats come in a variety of sizes and styles. The standard Western saddle seat for adults measures 15 inches from horn base to cantle (seat) edge; 16 inches is the standard large size; and seats up to 18 inches for very large riders can be custom made. Seats with more "pocket"—those that slope upwards toward the front—are a bit more secure. High cantles (4 inches or more) complete the pocket. Low cantles (3 inches or less) may be just as comfortable but are less secure. Wide swells (12 inches or more) provide some lateral support for rough riding. For show events in which riding skill is judged heavily, a deeper pocket helps keep the rider's bottom stable, thus giving the appearance of controlled riding skill.

Western saddle seats have come almost full circle since the early 1900s. Old-time pictures show flat, high-backed seats with either a slick fork in front or a medium swell. High cantles and flatter seats let the rider sit forward on the horse. By the 1950s and 1960s, seats sloping back to flat cantles were popular, but these were made for getting out of the

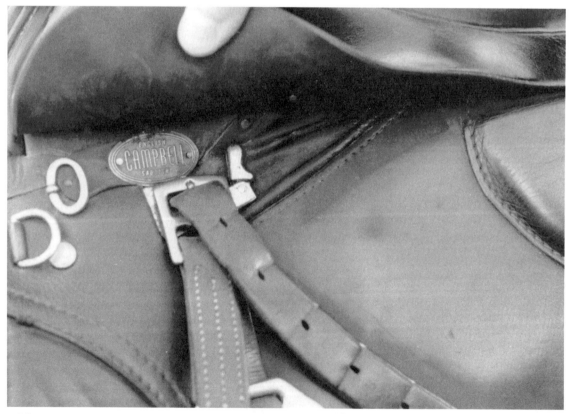

While Western saddles can be fitted with the optional breakaway stirrup, quality English saddles are constructed with the breakaway as an integral part.

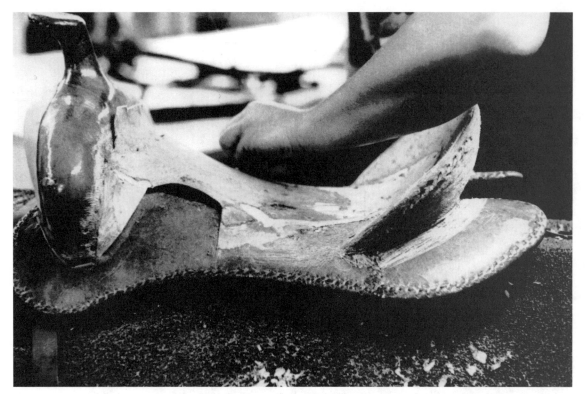

A craftsman shapes the groundseat of a saddle. The groundseat is the hidden but critical foundation of rider comfort.

saddle quickly in a calf-roping event. For more general riding they were replaced, over the next couple of decades, by higher cantles and deeper pockets.

Finally, inspect a saddle for overall construction quality. The best saddlers use nails to hold leather pieces in place and add screws for superior strength. Some use staples instead of nails (staples are quicker during construction). Staples should be viewed with suspicion: they work their way out easily, and if their crossbars wear out they're useless.

Good hardware is stainless steel or solid brass; cheap hardware is nickel plating over pot metal. Real silverwork is very expensive. What looks like silver on an otherwise inexpensive saddle is almost certainly not authentic.

Be suspicious of efforts to cover construction with fancy tooled patterns and metal trim. While tooled leather can be beautiful, there are degrees of quality in tooling. An intricate design might take fifty or a hundred hours of meticulous handcrafting. Some "tooling," however, is done by a machine stamp before the leather is put on the tree. Claims

of hand tooling on cheaper saddles are probably bogus. Consider also that tooled leather is harder to keep clean because dirt and saddle soap fill in the tiny crevices.

Some saddles are made entirely of synthetic materials. Since I have a traditionalist's dislike of these, I can't be unbiased on the subject. But those I've seen become ragged relatively quickly, and I do question their strength.

Saddle Fit

In determining whether a saddle will fit your horse, the first critical measurement is gullet width, the distance across the front opening of the tree bars. Wide bars, called "full-quarter horse," can measure 7 inches or more. Medium bars, called "quarter horse" or "semi-quarter," measure 6½ inches, while narrow, or regular, bars measure 5 to 6 inches.

On horses with narrow withers, a wider gullet contacts the withers bone, obviously a painful fit for the horse. Conversely, on horses with wide withers, narrow bars will ride up high, so that only the sharp

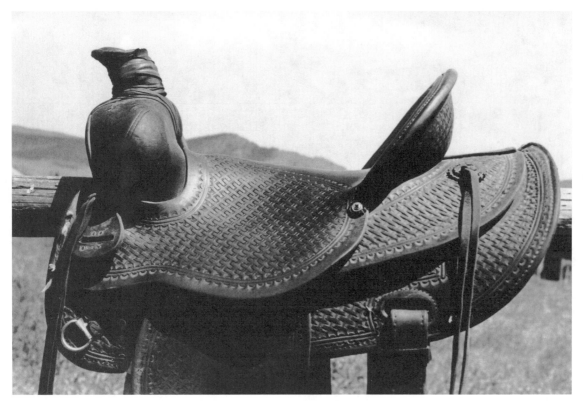

The deep seat in this modified Association tree is similar to saddles from the early 1900s. The Association swells are 14 inches wide.

This saddle, with the flat cantle and sloping seat of the 1950s, is harder to stay in but comfortable as can be.

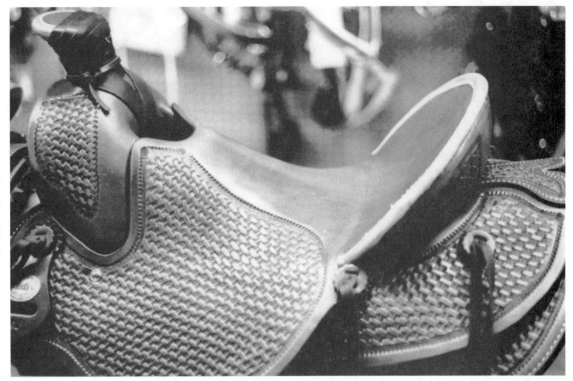

A buckaroo special, with a deep seat and "slick" fork (swells only 9 or 10 inches wide). Note the precision and depth of the hand-stamped basketweave design.

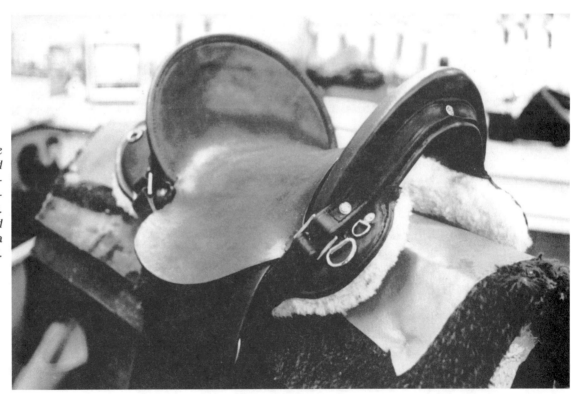

An endurance saddle patterned after Army saddles of the nineteenth century. Light, strong, and secure, with a deep seat.

lower edge of the bar encounters the horse's back. Again, it's painful for the horse.

By turning the saddle upside-down and pressing firmly against the woolskin, you can locate and measure the length of the tree bars. Short bars are 19 inches or less, while full-length bars are closer to 22 inches. With new saddles, these specifications should be available on sales information. Longer bars distribute weight better, but they may not fit well on small horses. Short bars can cause nasty sores on bigger horses, especially with heavier riders.

Beyond gullet width and bar length, there are points of fit that even some experts find difficult to analyze without some hours of using a saddle on a particular horse. For instance, some tree bars curve more abruptly than others. These sharper curves bruise a flat-backed horse, like the rockers of a rocking chair on a flat surface. Conversely, on horses with curved backs, flatter bars "bridge" the gap, leaving the rider's weight pressing down at the front and rear tips of the tree.

But even if you buy a custom-built saddle on a custom-built tree for each individual horse, you would still not solve all the possible problems with saddle fit, because as horses age, or as they gain or lose even modest amounts of weight, the back changes shape. Thus, what you need is a quality tree that fits a variety of horses.

That means if you're riding Arabians, you shop for a saddle with shorter bars or, better yet, a specially designed Arab tree. Then you add or subtract padding to accommodate individual horses. If you're riding lean, lanky horses, you might need a special saddle with a narrow tree, but you also might get by investing in a set of specialized pads to use under wider bars. If you're likely to be riding only wider horses, wider bars and thinner pads are called for.

Overall, a saddle with semi-quarter horse bars, combined with more or fewer pads, offers the widest range of possible fit. One precaution: no amount of fiddling with pads will make up for a saddle tree that is a truly bad fit on a horse.

Saddle Care

If you don't want to replace your saddle more often than necessary, clean and oil it once a year, or more often in a consistently damp climate. Pick

A gullet approximately 7 ½ inches in width

26

This very old bare tree has a gullet approximately 5 inches wide.

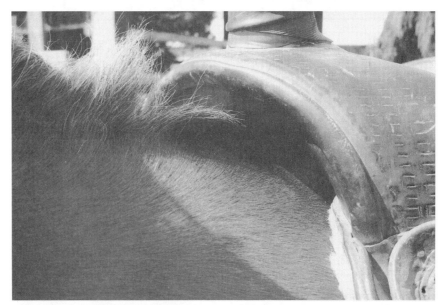

A wide gullet on a small horse contacts the withers. Heavy padding is needed to fix this painful arrangement. Better yet, this saddle should not be used on this horse.

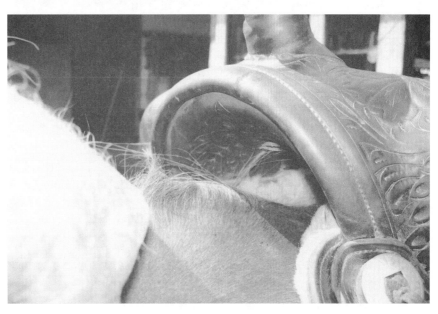

A narrow tree rides too high on this horse. Padding will only make it worse.

a miserable winter day when you have nothing productive to do, and bring your saddle indoors to let it warm thoroughly for several hours. (In both winter and summer, all leather gear should be stored where it remains dry and out of the sunlight.)

Leather can be scrubbed thoroughly with a soft sponge and saddle soap, glycerin soap, or (sparingly) a mild liquid detergent. Pay special attention to the crevices that collect dirt and to surfaces that come into contact with horse sweat. To get into those crannies, undo strings and screws. Rinse thoroughly after scrubbing.

After rinsing, let the saddle dry thoroughly and then apply preservatives. Parts soaked with horse sweat can be oiled liberally, while the parts you sit on need very little. Pull stirrup leathers down to oil the bend where they crimp around the tree bars or hangers, and also oil those leathers in the bottom bend where the stirrups hang and moisture collects. Cinch latigos and girth fasteners should be cleaned but oiled only lightly, since latigo leather gets weak and stretchy if oiled too much. Finally, oil the saddle strings.

There are too many good leather preservatives to list here. I'll list some pros and cons of products I have used.

It's hard to beat pure neatsfoot oil, though it does open pores and thus allows dirt to collect, and it does darken leather. I use it liberally on the horse-side of saddle fenders. My favorite product for conditioning leather is a saddle butter available directly from Ray Holes Saddle Company in Grangeville, Idaho, and elsewhere. It darkens the leather, but it leaves the best feel I'm aware of, and it buffs to a dull shine. Leather should be warm, and the butter softened, before application. A little goes a long way.

I also like Weaver Leather Company's saddle cream. It also leaves a nice feel, and it doesn't darken leather, but too much leaves a white residue in crevices. Both the butter and the cream rub off on clothing, but only for the first couple of rides.

Farnam's Leather New is an all-in-one cleaning and preserving glycerin product; it's available in spray bottles so it's easy to use. It leaves a waxy feel and doesn't darken leather. If leather is really dirty, however, I scrub with soap before using the Leather New. The only drawback I've seen with this or any other glycerin product is that if it's applied from one of those spray bottles onto extremely dry

leather, it leaves speckles that remain visible for a long time.

Saddles need continual safety checks. Screws work loose, riggings wear thin, stirrup leathers become ragged, woolskins collect debris, and, on factory-built saddles, woolskin may even conceal nails or staples working loose. It's a good idea to do a thirty-second run-through of these items at every saddling and at cleaning time.

While you are cleaning your saddle, clean bridles and reins, too. The bent ends of reins and headstalls, at the point where they attach to the bit, are especially prone to rot since they collect a lot of the horse's slobber. Reins are prone to weaken where they touch the horse's neck. Both areas need preservatives and safety checks.

Cinches also need periodic cleaning, not only for looking sharp, but to remain nonabrasive to the horse, and to avoid carrying bacteria that can cause rashes or spread ringworm. Stretch cinches on a board and hand-scrub with soap and water. Rinse thoroughly, as detergent residue can burn skin. Leather or neoprene girths can be hand-scrubbed, while fleece girth covers wash easily in a washing machine.

When reins begin to show cracks or thin spots, replace them. The same is true of cinch latigos and billets (the leather attachment straps between saddle and cinch). Replace cinches when individual strands start breaking or when the whole cinch becomes narrow or stiffened. Your life is on the line if any of these items break at the wrong time, so there is no excuse for keeping them when they show wear.

Bridles and Bits

The terms *bridle* and *headstall* are sometimes used interchangeably, but technically a bridle is a headstall with a bit and reins. While any headstall will hold any bit, subtle differences of style and use have evolved. Horse magazines are a good source for learning what headstall types professionals are using for different bits and different events.

Nosebands, originally used to keep the horse from opening his mouth when pressure is applied to the bit, are not essential on headstalls, though they can serve as a light, humane tie-down, also called a standing martingale. Tie-downs set an absolute limit as to how far the horse can raise his head. They're used for some speed events for the horse to brace against, but also generally for a horse that shows resistance by throwing his head up. You'll sometimes see tie-downs of cable or other stiff material, but these don't cure head throwing any better than softer materials. They just hurt the horse more. A running martingale, sometimes called a training fork, doesn't limit head position. It simply ensures that all rein signals come to the snaffle bit from the same angle, regardless of how the rider's hands are positioned.

Leather headstalls need occasional cleaning and preserving like any other leather gear. There are headstalls made of strong, colorful, and easily cleaned synthetic materials, and these, too, can do the job nicely. Synthetic headstalls, however, don't appeal to traditionalists and probably won't gain any points at show time.

On the subject of bits I'd advise two things: First, keep it simple. Second, read far more than this book on the subject. Bits are complicated precision tools that can easily be abused. A common misperception is that a bit is for "holdin' 'em," when in fact it's for "talkin' to 'em." Making this distinction knowledgeably for every choice of bit and every touch on the reins is a major advancement of horsemanship.

For initial training of a young horse, you can use the Spanish bosal hackamore (not the mechanical hackamore), an English caveson, a "side pull," or even a halter. Any of these tools allows basic driving and schooling without pulling on the horse's mouth.

While novices can get some use from the bosal, long-term use is intended to produce the truly finished "bridle horse," following the tradition of the Spanish vaquero. This means eventual transition to the spade bit, which alone can cost several hundred dollars. Even if expense isn't a problem, the spade bit is absolutely only for riders who have mastered that specific tradition.

Once the horse knows to turn left and right, stop, and back just a few steps, the snaffle bit comes into use. Snaffles are mild training bits used for both Western and English riding. One with a thick mouthpiece (very mild) and one thinner (slightly more severe), along with a running martingale, will serve for most schooling purposes. Used properly, the snaffle can carry a horse through years of schooling and other work.

When the horse is ready to move beyond the snaffle, some form of curb bit is used next. Curb bits can be confusing because both severity and

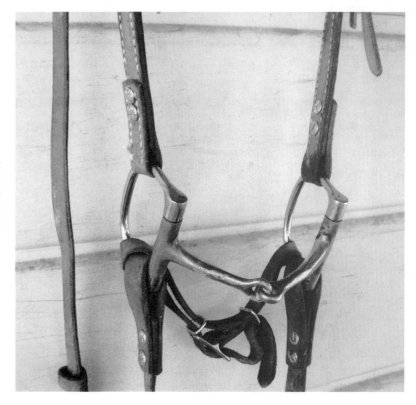

A simple D-ring snaffle with a copper mouthpiece. It is a mild bit, though a thicker mouthpiece would be milder yet.

29

effectiveness are influenced by the thickness of a horse's tongue, the thickness and style of the mouthpiece itself, the length of shanks above and below the mouthpiece, construction materials, and looseness or rigidity of connecting points. Myler is a reliable bit manufacturing company that gives the best explanations I've seen on this subject, in a succinct yet comprehensive little book entitled *A Whole Bit Better* (Toklat Originals, 2000).

Shank length both above and below the mouthpiece is the most obvious clue to severity. Generally, the longer the shank, the more severe the bit, since more leverage is available to your hands. This is also true of shanked snaffles, which are often misconstrued as mild bits. Anything with shanks operates as a curb, applying constricting force to the tongue, to the tender bars of the lower jaw, and to the underside of the jawbone. For a well-broke horse, you shouldn't need more than 4 or 5 inches of shank below the mouthpiece, and 2 or 2½ inches above.

Popular horse lore holds that copper mouthpieces promote salivation, which translates to comfort, which translates to better communication between rider and horse. But copper isn't the only good material for mouthpieces. Stainless steel is fine, as is old-fashioned "sweet iron," which rusts harmlessly. Avoid cheap bits plated with a chrome-like substance; the surface material flakes away, exposing whatever poor quality metal is beneath.

One popular tack catalogue pictures approximately 175 bits, mechanical hackamores, and bit/

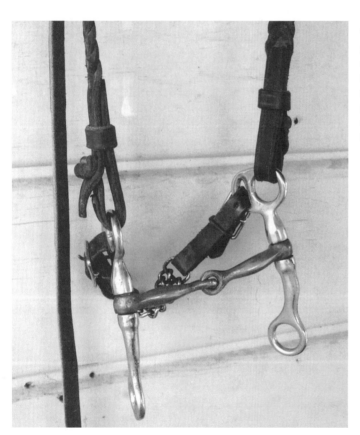

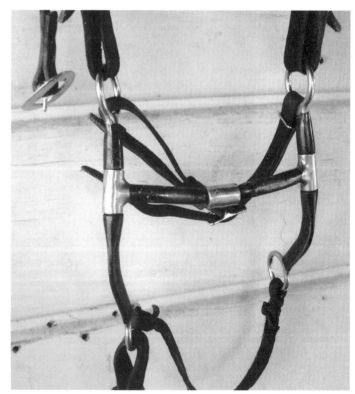

The popular Tom Thumb, considered a snaffle because of its mouthpiece. However, its shanks and curb strap make it operate as a curb bit. Its popularity may be undeserved because the mouthpiece joint doesn't swivel far enough to allow the shanks the looseness needed for direct reining. Pulled one rein at a time, the Tom Thumb, like other curbs, tends to tip over and poke at the horse's face.

A Billy Allen shanked snaffle. Its longer shanks are more severe than the Tom Thumb. It is somewhat better than the Tom Thumb for direct reining, because the barrel-jointed mouthpiece allows more complete swiveling.

A pull on the snaffle contacts the soft corner of the horse's mouth. On the opposite side, the ring of the bit "pushes" the horse's face.

The running martingale, used with a snaffle bit, ensures that all signals come from the same angle, no matter where the rider's hands are held. This one could be adjusted slightly longer. The running martingale is sometimes used—erroneously, and perhaps dangerously—with curb bits.

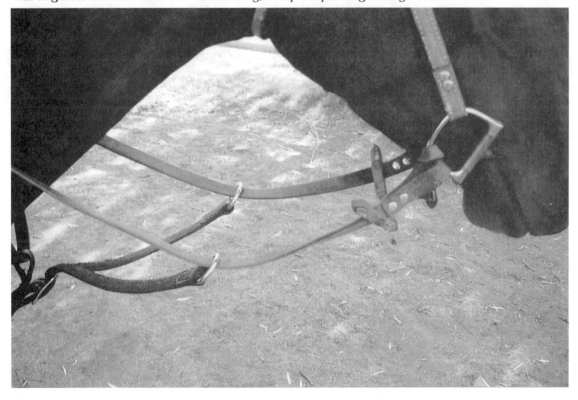

• Snaffle bits initially pull directly on the corners of the horse's mouth, and are intended for direct reining (two-handed reining). When a horse is collected (flexed), snaffles do contact the bars of the lower jaw and do squeeze the tongue. Direct reining is done with alternating tug-and-slack rather than by pulling on both reins simultaneously.

• Curb bits can apply constricting force to the tongue, the bars, the palate, the nerves behind the jaw, and the poll (just behind the ears). They are less effective for direct reining than snaffles and are generally more severe.

• Any bit with shanks is a curb, even though it may be called, for instance, a Tom Thumb snaffle, a shanked snaffle, or a Billy Allen snaffle.

• Longer shanks above and below the mouthpiece provide more leverage, and more severity.

• Longer shanks above the mouthpiece increase pressure on the poll.

• Below the mouthpiece, severity decreases as shanks curve toward the back.

• Thinner mouthpieces and significantly higher ports (center "bump") are more severe.

• Curb chains are more severe than leather curb straps. Tight straps or chains are more severe, while neither accomplishes anything if left loose.

• Aluminum mouthpieces are rumored to dry up saliva. Sweet iron and copper both encourage salivation.

• Heavyweight bits are not necessarily severe. Weight helps balance or "feel."

• Generally, the more complicated and exotic the bit/hackamore combination we use, the more likely we don't know what the horse really needs.

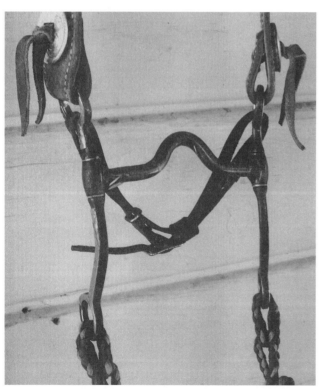

A plain curb with a mild port (bump) for tongue relief when there is pressure from the reins. This port will not contact the palate in most horses.

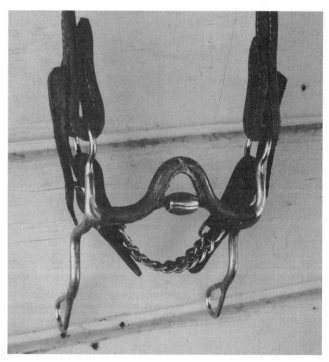

This curb bit has a thick (mild) mouthpiece, a higher (slightly more severe) port, medium-length shanks, and a roller (a type of pacifier). While this bit may look sophisticated, the roller eliminates space for tongue relief and thus may annoy some horses.

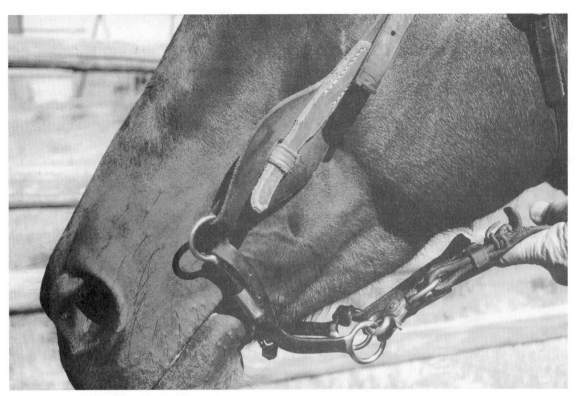

Adjusted too loosely, the curb strap allows this bit to move too far back, creating a direct pull instead of the constriction that is the advantage of curb action.

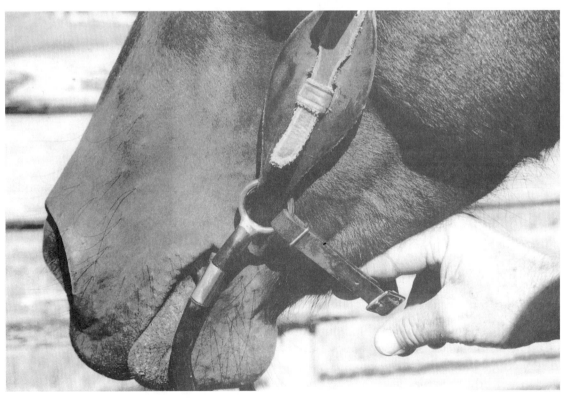

The two-finger guideline for adjusting the curb strap. This headstall could be adjusted one notch shorter, raising the bit against the corner of the mouth, but if the horse carries the bit quietly at this level, it's workable.

hackamore combinations. Perhaps half are duplicated, differing only in brand or quality, but even at that, the buyer is left seriously confused. And it isn't only the number of choices that's confusing. It's the descriptions. They're creative and exaggerated, each promising performance you've only dreamed of. But the bare truth is that most of the horse's performance is in the rider's hands, not in the bit.

Other Tack

Good quality gear is always important, but it is especially so when it comes to the items that lash your saddle to your horse. A girth, or cinch, of poor quality or poorly maintained can annoy a horse to the point that he causes you trouble—or worse yet, injury. There are so many good materials and styles available that there is no reason to scrimp.

Unless you're roping, the rear cinch on a ¾-rigged Western saddle is excess baggage. On a full-double rig, however, it should be used at all times and pulled tight. The short hobble strap that attaches the rear cinch to the front is essential. Without it, that rear cinch creeps back until it becomes a flank cinch—the item that encourages bucking at rodeos. Since rear cinches make contact all around, they should be smooth, 2 inches or more in width, and cleaned periodically.

Halters are the simplest items of basic gear, but halters, too, should be chosen and maintained carefully. Nylon web halters, doubled or tripled in strength, with brass or stainless steel hardware, are very strong, but the buckle holes do fray. Frayed holes can be repaired by using a torch to heat a nail, and then using this nail to re-scorch the holes. Avoid single strength halters with thin buckles; the buckles can break easily, and when they do, they can cut. Some quality halters close with a heavy snap, which is convenient, but I've had snaps twist apart under strain.

Quality leather halters are almost as strong as and considerably more attractive than nylon. The disadvantage is that they require more care than nylon does. Treat them as you do all leather gear.

Rope halters, usually made of light, doubled, synthetic rope (similar to climbing rope) have become very popular and, since they have no hardware, can't cut or bruise. However, the cheap ones stretch and are likely to snag on fences or other protruding objects. Never leave a halter of any kind on a horse when you turn him loose.

Lead ropes with heavy snaps are popular, but I've come to prefer ropes with a braided-in loop, as backcountry expert Smoke Elser recommends in his book *Packin' In on Mules and Horses* (Mountain Press, 1980). Snaps break under heavy strain, and when they do, they're deadly projectiles. I'm often leading another horse or two when I ride, and at a steady walk those snaps sometimes swing and bang on the horse's jaw. Also, some styles of snaps disengage if twisted.

As with other gear, there is a wide variety of what can go between your horse and your saddle. There are many quality choices that simply were not available years ago, such as gel-filled or air-bubble pads that conform precisely to the horse's back. Real wool and washable hospital fleece are expensive but trusted basic materials. A good combination is a light wool blanket on the horse's back, with a good quality pad on top of the blanket. The blanket is more easily washable, and wool wicks sweat away from the skin.

Cheap pads made of foam rubber squash flat in a few months and are extremely hot on the horse's back. Pads and blankets of unspecified reprocessed fibers should be avoided. They may be extremely hot or abrasive on the horse, and they might also deteriorate and create lumps under the saddle.

Some riders use up to 2 inches of padding. This may be necessary in a few cases (steer roping, for instance) but generally isn't a good idea. Too much padding moves the rider higher off the horse, making the load more top-heavy than necessary. Also, too much padding makes the horse rounder, which means the cinch needs to be extra tight to keep the saddle from rolling. A ¾- or 1-inch pad is a reasonable starting place.

Western pads are often too heavy to be washed in regular washing machines, but can be cleaned nicely with a power washer. Cleaning chores can be made easier by using a single-thickness blanket under a pad, or a ¼-inch "underpad" between the horse and the main pad, especially when the horse is shedding winter hair.

CHAPTER 4
Transportation

Horse transportation may sound somewhat redundant, since horses themselves are supposed to be the transportation. Be that as it may, almost no backyard owner can get by without hauling horses, if for no other reason than because homes are most often located some distance from trails, practice arenas, and shows or other competitive events. Although years ago it was common to jump a horse or two into a stock rack on any old pickup truck, that practice was reasonable only for short distances, back roads, and slow speeds. For most situations and for reasons of safety and convenience, "hauling" nowadays means owning both towing vehicle and trailer.

Towing Vehicles

Any time you pull onto a busy highway, you're entering a risky world. These risks increase even more if you make a poor choice of towing vehicle. Right off the top then, making a good choice means you probably shouldn't be towing horses with any vehicle rated less than a half ton. This definitely includes minivans and compact SUVs.

Some of these vehicles may be tempting as tow rigs because they're on hand, or because they get better fuel mileage than bigger rigs, but the bottom line is they are inadequate because they lack power and braking capability, and because their light weight makes them unstable at highway speeds. Even a two-horse trailer load can be heavier than the towing vehicle and thus can overpower that vehicle. And smaller engines, while they may seem to get going adequately, simple are not built for towing stresses.

Thus, the full-sized half-ton pickup truck or comparable passenger van is the minimum towing vehicle. Equipped with a transmission cooler and augmented suspension (often noted as "tow-

ing package" or "off-road package"), these vehicles work well for two-horse hauling. The newer 5.3-liter gas engines, and anything larger, get reasonable fuel mileage and have adequate power even on hills. The older 5-liter or 300-cubic-inch engines, and anything smaller, are adequate only on flat ground.

Up until the late 1990s, no foreign pickup trucks qualified as full-sized half-ton. However, at least two foreign manufacturers have since entered this market niche. Given their existing reputations for reliability, foreign trucks are worth considering in the half-ton category if their engines are large enough.

Older half-tons with a 350-cubic-inch gas engine or larger also make good two-horse haulers if equipped with the towing package. Fuel mileage is often poor, but for occasional use these remain a good buy.

Since the early 2000s, new half-tons have been advertised for towing nine thousand pounds or more, a load comparable to four or five horses in a large trailer. But when your load is that heavy, you do have to ask: How many times can it tow that much weight before engine bearings or drive train give out? And, how do I get this juggernaut halted?

Vehicles in the three-quarter-ton category have stronger axles, bearings, and drive trains, plus heavier tires and larger brakes. Thus, even with the same engine as a half-ton, the three-quarter is somewhat safer and certainly better able to stand the stresses of towing. Nevertheless, "towing power" is still decided by engine size, not by truck size.

Equipped with a newer 6-liter or larger gas engine, or with an older 400- to 460-cubic-inch gas engine, or with almost any size diesel engine, the standard three-quarter-ton truck will nicely tow four horses in a lighter trailer or three horses in a heavy trailer. For the heaviest loads, however, such as a 20-foot gooseneck trailer with five horses, a "super-duty" three-quarter is required. Better yet, this load should be towed by a one-ton.

The towing arrangement you choose will, of course, depend on how you intend to use your horses, plus the miles and terrain you travel regularly. But whatever you decide, there are some universals that shouldn't be ignored:

• Smaller engines might pull the load, but when they do they're operating at the far end of their capabilities. Engines shouldn't be run at maximum stress on a continuing basis.

• An underpowered vehicle is guaranteed to become a frustration, and it can be a significant safety problem if you run out of power on steep roads.

• A choice of truck should never be made with the intention of trailering horses at the same speeds and non-stop distances as you drive a sedan.

• Being able to stop is far more important than being able to get going fast.

• It's better to have more truck than you need than to have more load than your truck is rated for.

• Reliability is more important than style.

Four-wheel drive has overwhelming advantages over two-wheel drive in certain conditions. However, four-wheel drive by itself should not be construed to mean more towing power, better braking, or foolproof safety on slick roads. On winter ice, Montana road ditches are continually invaded by four-wheel-drive owners who refuse to slow down.

The old argument about automatic versus manual transmissions has been moot since perhaps the 1990s, at least in the three-quarter-ton and larger trucks. Standard transmissions do retain a modest advantage for steep downhill work, but perhaps not enough to be significant for most backyard horse owners.

Drafting this chapter, I consulted a local automotive dealer and entrepreneur who not only sells towing rigs but uses them extensively. He has a keen eye for what others are doing in the towing world. This gentleman told me that, despite major improvements in capacities and qualities of both trailers and towing vehicles, many of the rigs on the highway are still dangerous, because owners still insist upon towing much more than their vehicles are rated for, and still insist upon driving much too fast.

Even these owners may not be as thoughtless as I once was, as a friend and I pulled up a steep, one-lane mountain road in a two-wheel-drive half-ton pickup with two horses and a homemade brakeless trailer on the bumper. You can probably guess what happened. The truck spun out. The truck brakes were barely holding. We tried to back down to a wider spot, but the trailer jackknifed. The horses thrashed frantically. We did get them out of the trailer, but very near a steep drop-off on the edge of the road. Once the trailer was empty, the truck pulled on up the mountain. We laughed about it later, but the truth is that we were within inches of killing our horses and ourselves.

Trailers

All sizes of trailers can be purchased with or without bells and whistles, ranging from plain interiors in the stock trailer styles, to air-conditioned, wall-to-wall padded, walk-through, private-stall luxury styles with living quarter for humans, too. My primary purpose here is to discuss practicality and safety.

I'll begin with the conventional two-horse trailer. These are easily maneuverable and easily towed. They require limited storage space. Prices of new or used are generally bearable, even for those who must pay on the installment plan, since with reasonable care these (and all other) trailers can serve twenty or more years.

While older conventional two-horse trailers can often be found in good condition at bargain prices, sometimes they are for sale simply because they are too cramped. The minimum size should be 6 feet tall (6½ is better), 30 to 32 inches wide per horse, and a full 8 feet from front to tailgate. These dimensions reflect the fact that an average-sized saddle horse can easily raise his head 6 or 7 feet high, is well over 2 feet thick, and is roughly 8 feet from tail to nose. Cramp him up in a smaller trailer space, and he's likely to show some form of resistance.

Some horses resist loading in conventional two-horse trailers more than they do in larger trailers, probably because they sense the confinement immediately. Also, these two-horse trailers require that horses back out, either by stepping down backwards or by backing down a ramp. While most horses can learn to do these things well, they're scary lessons at first. Thus, with these trailers your

Horse shows offer an opportunity to study trailers at length.

horses need careful, incremental trailer training for both loading and unloading.

One minor drawback with two-horse conventionals is that the narrow stalls make it hard to haul saddled horses without jeopardizing your gear. You might need to do some advance planning if, for instance, you're heading to an activity where other riders arrive with their horses already saddled. It's a little embarrassing to have people waiting while you dash around getting ready.

I have seen single-axle two-horse trailers that appear to be heavy duty, but my personal view on these is that if one tire blows, you're done for. Tandem axles (four wheels) give that extra margin of safety. I've also seen one-horse conventional trailers, but the reality is that sooner or later you'll want to haul more than one. You might as well spend a bit more right up front.

The two-horse slant-load trailer is the updated version of the conventional trailer discussed above. These have the same advantages, along with wider dimensions that allow the horses to stand at an angle to the direction of travel. Horses are more relaxed riding in this position. Depending upon interior construction features, some of the widest models (6 feet or more) allow average-sized horses to simply turn around and step out rather than having to back out. Slants generally have a nice front compartment for tack or feed. The only disadvan-

tage I'm aware of is that slants are slightly heavier than conventionals.

Utility-grade stock trailers range in size from 5 feet wide by 12 feet long to 6 feet 8 inches wide by 20 feet long. Inside height starts at barely 6 feet and ranges on up to at least 7 feet. There are thousands of these trailers on the roads, all of them looking pretty much the same—round nose, steel slat walls with open spaces between slats, and a small escape door on the front right side.

Because these trailers look so similar, they can be deceiving. Compare their minimal sizes to those of a conventional two-horse trailer, and you'll see that the 5-foot-wide by 12-foot-long by 6-foot-high trailers are inadequate for hauling horses. They look like they hold four horses, but they don't. For four horses you need at least 16 feet of length, 6 feet of width, and preferably 6 feet or more of height.

Utility-grade stock trailers are heavier to tow than smaller trailers, they are not as maneuverable, and they require more storage space. They do not have complete weather protection. Many do not have separate tack compartments.

However, they have advantages. Horses seem to load willingly into these trailers, probably because they can see out through the slats. Saddled horses can be hauled, and unloading is a snap because horses can turn around and walk out. And because they are utility trailers, they serve well for many

37

purposes. Those without permanent dividers can be used for hauling all kinds of home needs.

Large horse vans (also commonly called trailers) are specifically designed for hauling horses. They may not be as versatile as the plain stock trailers, but the vans have far more safety, comfort, and convenient features, some standard, some optional. These trailers are completely weatherproof.

Within this van category, slant-loads are again the updated, popular version, and for good reason. While the original straight-load vans with individual stalls were workable, they were heavier, more cramped for the horse, and clumsier for loading and unloading.

Horse vans can include larger tack compartments, sleeping space for humans (everything from just plain floor space up to luxury RV features), and stall dividers that reach the floor. This last feature is for safety, ensuring that nobody gets a foot under the divider, even if he happens to lie down on a long trip. Of course, all these extras mean more towing weight that isn't strictly equine payload.

The debate about which is better—the bumper-pull or the gooseneck hitch—isn't really an argument worth getting into. Ask anyone who tows more than a few miles a year, and they'll tell you the gooseneck hitch is superior. It is more maneuverable in tight quarters, though it takes a bit more practice to learn to back up. By distributing trailer weight farther forward on the truck, the gooseneck stabilizes steering and braking, and it smooths the ride for both equines and driver.

That doesn't mean bumper-pulls are all bad, however. They're less expensive and somewhat lighter with comparable payloads. Set up with a load-equalizer hitch system (in my opinion, an absolute necessity), they travel and brake with little or no sway. But when loads get really heavy (four or more horses plus living quarters, for instance, or simply five or more horses), bumper-pulls quickly become questionable for safety reasons—unless towed by a monster truck.

The term *bumper pull* is actually a remnant of the early—and scary—practice of pulling from a ball hitch screwed onto a truck bumper. No horse trailer should actually be towed this way. A load-rated receiver system, properly mounted to the vehicle frame, and the load-equalizer system already mentioned are critical items. In some states they may be legal requirements, too.

Whatever type of trailer you use, one seemingly minor construction feature that is actually very

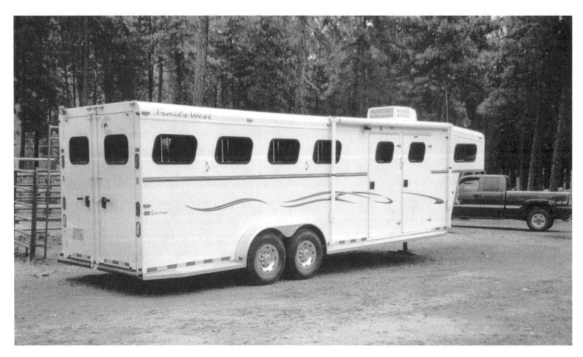

A four-horse slant-load trailer with a gooseneck hitch, a tack compartment, and a small sleeping compartment. This is a professional's first-class rig, best towed with a one-ton truck.

important is the edging at the rear of the trailer floor, right at the entrance. On my trailer, that edging is round, large-diameter steel pipe; on better rigs, a thick rubber bumper covers the metal skeleton. Either one prevents the nasty bruises that come from plain angle-iron edging used in some trailers. In fact, that sharp angle iron not only can injure the horse, it can make him fearful of loading.

Trailer ramps have good points and bad. They're advantageous when backing horses out, but some horses seem more afraid to load with a ramp than to simply step up. A ramp also adds weight and some risk of injury if a horse steps off the high edge. Some owners don't like to have their horse step up and down from the larger rampless trailers, but horses (even foals or yearlings) trained carefully do learn not to fear or hurry this step. My advice would be to discuss this specific item with a number of trailer owners before deciding.

I haul three horses in a 6-foot-wide by 16-foot-long by 6½-foot-tall bumper-pull stock trailer. It has a small front tack compartment, leaf springs, a front escape door, and tandem axles with 6-ply tires. (Newer trailers use torsion bars instead of leaf springs, giving a more stable ride.) I use a two-bar equalizer hitch system. The inside walls of the trailer are smooth bare metal with no pads. I've serviced or replaced wheel bearings, floor, tires, and some wiring.

I store my trailer out of the weather. I seldom haul more than a thousand miles a year, and that mainly on back roads at less than highway speeds. I haul without solid dividers, separating horses with rope snapped at an angle across the trailer. There's plenty of room for three fully saddled horses; I'm ready to ride when I get to a ranch or trailhead. Unloading, I turn the horses around one at a time and walk them out.

Occasionally I set in the front divider with butt chains and haul four horses. I don't like this arrangement even though this trailer is designed for it. Hauling four means both rear horses have their noses on the fanny of the front ones. If somebody's a biter or a kicker, there's going to be trouble. Also, the last horses in must be foolproof, independent loaders, since it isn't really safe for me to crowd in with them directly behind the two front horses. And, I don't like towing this much weight—at least five thousand pounds plus the trailer.

This basic trailer—what I call a utility/stock trailer—works well for me. However, if I were show-ing or otherwise competing, or if I lived where I was forced to haul more miles, even for my small operation I'd need to upgrade to at least a weatherproof, three-horse slant-load bumper-pull for reasons of safety, horse comfort, and my own convenience.

It really isn't wise to buy a worn-out beater or a homemade trailer, however tempting the cost may be. At the same time, it's silly for a backyard owner of two horses to pull into a show with a four-horse trailer complete with living quarters, bar, and hot tub. The monthly payments on those frills could be buying hay. Besides, the bigger and more complex the equipment, the more there is to go wrong. The size of the payments doesn't prove the skills of the rider.

Trailer Maintenance

Whether you are buying a horse trailer or just looking yours over before the season begins, a few items need careful checking.

Welding can develop stress cracks, which may or may not be easily seen. A welding technician can inspect this for you and reinforce, reweld, or replace as needed.

Wheel bearings are inexpensive items that can cause expensive problems. They are easy to check, lubricate, or replace. It's a good idea to carry a prelubricated spare bearing or two. If you burn out a bearing a hundred miles from home, it's not difficult to jack up the trailer and replace that bearing using a large adjustable wrench, a screwdriver, and a pair of pliers.

Trailer tires suffer the same stresses as those on the towing vehicle, but you do see people who let the trailer tires wear awfully thin. That's just not smart. Tire inflation, good tread, and proper rating for the load are essential. Tires that are out in sunlight year-round deteriorate faster than those kept under cover. Weather cracks can develop on tire walls in just a few years, even on tires that appear to have deep tread.

Manure and urine rot trailer floors rapidly, especially if mats are left inside to hold moisture. Some longevity is gained by thoroughly cleaning and drying the floor, then soaking liberally with hot linseed oil. An alternative is to use rubberizing spray, though shod hooves will cut and scratch through this.

Trailer floors constructed of dimension lumber or plywood are installed with the intention of being replaced periodically. High-end trailers have sealed, rubberized floor systems, which take a lot of abuse yet still protect horses from concussion and floorboards from deterioration. Even at that, you don't know what that floor system is covering unless you look.

To check the wood integrity, occasionally rap on the floorboards with a hammer. Good wood raps right back, while poor wood absorbs the hammer blow. If you suspect rot or poor-quality lumber, replace the whole floor. Most floors are bolted down and are not hard to remove. The bolts may be rusty, but a grinder takes them off and the boards can then be pried up. Replacement lumber should be 2-inch-thick hardwood, or the hardest of the softwoods such as Douglas fir or western larch. Leaving drainage cracks between the boards helps the floor last longer.

Surface rust is inevitable on steel trailers. At some early stages it's simply a cosmetic problem, but deeper rust eventually means safety and cost problems. Feeding grain in the trailer allows stray grains to hold moisture down in the tiniest of spaces, and this is one common starting point of rust. Another is any little dent made by a horse's pawing. Mats or plywood add-ons can prevent the latter. Trailers stored out of the weather will rust far less than those left outside.

Regular maintenance should include checking all surfaces for anything that could cut, scratch, bruise, or entangle the horse, whether he's inside or tied to the outside. Loose trim moldings, vents, protruding latches, bent license plates, and angle braces are all common culprits.

CHAPTER 5
Backyard Facilities

Planning and building your facility before you bring home a horse might sound like common sense to you, but if so, you may be in a minority. Too often in the excitement of a horse project, adequate facilities get pushed way down on the list of priorities.

For instance, I've seen a horse picketed by the neck in a weedy lot for a whole summer while the owner wondered about a more permanent place to keep him. Recently I bought a mare who had spent four winter months on the end of a 30-foot rope; the owner had no facility available when winter struck. Then there was the local tale of a half-wild mare and her foal who broke out of a temporary holding pen for a month-long frolic in the mountains and were finally captured when they returned looking for water. And once I hauled two young horses a hundred miles to my uncle's farm for summer use by my cousins. Overnight the two colts walked out of a makeshift fence and disappeared. Days later we found them forty miles from where they'd started. These types of mistakes are usually made by novices, but there are plenty of people years into their ownership who still don't have adequate facilities.

Lack of preparation is one result of romantic perceptions taking precedence over the practical considerations of ownership. It's much more fun to think about the horse than it is to think about such mundane details as fences and gate latches, shelters and manure disposal. But reality closes in fast when the horse arrives, and if we attend to the mundane first, we (and the horse) will find ownership far more enjoyable.

Time

Before buying, you should honestly assess how much time you have to devote to horses. If your life is already too hectic, you can't expect to add horses

Perhaps your backyard horse facility will never be thirty acres of irrigated lawns and white fences spread out between a river and a few hundred thousand acres of mountains. But with careful planning and a steady building and maintenance program, you can be proud of what you do have.

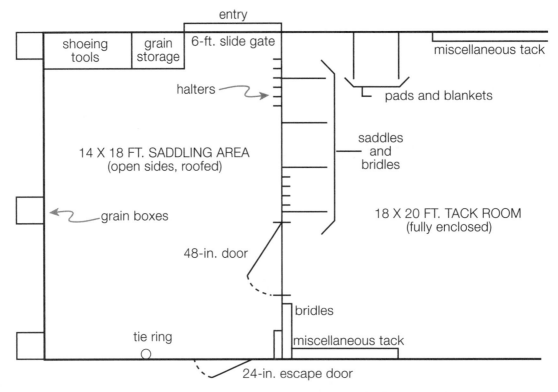

shoeing tools

grain storage

entry

6-ft. slide gate

miscellaneous tack

halters

pads and blankets

14 X 18 FT. SADDLING AREA
(open sides, roofed)

saddles
and
bridles

grain boxes

18 X 20 FT. TACK ROOM
(fully enclosed)

48-in. door

bridles

tie ring

miscellaneous tack

24-in. escape door

The author's tack room and saddling area—an example of efficiency and convenience

to the mix and do it well. It takes time to feed them, haul them, clean equipment, clean facilities, mend fences, and so on. A half-hour ride will take at least an hour, since you need to catch the horse, groom him, saddle and bridle him, warm him up, check him out, all before doing any training or exercising. After the ride you need to cool him down, put up the equipment, and maybe change your clothes before getting on to the next thing. And a half-hour ride isn't really adequate for exercise, though it will be adequate for some kinds of training. To keep a young horse learning or a finished horse fit, he needs several rides per week of an hour or more.

I can't tell you how many times over the years I've commiserated with friends or fellow workers about not having time for a particular horse event. Now that I'm retired, some of that problem has been cured, but not all of it. I've kept a log of my activities and found that annually I average about 160 hours of riding time in about 70 saddle-up days. To do my horses justice, I should be doubling those riding hours. But writing, yard work, minor civic duties, family responsibilities, travel, and other nonhorse hobbies combine to fill up most days before I add in horse time.

In the northern states, we tend to retire our horses from about November to March, though some people do have access to indoor riding. But even without the incentive of riding, there still are horse chores year-round.

I'm not telling you that if you already have a busy life, you should forget about horses. I am saying that whether employed or unemployed, young or . . . seasoned, you need to assess the situation realistically. If the time isn't there, or if you simply cannot make the time by dropping something else, you need to do the right thing. If you find yourself saying, "I don't have time for this," you need to be careful that you're not referring to your horses.

Efficiency and Convenience

Part of having time for horses comes from planning a facility with efficiency and convenience in mind. In planning the layout of your horse facilities, you need to think about where you will ride, pasture, shelter, groom, feed, and water your horses, as well as where you will store your tack, stack your hay out of the weather, store grain, park your truck and trailer, and dispose of manure. Some arrangements will evolve over the years, but some can be planned up front. I'll use my own layout as an example.

Before I catch a horse, I first place grain in a feed box approximately 15 feet from my tack room door. The grain is stored in a locked, mouse-proof container 3 feet from the feed box. I open a gate from my holding pen and the horse goes straight for the grain. While he's eating, I halter him and brush him. I never have to play "catch-me" games because he'll stand at the grain until he's done with it. Then I lead him the 15 feet into a plank-floored, roofed, enclosed 14- by 18-foot saddling area adjacent to the tack room door. Inside that door, immediately within reach, hang bridles and saddles. At the most I take five steps between horse and saddle rack. For doctoring or shoeing (I do my own shoeing) I use that same shelter. It's shaded, dry, and secure.

I can catch, groom, and saddle three horses in twenty minutes. This arrangement evolved over the course of many years as I tried one setup or another, each resulting in such questions as: Why did I build my saddle racks 20 feet away on the far wall of my tack room? Why are my halters inside, on the far side of the bridles, rather than in the saddling area, right where I can grab one directly on my way to the horse? Why are my grooming tools on a shelf by my workbench, rather than on the wall 3 feet from where I tie the horse for grooming?

I've sketched the layout of my tack room and saddling area not because they're perfect, but as food for thought. Dragging saddles 50 feet between trailer and hitch rack, leading horses back and forth an extra 150 feet between poorly arranged pens, hunting down brushes that don't have a permanent home—all of it subtracts from our real purpose: enjoying time with our horses.

Every site will need its own adaptations, even if that means cutting a side door in that brand-new garage. And your system will inevitably change as your needs change. But if you plan ahead better than I did, you'll like your system better from the beginning.

Shelter

Some owners like to keep their horses in an enclosed barn. In northern Minnesota, where I was raised, winters are commonly . . . how should I put it? Awful? Brutal? Deadly? There we kept a half dozen horses tied for days at a time in a small barn, packing water and food to them and pitching manure away from behind them, while subzero temperatures and cutting winds ruled outdoors.

Author's roofed, enclosed saddling platform attached to the tack shed

43

A nice tack room and saddling area attached to a garage/shop

Even in that harsh environment, however, indoor sheltering probably wasn't necessary. Horses are incredibly durable in cold weather. They do need good windbreaks, a roof to keep them dry, extra feed, and perhaps a good blanket during the coldest periods. But keeping horses indoors can be unhealthy. Breathing hay dust and ammonia can lead to respiratory problems, and no amount of shoveling can prevent stalled horses from standing in their own manure.

Adequate shelter can be had for far less expense than that of a complete barn. A barn provides benefits such as appreciation of property value, space for efficient saddling and grooming, and storage, in addition to complete shelter, but it doesn't have to be the first consideration in horse owning. Your primary considerations in planning and building a horse shelter should be:

• protection from prevailing winds, cold rains, hot sun, insects

• space enough for submissives to be safe from dominants

• prevention of injuries from construction methods or materials

• convenience for humans

• cost, use of space, longevity, appearance

A simple flat roof or a lean-to roof against a shed or garage is a good beginning. A roof should be 7 feet tall at its lowest point and cover about 10 by 10 feet per horse. Still another alternative is an L-shaped building, both outer walls against prevailing winds, and the partial "courtyard" completely open.

I suggest a three-sided shed for a good starter horse shelter. With the long wall against prevailing winds, the shelter will provide shade in summer, protection from wet weather, and space enough to allow the submissives to escape the aggressives. You can extend the roof beyond the walls for more protection.

I have used this simple design for many years. The horses themselves decide when they want to use it, and I'm still surprised about how little shelter they really need, even in winter. Mainly, cold winds combined with rain, or unusually hot days, or unusually pesky flies will bring them inside.

My shelter is 8 by 24 feet, sectioned with simple pole dividers into three 8-by-8-foot stalls (I'd make stalls much larger in a fully enclosed barn). When I introduce a new horse, it takes a month or more for the indoor pecking order to get established, but eventually each horse seems to claim his or her favorite stall.

44

Slightly more complicated but even better than the simple three-sided design is a series of 90-degree zig-zagged walls, 8 or 10 feet each, with a roof over the whole thing. This gives wind protection from any direction and provides each horse a bit more protection from other horses. This design, when viewed from above, looks like a roofed-over letter W, and can be extended to as many wings as needed.

Whether commercially manufactured or home-made, shelters are built of anything from steel or vinyl to conventional stick-framed wood or "pole-barn" construction. Steel buildings are popular for horse shelters and some can be purchased as pre-cut packages. Steel has the advantages of being quick to erect, relatively inexpensive, and durable, but the disadvantages of being cold and damp and often not matching the property's other buildings in appearance. Steel also has safety disadvantages: exposed edges are extremely sharp, and horses can kick through exposed steel siding. Steel roofing must be installed on a completely sheathed roof, or at least with heavy roofing paper between steel and rafters. Without this, condensation drips on cold mornings.

Vinyl tarp shelters are also marketed. They're easy and quick to erect, but they do look a bit tacky,

and I can't imagine they hold up well to either weather or horses.

Dirt floors are practical any place horses stand a great deal. Dirt, however, makes it hard to keep a shelter clean. My own horse shelter has a raised floor of 6 inches of gravel, giving horses a dry place to stand in muddy weather. The drawback is that manure mixes with the gravel so thoroughly that the manure can't be removed. Also, the gravel does track out and gradually disappear.

Concrete is easier to clean, but it's dangerously slick and hard on horses' legs. Wood floors are better on the legs but can also be slick, and wood won't last if soaked with urine. Wood or concrete surfaces can be improved considerably with rubber mats manufactured specifically for horses. These are an additional expense, but they alleviate the disadvantages.

Whether we build a simple shelter, a shed, or a barn, the considerations are cost, space, wind protection, dryness, safety, durability, and looks. The horse won't care about the last one, but you should. We want to spend money on facilities that not only do the job, but also enhance the value of our property. Unfortunately, there are horse owners everywhere with ramshackle facilities. It's an image we need to eliminate.

A three-sided shed, 8 by 24 feet, with its back to the prevailing wind. There is room for three if they don't argue. The waste-wood siding does work, but it's neither attractive nor durable.

Feed and Water

Having feed on hand for your horse seems elementary, but it isn't uncommon to hear from people desperately seeking a few bales of hay to carry them just another week. While I pride myself on being smarter than that, in the spring of 2004 I wound up needing half a ton of hay, having miscalculated the previous autumn. Luckily, a local farmer obliged me.

Horse feed is a commodity that needs to be thoroughly understood for your area before your project begins. There are several key questions to ask yourself.

How much pasture time will I have? When can I begin using that pasture in the spring? Is the grass adequate for that entire time, or will it be stressed if I use it too early in the seaason?

How much hay will I need at a minimum of 20 pounds per day per animal? What will it cost? When is it available and when is it not? Am I set up to feed hay without wasting any, or do I need to buy extra to accommodate waste?

Where do I buy grain, how much will I need, and what will it cost?

How will I store hay and grain out of the weather, in a convenient place, and away from horses? How much space is needed?

If I have to be gone overnight, or for vacations, how will the feeding get done? Can the neighbor kids do it? Reliably?

How will I water my animals? Can I set up self-watering for them? Is my water supply foolproof year-round?

Water is a life-or-death necessity that can become critical almost overnight. In the early 2000s at Montana State University, students found several horses dead of dehydration in late winter. For the first time in known history, the university farm's spring-fed water supply had dried up, unbeknownst to anyone.

In hot weather, horses will want water two or more times a day and will consume five or more gallons each time. If you want to build muscle (on you, not the horse), plan to haul water in buckets. But remember you'll be packing that water several trips per day, every day, all year long. If you go on a vacation, can you con your friends and neighbors into doing the job?

Even in snowy winters, horses require fresh water daily. They'll sometimes colic if they get dehydrated while living on hay. They cannot be expected to survive by eating snow.

Install a water tank and hydrant for horses before you bring them home, or run your fences down to the creek. You'll save yourself a lot of grief. Zoning or environmental land-use regulations sometimes restrict or prohibit livestock in creeks or ponds.

Space

Horses like to roam the countryside. Turn them out into a new pasture, and the first thing they do is head out at a trot to inspect the boundaries.

Unfortunately, backyard horsemen can't afford ten square miles for each animal; and besides, catching horses in big spaces is a little annoying. Something less will have to do, but how much less is open to argument. Horses adapt to confinement quite well, but you should be aware of the physical and mental effects of confinement on horses and take steps to counteract the limitations.

I'll start with the one-acre plot. To tell the truth, while plenty of people do keep horses on this bit of ground, it really isn't enough. It can be workable for one or two horses—after all, moving around on one acre isn't nearly as crowded as being in a barn stall year-round, and plenty of horses endure that (although plenty of these also become neurotic). But a horse or two on one acre will feel so confined that they'll chew anything that doesn't hurt their teeth, and they may become grumpy, too. Owning just an acre might be a good reason to board out a horse, or to consider not owning horses at all.

If you do keep horses on one acre, remember that their favorite stamping grounds are near feed and shelter. This is also where flies and manure collect; thus horses and your house should be kept as distant as possible.

Regular exercise is the one thing that makes cramped quarters bearable. Too often, horses that have been confined for months are dragged out for a spur-of-the-moment, all-day trail ride. Most horses survive this just as they survive other poor handling, but not because this type of exercise is good for them. On a one-acre plot it takes more planning and commitment to provide your horse with regular exercise than might be the case on larger plots. Placing food, water, and shelter in three different corners of pens or other holding areas will help keep horses moving around, but it's still not enough to maintain physical conditioning. Using a treadmill or a hot walker can improve the situation dramatically without the need for significant space.

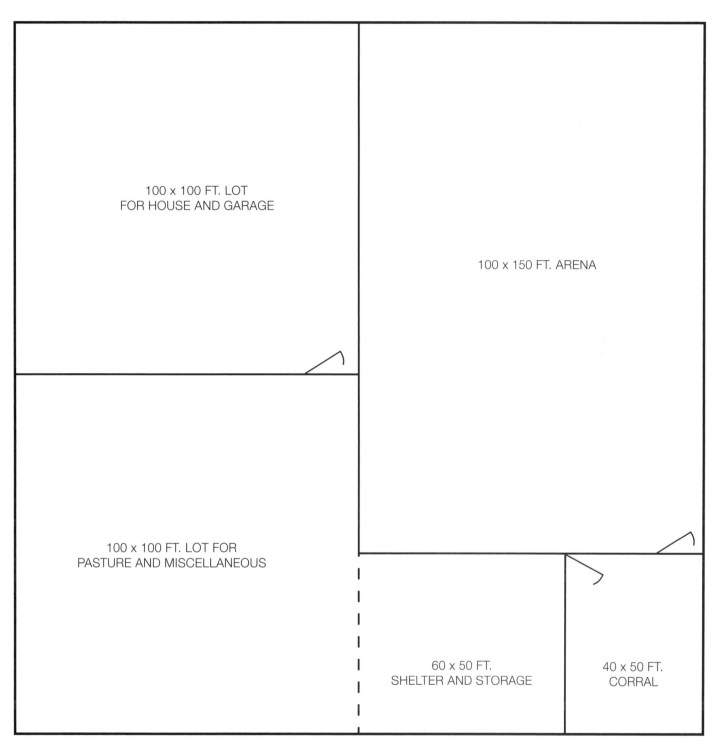

100 x 100 FT. LOT
FOR HOUSE AND GARAGE

100 x 150 FT. ARENA

100 x 100 FT. LOT FOR
PASTURE AND MISCELLANEOUS

60 x 50 FT.
SHELTER AND STORAGE

40 x 50 FT.
CORRAL

Sample plan for one acre. This arrangement provides enough space for two horses who get regular exercise and frequent changes of scenery. The small pasture would not support a horse, but if well cared for it could feed two over a long weekend once or twice a month.

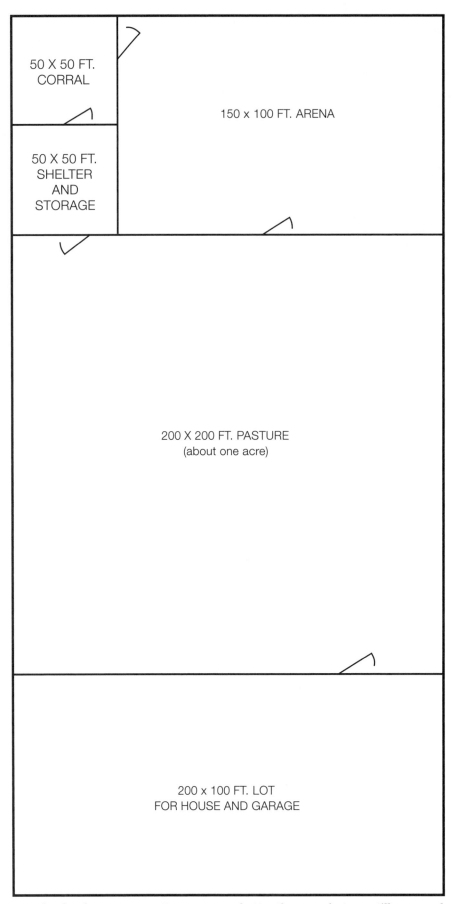

Sample plan for two acres. Two acres are better than one but are still cramped.

On two acres, things improve a little (assuming the plot is all useable ground). There is room for buildings, room for an arena and small pasture, and room enough for one or two horses to romp when they feel like it. But it isn't enough to satisfy their inborn love of big spaces (Yellowstone National Park is more what they have in mind). Nor will it be enough space to pasture them on a regular basis.

To complement a small space, consider renting a larger pasture for the winter months. Be aware, however, that sometimes "winter pasture" may be just space: If it was used as summer pasture, there may not be much grass left. Or the grass quality may not be adequate to sustain horses that must paw through the snow for it. Winter pasture usually must be supplemented with a full ration of feed. Also, depending upon where you live, you will have shelter arrangements to consider.

Keep in mind that if horses are turned out in a rented pasture with unfamiliar horses, there will be some running battles until they clarify the pecking order, especially if some of the horses already "own" the range. If a horse is injured, it will be herd instincts—not the landowner—that is to blame.

A five-acre plot is ample space for two or three horses. There is room for pens, corrals, shelter, and perhaps a couple of months' pasture, or a few tons of hay for cutting. If the pasture has good quality grass, it can support a few horses for a couple of months, especially if they are kept off the grass part of the day. But five acres are not enough to just turn your horses out and forget about them. They will eat the grass down to dirt in a few weeks, become overly fat in the process, and then begin starving. For a plot of five acres or less, you will need a pasture management plan (see chapter 2).

Plots of land larger than five acres begin to have possibilities for pasture rotation or hay crops in addition to the other facilities I've mentioned. Owning twenty acres, however, doesn't mean you have room for twenty horses. It means you can take better care of your land.

In addition to planning for pasture space, you also need to analyze the space available for riding. This is especially true where children are concerned, both for reasons of safety and for maintaining interest. Kids will quickly grow bored with riding if there is no variety. And if kids can only ride around the nearest two homesites before they're endangered by freeways, railroads, city traffic, or industrial plants, the risks are too high and the interest won't hold. Other arrangements will need to be made, and that may include something as drastic as abandoning plans for horses at home.

For adults who plan to engage in a specific kind of competition such as dressage, jumping, pleasure-classes, or just basic training, a home arena or a nearby facility will be adequate. If you want cross-country riding, however, think seriously about where you will ride. If you have to trailer up and fight traffic for an hour just to accomplish an hour of riding, chances are interest will wane once the newness is gone. Boarding out can lead to the same travel predicament.

If you can ride in only one direction from home, and that down a fenced lane with traffic whizzing by in both directions, you soon won't ride much. Even if there's plenty of open ground but it's all privately owned, investigate crossing agreements before investing in horses. If those other landowners don't like hoofprints, you could be all dressed up with no place to go.

Fenced Areas

It's hard to keep even one horse without having at least one strong, safe corral. A corral is a small, sturdy enclosure 5 to 6 feet high, with an area up to approximately 50 by 50 feet. One corral should be round, 40 or 50 feet in diameter. If there's room for only one corral on the property, build it round rather than square. A corral is where you lure a hard-to-catch horse so you don't have to chase him around for half a day. A corral is where you lock up your horse for vet work, introduce anything new or spooky during training, keep new horses until they're accustomed to you, allow beginning riders to become acquainted with your horse, and separate new horses from those familiar with the place, thus avoiding the worst dominance battles.

A pen is a square or rectangular fenced area larger than a corral. A pen doesn't need to be as sturdy as a corral, but it should be. More a holding place than a training place, a pen may be almost any larger size, depending upon the space you have, the number of horses, and the arrangement of buildings. Horses penned too tightly will fight over feed, or just out of cantankerousness, so pens for two or more need to be large enough to allow the submissive ones to stay clear of the dominants. My 30-by-75-foot pen seems to be room enough for two horses for a few hours, but three crowds it.

In my 75-by-175-foot pen, which has a shelter at one end and water at the other, three horses can be held comfortably for indefinite periods. You might see fifty horses jammed into a pen not much larger than this on a rental string or guest ranch, but these horses generally work all day, so when they get the chance they usually stand quietly. Also, they usually all know each other and have established pecking orders among individuals and groups. But even under these circumstances, crowding can provoke dominance fights.

An arena—or access to one—is also a must for training and light exercise. Arenas vary greatly in size and strength; a minimum size is 75 by 150 feet, enough room to work at a slow lope. If you don't intend to use your arena for roping cattle, it

Two views of a corral built of railroad ties and rough-sawn planks. At 5½ feet high and with good gates, it will hold all kinds of trouble.

can be made of light poles and posts. However, if it doubles as a holding pen that has continual traffic, it needs to be as heavy duty as you can afford.

If you have access to an adequate arena nearby, you're ahead of the game. If not, consider building one on level ground at home. Ideally, the surface of an arena is kept clean of manure and worked up soft to a depth of 2 or 3 inches to alleviate concussion on horses' legs. But, realistically, we often can't get that done.

My 75-by-175-foot pen doubles as my arena. About a dozen trips around its perimeter will equal a mile, and an hour of walking, trotting, loping, and schooling in this space is worthwhile exercise. This combination pen-arena has several weaknesses, however: It isn't wide enough for speed work; my horses quickly become bored working in it because it's so familiar; and the surface is pounded hard by continual occupation.

Corral and Pen Construction

Wooden corrals should be constructed of heavy 8-foot posts at least 6 inches in diameter, set 36 inches into the ground no more than 8 feet apart. Good railroad ties make excellent corral posts, and I've used them a great deal, but there's no getting around the fact that they are ugly. Treated 6-by-6-inch timbers are great, with the advantage of flat surfaces for attaching rails, but with the disadvantage of being expensive. Also, sawdust from these is laden with arsenic.

Wooden corral rails should be of dimension lumber (2-by-6s or 2-by-8s), or of 3- or 4-inch poles, about 9 inches apart so a horse can't stick his head between them. The bottom rail should be 12 to 16 inches above the ground so a horse can't get a leg stuck underneath. Round rails tend to roll off the post, a problem that can be rectified by flattening surfaces that touch each other, and by using lag screws rather than nails for attachment.

For corrals, four rails are the minimum, but five are better, with the top rail 5 feet high or more. Rails are mounted on the inside of the corral, with ends butted together to avoid protrusions that can be dangerous to riders' knees (see photo below). Posts should not protrude above the top rail. Gates should be as tall and as strong as the wall, with no protruding wires, latches, nail heads, bolts, or anything else that could injure horse or human. A nail head jutting a quarter inch can rip a horse deep enough to cripple him for a month and scar him for life.

Any wood construction needs frequent applications of a preservative, especially on surfaces or crevices that hold moisture and dirt. I've had good

Traditional wood post and rail corral fencing. The doubled post is a tie station.

service from a relatively inexpensive petroleum-based preservative called shingle oil, available from some automotive service stations.

Steel panels have become popular for pen and corral construction. Although they are considerably more expensive than some wooden structures, they have significant advantages. They're durable, easy to build with, safe, attractive, and low maintenance, with specifications that have evolved specifically for horse use. They're sold with matching steel gates.

I've seen only two drawbacks to steel systems. First, the narrow space between gate and gatepost must be covered because horses will find a way to hang a foot in that space. You can build your own solution, or purchase a product that does it for you, such as those available from www.panelcaps.com.

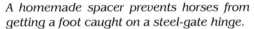
A homemade spacer prevents horses from getting a foot caught on a steel-gate hinge.

Second, it occasionally happens that a horse reaches over the top rail and fiddles down on the second rail with lips or teeth, then hooks his lower jaw over that second rail. Not smart enough to tilt his head and unhook, he pulls straight back and in seconds hangs himself.

Very attractive, strong, and safe corrals or pens can be built with steel-mesh fencing, with the mesh kept taut by attaching it to 2-by-6-inch horizontal planks at top and bottom. Posts for this construction should be set 8 feet apart. Mesh must be super-strong with very small openings (2-by-2 or 2-by-4-inch), for the bottom half at least, so horses cannot stick a hoof through. Less expensive 2-by-4-inch steel-mesh fencing built for dog pens or other light-duty purposes is available, but it will not be safe or durable for horses. Also available are very strong steel-mesh panels that in Montana go by the name "hog panels." These would make excellent horse-corral material except for one drawback: some designs leave the mesh spacing 6 or 8 inches throughout, large enough for a horse to shove a foot through.

Vinyl posts and rails are also popular. Probably the most expensive of readily available materials, vinyl is arguably also the most attractive, and it certainly qualifies as safe and weatherproof. There are various grades, some of hollow-core vinyl, others of vinyl-wrapped wooden planks. The plank version may be stronger unless a poor grade of lumber is inside. While the other products described have their weaknesses and strengths out in plain sight, that is not the case with vinyl. Thus, vinyl takes more research, particularly on the subject of strength, yet it has the potential to be the best investment, too, because of longevity and aesthetics.

Whether of wood, steel, wire-mesh, or vinyl, corral construction must be aimed at safety and strength. It isn't likely we backyarders will be busting five-year-old range broncs. However, any horse work has the potential for an occasional dustup, and the last thing we want is for a horse to go through a makeshift corral, not only tearing it apart but also injuring himself. Picture twelve hundred pounds banging into the walls at high speed, or perhaps trying to go over the top. That's the potential.

Pens and arenas are intended for holding rather than working and are less likely to contain violence; therefore, they don't need to be quite so heavily built. Like corrals, pens and arenas must be at least 5 feet high and strong enough to hold

Prebuilt, fitted steel-panel arena fence with treated wood posts—expensive, but durable, versatile, and well worth the cost.

horseplay that gets clumsy or boredom that gets pushy. Safety is still important—no protrusions, and definitely no barbed wire.

In the early 1990s I stumbled upon a free life-time supply of soft no. 9 steel wire, and I've since used it to rebuild my large holding pen. I set 6-inch posts 10 feet apart, stretched six strands of the wire at 8-inch intervals, each with a turnbuckle at one end, and I electrified the top, middle, and bottom strands. The turnbuckles allow easy tightening if a horse happens to hit the wire and stretch it. This has worked very well for me. The one problem I've had with this system is remembering to switch off the fence charger before I ride within reach of the wires. The horses know better than to touch the wires, but they'll brush close enough that my leg can make contact.

The previous construction of my holding pen was wooden rail, which worked fine, too, except that in high-traffic pens it seems you're always finding a rail chewed up, knocked down, or rotting away faster than the rest.

Fence Construction

It's a worthwhile goal to rid your horse facility of all barbed wire. If that's impossible, at least get rid of barbed wire any place horses are confined. That's a reasonable goal even if you keep a few cows, by the way, because those barbs won't hold cows either, once they've decided they have a mission on the other side. And while cattle almost never get hurt from barbed wire, horses can walk past one loop of loose barbed wire and end up sawing off a hind leg.

There are far better alternatives for horse fences. Vinyl, already mentioned for pens, is a good alternative. Vinyl is the modern version of the old white-painted fences that grace the horsey estates of the wealthy, but vinyl eliminates rot, warping, and repainting. Since fences need be only 4 or 4½ feet high, whatever the material, the three-rail version of vinyl will do nicely, and it will be somewhat cheaper than four- or five-rail construction. Again, however, strength specifications for livestock use must be verified. (Vinyl's strength can be multiplied substantially by adding one electric wire.)

Fences can also be made of wooden post-and-rail systems. Like vinyl, these are safer than wire and more aesthetically pleasing. Posts don't need to be as heavy or as long as those for corrals: 4- to 5-inch diameter, 7 feet long, and 30 inches in the ground is sufficient. But round rails have problems. Most species of wood sag after a couple of years if posts are spaced more than 8 feet apart. That means digging roughly twice as many post holes as with wire fence systems. Also, round rails hold enough moisture on the top surface to rot quickly unless preservatives are applied frequently.

Dimension lumber is a strong, safe, nice-looking variation of the post-and-rail system. Common 2-by-4 rails are not strong enough, so 2-by-6s or 2-by-8s are needed. If you can purchase rough-sawn lumber, you might save some money. Drawbacks of wooden rails include the need to paint or stain repeatedly. Also, any wooden rail system tempts horses to chew when they're bored. Some preservatives will forestall this (shingle oil seems to help) but some won't, so they'll ingest the preservatives as well as the wood.

One-inch lumber for rails is a waste of time and money; it will not stand up to the abuse horses will dish out. And any post-and-rail system begins to look like a huge investment of time and money when you're dealing with more than a couple of acres.

I like electric wire fence for horses. While they'll periodically test the wire and quickly become disrespectful if they don't get zapped, most learn to leave it alone for months at a time. This means less worry about escapes and injuries. Even panic-stricken horses will turn away from a hot wire if they know it's there.

The advantages of electric fences, however, aren't gained simply by stringing a couple of strands of 16-gauge wire here and there across some little step-in posts. An electric fence needs to be as safe and strong as if it were not electrified. Three or four strands of 9-gauge wire 12 inches apart on wooden posts is the standard. Wire any lighter than this can be broken even by a passing whitetail deer. Only top and bottom wires need to be charged, to keep horses from reaching over or under.

I recommend wooden posts. The tiny steel or fiberglass posts sold with some electric systems seem to me just waiting for the opportunity to impale a horse. While standard steel T-posts are stronger, they're not much safer, although I do sometimes use them in low-traffic areas. One good push bends them over. When fences are made only of steel, eventually all the posts are pushed outward.

Another safety concern of steel posts is that a horse can gouge his face when doing some innocent scratching. That said, there are at least two vinyl products made to soften the dangerous ends of steel T-posts. One is simply a small cap that slips down onto the top of the post. Safe-T-Post Caps is one brand name; information is available at www.cze.com. Another common type of cap, available from fence-material suppliers, is larger and mushroom shaped, with a clip to hold a wire.

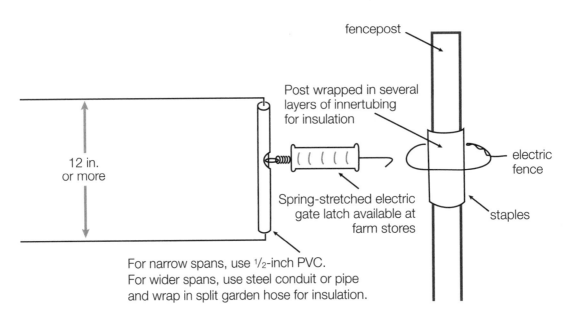

Plan for a two-strand electric gate. For narrow spans, use ½-inch PVC. For wider spans, use steel conduit or pipe and wrap in split garden hose for insulation.

54

There are commercially made electric fence systems that use a very strong, highly visible electric "rope" stretched long distances between conventional wooden posts. ElectroBraid is one reliable brand name. Since digging and tamping post holes is slow work even with machinery, this system is advantageous in that it needs fewer posts. The drawback, in my opinion, is one of appearance. If your taste runs to more traditional fencing, then these high-tensile systems look like something is missing, until you get accustomed to them.

Other electrical fence systems use a plastic "ribbon" 3 or 4 inches wide, also strong and resilient, but with posts closer together. With three or four ribbons it is somewhat like post-and-rail fencing in appearance. Some brands are available with a choice of ribbon colors. This type of fence has the advantages of modern products with a more traditional look.

Another good option is the basic wire fence. I've mentioned plain 9-gauge smooth wire as the standard for electrical fences, but it can also be used without electrification. It's strong enough to take a lot of abuse, and while a serious entanglement in it might bring injury, that injury will be far less serious than would be the case with barbed wire. An alternative is twisted, doubled, galvanized, barbless fence wire. It will last for generations. It's relatively safe, repairable, reusable, and inexpensive. Four tight strands between posts 12 or 15 feet apart will hold horses or cattle (at least until the cow decides the grass is greener on the other side). Of course, electrifying the top and bottom wires multiplies effectiveness.

Building good fences takes some thought and effort. Nails, staples, or bolts should be heavy and long; braces should be numerous; wires should be stretched tight with provision for retightening. Fences should be straight. Run string along your fence lines and dig holes along the string. Rails should be leveled and paralleled.

Deciding on fence materials is one decision; using those materials properly is another. If you are going to the trouble of putting posts in the ground, you may as well make them big enough and deep enough to last. I once lived at a place that had nice white board fences, but the posts were untreated and sunk just over a foot into the ground. One March evening a brisk wind blew it all down. Rotten posts had weakened it, and those still sound weren't deep enough to withstand the strain.

Commercially built tightener for smooth-wire fencing

55

Gate Construction

Gates are the weak link in the corral/pen/fence chain. There are two alternative scenarios with gates: One, every time you go through, you argue with the latch, wrestle the gate open, wrestle it closed, and argue with the latch. Two, every time you go through, you touch the latch, walk through, and touch the gate closed almost without pause. The second scenario is well worth the effort it takes to make it happen.

The vinyl fences discussed earlier have their own gates as part of the system. In these, the main concern is the strength of hinges and latches. Horses quickly learn what gates are for, and they tend to hang around, and on, the gate. If hinges and latches can't take the weight, the strength of the gate itself doesn't mean much.

Steel panel systems also are manufactured with their own gate arrangements. A common latch for these is a chain that drops into a slot. This is adequate, but sloppy, and I get tired of fiddling with that chain. Better latches can be built or purchased. I like lever-style latches with a short handle

protruding above the gate. Yes, this violates my aversion to protruding objects, but these latches can be opened and closed while you're mounted. As mentioned previously, with steel you do need to worry about the space between gate and gatepost.

If you lean toward do-it-yourself projects, you can build your own gates for some applications. I've built gates of 2-by-4-inch lumber that, if coated with preservatives occasionally, have served for twenty or more years. They're strong, too: I had two mares argue one day, with the result that one tried to leap over a 4-foot gate. She high-centered and I had to saw the gate out from under her to get her down. I have a couple gates of this type over 6 feet wide, but at this length wood's weight-to-width ratio becomes inefficient, and inevitably these gates sag. I've had to brace them with diagonal cables on turnbuckles. That weakness aside, with sliding 2-inch-thick latches, they've worked effectively for many years.

That weight-to-width ratio also gets skewed with steel gates when they approach 10 feet. You can put a wheel under the free end of the gate, but that

Common steel gate. It is easy to mount and use; however, the chain latch is inconvenient and loose.

56

This latch system for steel gates is stronger and more convenient than chain. (Note: the chain in this photo is not part of the latch.)

A 48-inch gate made of 2-by-4s bolted together and painted with a preservative.

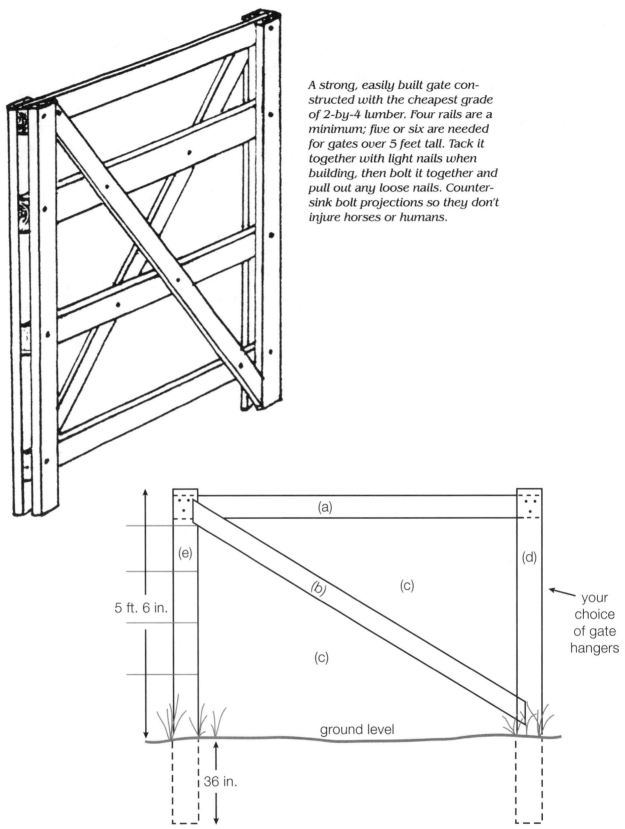

A strong, easily built gate constructed with the cheapest grade of 2-by-4 lumber. Four rails are a minimum; five or six are needed for gates over 5 feet tall. Tack it together with light nails when building, then bolt it together and pull out any loose nails. Countersink bolt projections so they don't injure horses or humans.

(a)

(e)   (b)   (c)   (d)

5 ft. 6 in.   (c)   your choice of gate hangers

ground level

36 in.

No-sag gateposts. Space (c) will be filled with wire, plank, or poles (the same material as the rest of your fence). Though (b) can be nailed or bolted to the outside of posts, it is stronger if inset. It should be a 2-inch plank or a heavy pole. Gate weight pulls down on top of post (d), but (a) transfers the weight to (e), and (b) braces it against the ground. Part (a) can be a plank lag-bolted on the side of the posts, hard no. 9 wire twisted between posts, or a heavy pole nailed to the top of the posts. The same system can be enlarged at post (d) for a taller, heavier gate.

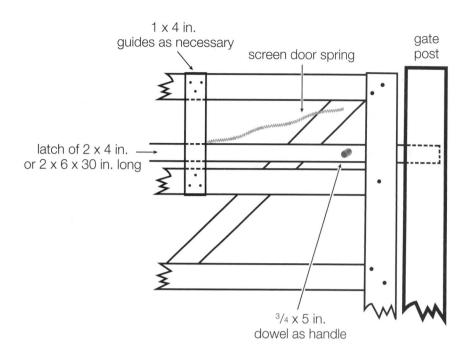

1 x 4 in.
guides as necessary

screen door spring

gate post

latch of 2 x 4 in.
or 2 x 6 x 30 in. long

$^3/_4$ x 5 in.
dowel as handle

Detail of gate latching method

Details of a sliding 2-by-6 gate latch; very strong and handy, though not very sophisticated

only works on flat ground, and not at all when the snow is deep. You can place blocks under the free end, one where the gate is shut, another where it is opened. This means you have to carry the free end back and forth to place it on either block, but you've taken the strain off the hinges.

If you don't like these alternatives, you can use two short gates for the same space. The disadvantage here is that there is no rigidity at the point where the two gates meet, though this can be partially solved by digging in a 30-inch length of 4-inch PVC pipe at that center point and dropping in a post, which can then be easily removed when you need to open both gates (though not so easily if it's frozen in).

The gates discussed thus far are necessary for any enclosure that gets a lot of animal traffic and heavy use. Gates for plain wire fence are simple: three or four strands attached to a moveable, lightweight post, which in turn attaches to a permanent post. However, even wire gates do need to be stretched between braced posts rather than simply between unbraced fence-line posts. At those places

where you cross frequently, a wire fence should have efficient swinging gates rather than the old stick-and-wire style. This is especially true if it's a location where you lead horses through. Sooner or later, you'll have a situation where you must drop the wire gate at the precise moment a horse steps into that space. Entanglement ensues.

Walk-throughs can be built where you most frequently cross your fences or pens. The small, protected opening of a walk-through allows a human being but not a horse to pass through the fence or pen wall. Walk-throughs work with pipe, wire, plank, or pole fences, and they save more time than even the most efficient gates. They are not a good idea, however, in corrals or training areas, where horses are likely to bump into them at speed.

Once you've accomplished all the preparation suggested in this chapter, you're far more ready to go looking for horses than most people who begin the project.

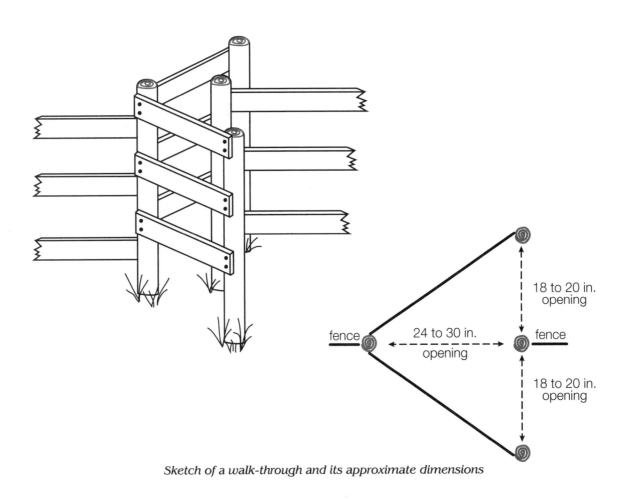

Sketch of a walk-through and its approximate dimensions

CHAPTER 6
Buying Your Horse

While the horse market is glutted with weanlings, yearlings, and untrained adult horses, there's a real shortage in one category—the well-trained, trustworthy, sound, middle-aged, "well-broke" horse with a modest price tag. There are two common reasons for that shortage: One, people who own such horses aren't about to part with them, and two, not enough horses get to that stage because they don't get enough use.

This shortage of well-trained horses is the first obstacle many horse buyers encounter—at least if they're shopping wisely. There are few good reasons for inexperienced riders, or even experienced nonprofessionals, to buy young horses. Nevertheless, young horses often are the backyard horseman's reality, so it is wise to be knowledgeable about them.

Basic Principles

The first principle of horse buying is to match the horse to your level of experience. For most people that means buying a well-broke, seasoned horse. Only experienced riders should consider buying a young horse.

You might well ask what would qualify you as an experienced rider. The criterion many people use to judge their skills is the amount of riding done in childhood and adolescence. This criterion just isn't reliable. Much childhood riding, at least outside of structured lessons, can be discounted as experience in anything except hanging on and having fun. It might be of some use on well-broke horses, but it's likely of no use for handling young horses. In fact, if those childhood memories foster a know-it-all

Three nice horses looking for a handout. What are the odds that all three are sound, safe, and sensible under saddle?

This young quarter horse shows the muscle delineation the breed is famous for. But he's untried and untrained, a gamble for the experienced horseman and probably not a smart purchase for the novice.

attitude, we might be less likely to progress than we would as an open-minded adult novice.

Here are some benchmarks to help you appraise your level of experience. Ask yourself these questions:

1. Have I had at least twenty-five professional lessons, on a variety of horses and for a variety of types of riding?

2. Have I spent a few years doing mounted ranch work on a variety of horses, under the eye of knowledgeable horsemen?

3. Have I been a serious show or rodeo contestant on a variety of horses in a variety of events?

If you can answer yes to any of these questions, you might survive a young horse. Whether there will be progress beyond survival is still open to question. Notice the emphasis on a variety of horses. Familiarity with one horse doesn't qualify as experience with horses in general. Some people have the good fortune to grow up with one good horse—fun, durable, and very safe. Years later memories may remain, but without any knowledge of what to do with horses that aren't like that childhood horse.

If you are a beginner, admit it, and buy a well-broke horse of middle age, somewhere between age five and fifteen. Don't try to learn riding skills

on a mount that is too much for you. It may be cheaper to buy a young horse, but if you run into problems and can't progress, or if you have to pay a professional to rehabilitate your horse, where are your savings?

Experienced riders who have been hurt or frightened by some bad horse experiences also should buy a seasoned horse, as should those who intend to begin a specific discipline—jumping, for instance. Learning to jump well is tough enough without having to train a horse at the same time.

The second horse-shopping principle is to set some riding and training goals before you buy. Simply owning a horse is not satisfying for long. Horses progress only when owners have goals, whether competitive, recreational, or educational. Owners become satisfied only when they and their horses accomplish something. Knowing where you're going is a big help in knowing what you're looking for in a horse.

The third principle of horse buying is to give all breeds consideration rather than starting out as a single-breed fanatic. Breed discrimination based on stereotypes is rampant in horse circles. For instance, Tennessee walker and Missouri fox trotter fans snort about quarter horses "walking all day under the shade of the same tree." And while there

A seasoned saddle horse doing two jobs at once: training a novice rider and ponying a colt.

is no doubt the quarter horse can't walk as fast as the other two breeds (they're bred for different purposes, after all), there are plenty of quarter horses that can maintain a stretchy walk uphill and down, all day long. If they couldn't walk, they wouldn't remain so popular with backcountry outfitters and big-country cowboys.

Quarter horse people return the insult by lumping gaited horses together and dismissing them under the name "stumblers." Yet gaited horses know where their feet are landing just as other horses do, and they're used successfully in the roughest terrain by open-minded owners. Quarter horse lovers also routinely dismiss Arabians as too dainty for "real work," yet Arabs continually prove themselves in ranch work, endurance riding, and a variety of strenuous show events.

Modern cowboys often reject Morgans, thoroughbreds, and appaloosas in favor of quarter horses, yet these older breeds contributed their genes to quarter horse success. Morgans were doing all the work long before the quarter horse was a recognized breed. Thoroughbreds were the foundation stock for quarter horses. And appaloosas are serious contenders in many strenuous athletic events.

This silly stereotyped thinking is based on the assumption that all breed characteristics manifest in all individuals of a breed. As any of us who engage in Western riding for show or work know, the quarter horse is the standard by which much of rural America judges what horseflesh should be. We like the stereotypical breed characteristics—quiet disposition, big muscles, medium height, and superior athleticism. But to assume that a quarter horse is what all other horses should be, or to assume that all quarter horses fit that stereotype, is both ignorant and naive. Within this breed or any other there is a wide variety of character and quality.

This variety occurs because genetics is a tricky science, even for experts. If this were not so, top-of-the-line professional breeders wouldn't cull from each colt crop so carefully. But they do cull, and their rejects are on the open market. The different ways horses are handled also produces a variety of traits. While some horse personalities tolerate poor handling and remain well behaved for humans, others go nuts.

In some cases there's no plan or knowledge behind the breeding, even of purebreds. We Americans are fortunate to have no government interference in such things. (I've read that the Norwegian government has controlled the stud book on Fjord horses for seven hundred years.) But the downside of our independence is that every year thousands

63

A Tennessee walker offers a smooth ride and versatility. The breed is less common than many others, but for backyard horsemen it should be among the most common if breed characteristics and intentions are considered.

A lovely Arab looking fresh and alert after more than thirty miles of trotting. This pair won a grand championship in a tough, competitive trail ride.

A fine example of the Morgan breed. The best of this breed compete in nearly any event, Western or English.

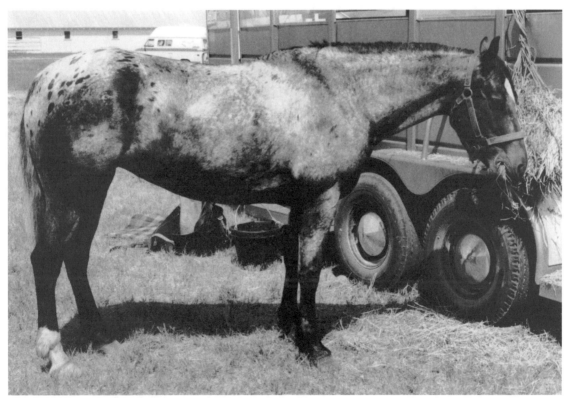

A light appaloosa mare, tough, quiet, and dependable—an ideal backyard horse. This one relaxes after thirty-five mountainous miles in five and a half hours.

Your first criterion shouldn't be breed or color, but rather what he can do, how he will act, and whether he is sound.

of horses are bred by owners who don't understand what it takes to breed good horses.

When you're shopping for a horse, you need to be aware that there's always a story behind the official story. After all, if breed organizations were completely honest they might advertise something like the following:

> The years 2004 and 2005 were not our best. We suspected a run of a genetically transmitted disease. About 30 percent of the colt crop is estimated to be positive carriers for both years, but there is no test yet to detect the disease until symptoms appear at approximately age five, at which time the horse must be euthanized.

Although this advertisement is invented, the problems it alludes to are not.

Breed characteristics and specific bloodlines may play a part in horse selection, especially as you become experienced. But when you're looking at a horse, the first question should not be whether it's the right breed, but rather whether the individual horse has the qualities you personally need.

There's even more silliness surrounding breed fanaticism. There are people who will sell a color-registered horse as if the horse had specific performance characteristics. The fact that a horse has papers declaring his coat spotted has nothing to do with soundness, disposition, intelligence, stamina, or capabilities.

Misinformation also arises with half registries. There are unquestionably some nice half-this and half-that horses. But, a horse born of the marriage of two different breeds doesn't necessarily inherit 100 percent of the ideal characteristics of each breed, or even a 50/50 split of those characteristics. Professional breeders who have made their reputations on the quality of their broodmares rather than on their stallions often state that offspring inherit as much as 75 percent of the dam's disposition, size, and athleticism (whether good or bad), and the rest comes from the sire. The half-breed horse

66

will be an individual, not necessarily the inheritor of the best of two breeds.

Similar to avoiding breed fanaticism, the fourth principle of horse buying is to give consideration to grade horses—those without registration papers or other proof of purebred breeding. If you are looking for a horse to fit your needs rather than a breed stereotype, grade horses can have significant advantages for backyard horse owners. One advantage is that there are usually plenty of available grade horses to choose from. Another is that grade horses are usually much less expensive than registered horses, even if characteristics are the same. While writing this I was aware of several registered Tennessee walker yearlings for around $2,000 each, while a half-bred walker was listed at $800 or best offer from the same location. As far as disposition and conformation, (the two immediately visible characteristics when we're guessing at a young horse's potential) the half-bred walker appeared to be as attractive as the purebreds.

Grade horses aren't necessarily mongrels. Many are purebred without registration papers, which is often the case when both parents are purebred but papers haven't been kept current on one of them. Others have only one registered parent and thus cannot be papered. Still others are intentional crosses between reliable horses by people who don't care about registration papers.

In fact, it's quite possible (though difficult to prove) that some grade horses might be more carefully bred than some registered horses. An acquaintance of mine used his registered stallion to win money in both cutting and roping. He repeatedly bred this stud to a particular unregistered mare simply because that cross threw foals with the right build and mind for what this owner needed, which was the performance, not the papers.

There are disadvantages to grade horses. Obviously, lineage often cannot be proven for breeding purposes. Another is that offspring will automatically be of lower value since they too are unregistered. Within the most popular breeds, this means that offspring are essentially worthless in monetary terms. Yet another disadvantage is that breed shows will be closed to the grade horse.

Still, if our goal is simply to improve our horsemanship, grade horses can be just the ticket. We can take an inexpensive horse as far as our capabilities allow and then move on, normally without busting our budget, and normally with as much satisfaction as with registered stock. Furthermore, if we do a good job with the grade horse, he will be worth something in the "well-broke" market. A well-started, unregistered four-year-old ranch horse at a Montana sale in May 2005 brought nearly $4,000 based on his own performance, while at the same sale, dozens of better-bred, prettier, registered yearlings were selling for $600.

Age

A two-year-old horse is old enough to be started by gentle methods but can tolerate only moderate loads and stresses for short sessions. Three is a better age because of greater size and strength, but it is still too young for prolonged work. Four-year-olds are headed toward maturity, but even these are not done growing. Full training of a four-year-old horse for polo, for instance, would be the equivalent of putting a large 16-year-old boy in the front line of an NFL team. The fifth year is considered the end of a horse's growth, but some continue to fill out for another year or two. A five-year-old is ready for hard work, but for something as strenuous as endurance riding age seven or eight is better.

By eighteen or twenty a horse is getting old. This doesn't mean that he is finished, however. He may be slower, and he may stiffen up after hard use, but reasonable care can keep him going for perhaps five to ten more years. And even though a thirty-year-old horse can't be competitive in the show ring or rodeo arena anymore, it isn't uncommon for one to be giving lessons to five-year-old humans.

Properly cared for, horses aged twelve to fifteen have the potential for up to ten good years of use. The fifteen-year-old might be a better buy than a five-year-old, given the amount of experience and use that should have occurred in the intervening years. The price shouldn't be the same, however. Sellers might not want to admit it, but at age twelve or fourteen, a horse is beginning to lose value, and by sixteen or seventeen that loss becomes significant. There are actuarial risks in buying the older horse, but those risks are probably no greater than the risk of buying a yearling and hoping to get him to age five healthy and well trained. The chances of immediately enjoying the older horse are much higher.

For children keep in mind the old rule: the younger the kid, the older the horse. Horses closer to age twenty might be what's needed, not only because there is a greater likelihood that the horse is more seasoned, but also because older horses are generally less apt to be flighty.

If horses are started and carefully schooled through their third and fourth years, and if they are ridden continuously after that as well, they are usually experienced enough to be predictable by age five or six. That means that their good and bad points are known. Most horses will have some annoying habits, weaknesses of training, or other "bad" traits. Some of these you can live with, and some will be minor challenges that you can enjoy working out over time, but others will ruin your experience. If sellers aren't mentioning any faults, you need to ask questions.

Particularly questionable is the horse that was started some time in the hazy past but hasn't been ridden for several years. "I haven't had time for him" may be an honest statement. "He just needs miles" may be true also. But perhaps the real story is that when the owner did ride him years ago the horse was unmanageable, due to either genetics or poor handling. If you are considering a horse like

this, perhaps you need to negotiate a return clause. You might try him out, perhaps even send him to a trainer for a time, but if the horse just doesn't work out, he goes back to the original owner.

Sellers of unregistered horses sometimes have a habit of not remembering age very well. A rudimentary knowledge of judging a horse's age by tooth condition might help save you from paying for years that have already passed. Many books on horse health have a complete chart of tooth aging.

Disposition

Disposition is the sum of personality and training. It includes behavior around other horses, manners while being handled from the ground, and adaptability to training demands. It starts with genetics but always proceeds with the qualifier that some genetic tendencies, more or less than others, either mesh with or conflict with human needs.

Disposition is extremely important for you as a buyer to consider, because disposition is the one characteristic of the horse that will determine

A well-broke horse will put up with all kinds of things, including kids, dogs, and spring runoff.

whether or not you actually like him. Although disposition in horses (as in humans) can swing from delightful to unbearable within one individual, generally a nice horse is a nice horse most days.

Some horses seem to really enjoy human contact, others are neutral, and others seem to dislike handling. If we intend our horse to be pet, friend, and confidante, the horse that enjoys human contact is the most desirable. However, many horses that prefer not to be handled make fine saddle horses. They may not seek human contact, but they don't mind working.

When buying, ask the seller how the horse gets along with others. Most horses settle in with other horses and live quietly after an initial adjustment period. A particularly submissive horse will do just fine if he's alone, or with two or three others. An aggressive horse can be a challenge since he may hurt other horses, himself, or you, but if he's going to live alone, that may be less of a problem.

Don't be impressed with the romantic image of a snorting, high-headed, wild-eyed wonder who cavorts in circles around humans. That may look great in Kmart paintings, but it isn't much fun to work with. Look for a quiet, alert disposition, both when riding him and when working around him on the ground.

Remember that it might take months of acquaintance before you have a clear picture of the horse's disposition, and that disposition will change gradually as the horse ages. Some horses sour with age while others outgrow their spoiled-kid act and become sweethearts. You can't blame a seller if some dispositional traits weren't visible on your visit; some may become apparent only with time or only in specific circumstances.

Bubba, for example, was a big, calm registered appaloosa whose lineage was primarily foundation quarter horse. He liked being groomed, liked standing right on top of me when I was fixing fence or shoveling manure, simply stood aside patiently if other horses got pushy about food or attention, and was always wonderful about simply "heading down the trail" when I went for a quiet ride. However, whenever I worked him at a canter he got hot tempered until he caught his second wind. He was a great horse with the exception of that flaw, which was not only hard to understand but invisible except in one particular situation.

Size

A horse is measured in hands, long ago standardized at 4 inches. Measurement is from the ground to the point of the withers. A generally accepted cutoff point between pony and horse is 14½ hands.

In Western events, a 14-hand horse is considered quite small, whether or not he's actually called a pony. Sixteen hands is considered large. In English events, 17-hand horses are common, and some are even taller. Within this 14- to 17-hand range, size may have more to do with whether we split our jeans while mounting than it does with the horse's ability to carry us. There are powerful and tough 14-hand horses, and there are weak 16-handers. I once used a 14½-hand, 800-pound Arab as a packhorse on an eighty-five-mile mountain trip. He carried only 15 pounds less than my other packhorse, a 16-hand Appaloosa weighing around 1,200 pounds. The little Arab easily accomplished everything the other horse did.

Furthermore, the bigger the horse, the more he eats and the less efficient is his strength-to-weight ratio. The most efficient members of the horse kingdom in terms of their size and strength are Shetlands and donkeys. Of course, there are laws of diminishing returns whenever extremes are approached. The fact that some small horses are powerful in relation to their weight does not mean a 6-foot-6, 240-pound man should ride a 14-hand horse. If you are over 6 feet tall you should avoid small horses to allow better proportion while you are mounted.

Common sense tells us that there are times when the more efficient small horse just isn't enough. But if a horse is easier to mount, lighter to shoe, cheaper to feed, yet capable of all the work you want done, height doesn't have to be the first priority.

Size is definitely an important consideration if you are buying a horse for a child. If you are considering a small pony (below 13 hands), here are some of the pros and cons.

Benefits of small ponies include:

• Kids can bridle, saddle, and mount small ponies independently.

• On a good pony, kids learn balance and handling skills that transfer to larger horses.

• Falls are not nearly as dangerous.

• Ponies of all sizes have few health problems, except for those that result from overeating.

• Despite a reputation for "orneriness," ponies are not necessarily bad tempered. Ponies can become favorite pets.

Possible problems with ponies include:

• Ponies can be troublesome because they are smart, tough, and independent, and they are often not well trained because they cannot be ridden by adults. And training ponies is seldom profitable even when it can happen, so it too often doesn't get done.

• Children will outgrow ponies faster than you can imagine.

• Small ponies usually cannot keep up with big horses on long rides, though this is more a matter of walking speed than of endurance.

• Small ponies have little resale value.

• Ponies convert food to fat so efficiently that they often suffer from obesity-related health problems.

Medium and large ponies (from about 13 hands to 14½ hands) are different from smaller ones in some respects. Some can carry older children or lightweight adults. Some have smooth gaits, though some have the choppy gaits you'd expect from short-legged animals. Some are big enough to pull a light buggy or sleigh. In other words, larger ponies are more versatile than the really small ones.

Color

Horse color is a complex subject, and could be the subject of an entire book (such as Ben Green's *The Color of Horses*, published by Mountain Press in 2001). Color may affect your initial impression of a horse. It may affect resale value as well. But color, like size, should not be high on your list of priorities, because pretty is as pretty does, and color does not affect performance.

Bays, sorrels, and chestnuts are common colors in several breeds, and at one time they were the most popular. Tastes change, however, and as I write this book horse buyers are favoring "color," which means "not bay, sorrel, or chestnut." Dur-

Reliable ponies are priceless and scarce.

70

ing the 1990s, black and white pinto coloring (particularly within the paint breed) was sure to bring premium prices. Dark grays bring extra money. Palomino lovers have parlayed the obvious beauty of their favorite color into a breed registry, but such registration certifies only color, not performance.

If you're concerned about resale value, color moves up on the list of priorities. There's no accounting for taste, but some uniformity is generally desirable, whatever the color. A uniformly marked pinto, for instance, will probably sell for more than one that is all white with a couple of freak black zags on his belly—unless, of course, you or a previous owner can prove impeccable performance.

Conformation

Deciding on color or size is easy compared to learning what constitutes desirable conformation—a horse's build, or physique. Each breed association has its own interpretation of good conformation. Studying breed literature and outstanding representatives of each breed does teach the eye what it needs to see. However, breeders and breed organizations make mistakes, too, especially when a show trend values a particular look which, sometimes arbitrarily, sometimes temporarily, is considered beautiful, regardless of whether that look contributes to performance.

There are, however, some universals that give us a foundation from which to judge a horse physically. Start looking at horses from the ground up. Don't be charmed by tiny hooves and legs on a horse of any size. Certain branches of the quarter horse world have bred for small hooves and skinny lower legs for a long time now, and for a long time these horses have had trouble holding up to hard use. It's a simple matter of pounds per square inch. A 1,200-pound horse needs some bone and hoof under him. I like to see a horse this size wearing a size 1 shoe, though unfortunately you'll see them as small as a size 00.

A glance at the frog gives a quick indication of hoof health. If it is 2 or more inches wide, dominating the space between heels, that's normal. If the frog is barely 1 inch wide and appears recessed below the heels, that means the horse has contracted heels, which, whatever the cause, will need rehabilitation.

Both of these hooves show healthy growth of horn (the outside covering) and frog (the triangular rear portion of the hoof). However, the hoof on the right is broader, with a thicker horn, making it superior in strength, particularly since it belongs to a smaller horse. Both of these hooves need a trim.

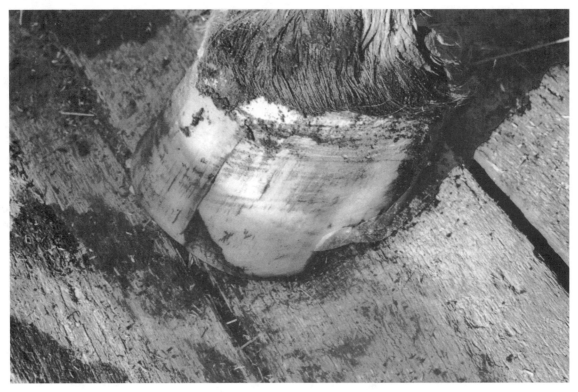

The vertical splits and the separated layers make this hoof a candidate for health questions.

Hoof walls should be free of major cracks. Since a hoof naturally trims itself by breaking off in small pieces, breakage does not necessarily indicate a flaw. Chipping is natural, but major splits may mean either a genetic, dietary, or injury problem.

Pasterns, the short sections of leg just above the hooves, should rest at approximately a 45-degree angle. If the pastern is nearly vertical, the ride will be rough and the horse prone to navicular disease. If the pastern is weak, it will be nearly horizontal when the horse is standing. Some variation is acceptable, but either extreme is a flaw.

Look the legs over carefully. They should be free of major scars, hard lumps, or soft swellings. If you look at a variety of sound legs, you will learn to recognize the oddities fairly easily. A horse can fully recover from some nasty injuries that leave unsightly scars but that may not affect soundness. Still, heavy scarring should be questioned. Older horses that have been used hard may have arthritic knobs on their front knees, and these will cause lameness. Splints are one exception to the need for wariness. These are round, hard, quarter-sized lumps a few inches below the knee on the front legs. Though they cause pain when forming, they do no harm after they have solidified, according to equine health texts.

Viewed from the front or back, legs should stand straight under the horse without angling in or out. The hind legs, when viewed from behind, will often be closer together at the hock than at the top or bottom. That's a common reality, but not the ideal. If this "cow-hocked" look is pronounced, it's a serious weakness.

A horse should have a sloping front shoulder and a sloping croup from the top point of the rump to the base of the tail. Some breeds emphasize the slope more than others, but in general a completely flat croup ("box-hipped") is a flaw. Hips that are higher than the withers look powerful but are not desirable for saddle horses.

The back should be roughly as long as the neck, and though some variation is acceptable, a short back and long neck, or vice versa, combined should be avoided. The proportion of neck to back can affect speed, balance, handling, and the ability to

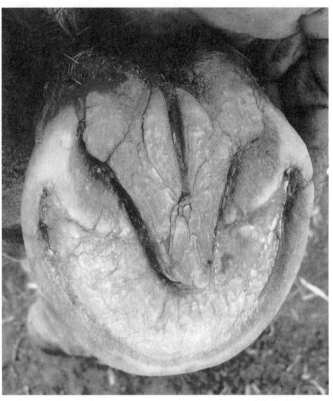

The underside of a healthy hoof, trimmed relatively short, edges rolled, showing good frog growth.

The upper view of a healthy hoof: no splits, no flared-out edges, no excessive length

bear weight. A thick, short, cresty (heavily arched) neck lacks flexibility. The opposite of the cresty neck flaw is the "ewe neck," which drops down significantly just in front of the withers, rather than rising out of the withers in a smooth arc.

While the back always dips a little just behind the withers, a pronounced dip (swayback) is undesirable. Saddles do not fit well on a swayed back, although specialized saddle pads or light loads (such as young children) might make this weakness workable.

Withers are considerably more important than they might seem. Much misbehavior from horses comes from poorly fitting saddles, and wide withers just about guarantee the saddle will have to be cinched down so tight that it causes discomfort. Fleshy withers also may hint of chronic laminitis, a debilitating illness discussed in chapter 7.

The Arabian head, with its small size, dished face, large eyes, and tiny ears, is an ideal, and there's no doubt about its beauty—on an Arab. But the look isn't pleasing on horses built differently than Arabs. Overall, the head should be in reasonable proportion with the rest of the horse, with some width between large eyes, and no unsightly bumps or cavities.

Conformation also needs to be observed as a whole. From a short distance, any horse should appear balanced, with body parts flowing smoothly into each other. Huge shoulders in front of a weak set of hams will skew that balanced look. So will short legs on a big, round horse, or a short neck attached to a long body, or tiny hooves supporting a big horse, or a barn-door-sized head hanging in front of a middle-sized horse.

When cartoonists draw caricatures, they simply combine commonly known flaws. An oversized head, long ears, pig eyes, ewe neck, box hips, ratty tail, and cow hocks all in one creature certainly destroy any illusions about the beauty of horseflesh. Fortunately this combination is not common.

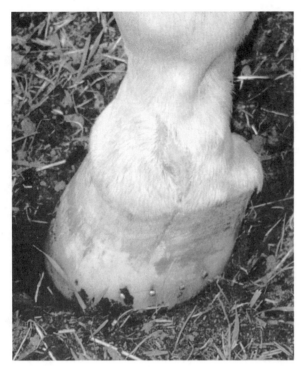

Scar tissue from a serious wound. It may not be a problem, since it has not affected hoof quality, but it should be questioned.

Soundness

A sound horse has no skeletal, muscular, cardiovascular, or digestive weaknesses that might interfere with working ability. Soundness is equal in importance to disposition. If a horse is sound, we can accept some conformation flaws and a few dispositional quirks. But if he isn't sound, a perfect build and disposition don't mean much. An unsound horse should not even be purchased for breeding purposes if the flaws are at all suspected to be genetic.

Though it may take months of use to be completely confident of soundness, there are simple and reasonably reliable tests of soundness to apply before buying.

• Have the horse led to you at both a walk and a trot, and watch the head "bob." A sound horse bobs his head in precisely regular beats. Bobbing that is more pronounced at one point in each stride indicates lameness.

• Have the horse led away from you at a walk and a trot. His hips should rise and fall evenly. If one hip drops more than the other, suspect lameness.

• Pick up each leg and bend all its joints up snugly for perhaps sixty seconds; then set the leg down and immediately have the horse either led or longed. A stiff start or uneven bobbing may indicate some joint lameness.

• Press sharply on the frog of each hoof with a hard object, such the claws of a hammer (nothing that would cut, of course) or a hoof-testing tool. If the horse flinches, there's a possibility of hoof disease, particularly navicular disease.

• Evaluate hoof quality. Poor hooves can often be rehabilitated with careful shoeing, or with vitamin and mineral supplements, or with "natural hoof care" methods. But if there are multiple deep cracks or deformities, don't buy the horse. Permanent scars on the coronet band (the gristly connection between hoof and skin) may grow down as permanent weakness of the hoof. If this is bad enough, deformity results, and deformity is likely to affect soundness.

• Lead the horse at a walk and a trot for a few minutes on a coarsely graveled surface. If the horse immediately appears to be walking on eggshells, he's tender-footed. Find out why. If the gravel test causes no discomfort, the feet are probably strong, as they should be. Good hooves will need shoeing, too, though perhaps less often, depending upon use.

• Have the horse exercised vigorously for a few minutes and then listen to his breathing. Raspy breathing or hugely distended nostrils, or an inability to quickly recover the resting respiration rate, might indicate lung problems.

Beyond these simple tests, it's a good idea to have a large-animal veterinarian check the horse. That may seem like an expense with possibly no return, but it really is the best insurance a buyer can get.

Small Quirks, Big Problems

There are some common traits in horses that may seem insignificant, but that, if they progress far enough, can become frustrations that lead to abandoning the horse project.

A horse that won't let you handle her feet is nearly useless. I had a lovely appy mare once who was difficult to handle from the knees down. I spent hours trying to persuade her that she was wrong. I failed.

74

When she finally went through the sale ring, she wore a wealth of scars from bashing her head on stall walls during my attempts to handle her feet.

It is possible to throw and hog-tie such a horse, and you should eventually learn how to do this. But throwing requires two people to accomplish safely, and it is always dangerous. Your friends won't volunteer for this duty more than once, and your shoer will charge combat pay for putting up with it. There are good training and corrective techniques for this problem, but they aren't foolproof.

Another annoyance is the horse that is hard to catch. Few things are more frustrating than a cagey horse who reinforces his own understanding of the rules every time he succeeds at eluding you. You cannot punish him when you do catch him because then he thinks he's being punished for being caught. For you, this is a no-win situation.

This is where a good corral or pen system comes in. When the horse can't get away, he begins to think this isn't so fun after all. In addition, expert clinicians have focused on this problem, and through clinics, videos, and written articles you can learn how to train this behavior out of the horse. Years ago this was a frustration that seemed to have no end. Nowadays, it's not a major challenge but is actually a fairly rational matter of reprogramming the horse. Even so, this quirk in a horse shouldn't be ignored at buying time.

A third annoying trait is the slow walk. While there is an acceptable variance of walking speed between the three-mile-per-hour hustle of a pony and the twelve-mile-per-hour poetry of the gaited breeds, the average horse, walking willingly, is in the three- to four-mile-an-hour range on flat ground. But some never do learn to walk briskly without constant kicking and spurring. Traveling with others, this horse lags behind, then jogs to catch up, then lags behind. Or he will only travel at a prancing jig. It's annoying, uncomfortable, and embarrassing because it looks as if you can't get even the most basic correct performance from your horse. If you intend this horse strictly for arena work, the naturally slow walk is of little consequence. But if you intend to use the horse for cross-country riding, then the best price, prettiest color, sweetest disposition and soundest feet won't make up for the slow walk.

Jigging is an annoying behavior related to the walking problem. A jigger has turned his unwillingness to walk into a bouncing, uncomfortable, slow trot that goes on and on and on. Give him slack and he charges ahead. Pressure the reins and he jigs some more. Spinning him to start over gets his attention, but only for a moment, and fifty spins in a ride gets pretty tiresome.

Many horses behave this way briefly at the beginning of a ride, especially if they're well fed and underused. However, most quiet down in a few minutes. A young horse started by soft methods generally won't develop the jigging habit even if he is hot-blooded. He may take more time to train but in the end will likely be worth the investment. An older horse, however, having perfected his ability to wreak havoc with the rider's peace of mind, may not be worth the hundreds of jaw-clenching hours needed to reverse the damage.

The horse that throws back against the halter rope when tied is a puller. A puller is dangerous. Straining against the rope, he'll thrash and scramble. If the rope doesn't break, he'll eventually leap forward, landing on the handler or bashing himself into a wall. If it does break, he falls. If you're too close during the performance, you could end up in the hospital. Properly handled, young horses learn to give to the contact of rope rather than pull against it. Those who become confirmed pullers do so because they were placed in scary situations before learning to give to contact. They did the only horse-logical thing: attempt an escape. If the halter or rope broke and they succeeded in escaping, they never forget it.

Horse shoppers can partially test for this trait by startling the tied horse, first obtaining the owner's permission and checking for safety. A puller throws himself back, leans against the rope, and perhaps throws his head back and forth violently. A nonpuller may jump around, too, but won't hover dangerously out on the end of a taut rope. There are gimmicks to alleviate this problem, but they aren't guaranteed. In an older horse this habit may be permanently ingrained. You may learn to live with it, but you won't ever like it.

There are several minor quirks called stall vices, which may not be immediately visible. Stall vices are neurotic habits that result from too much confinement or from living without other horses. Chewing wood, cribbing (grabbing a post or rail with the teeth and then sucking wind), weaving, mindless pacing, crabbiness when approached, all are commonly known. Few cures are permanent if the horse is kept confined, but stall vices may fade if he has room to roam. Few unconfined horses have these quirks.

Several minor items that have to do with the general condition of the horse are often overlooked. If a horse is continually obese coming off of sparse forage, he'll be prone to grass founder (chronic laminitis), in addition to difficulty with saddle fit. Owning him will mean keeping him fit by methods more sophisticated than semistarvation. If a horse is skinny on good forage, he may have internal or external parasite infestation, gastrointestinal problems, or vitamin/mineral deficiencies.

On a gray or white horse, wartlike protrusions or unexplained lumps on the body can be red flags. Gray or white horses can live healthy lives as long as horses of any other color, but the generic term "white horse disease" is based on a higher predisposition to cancerous conditions.

If the horse's attitude is particularly listless, if his coat is unusually shaggy in winter or doesn't shed off by late spring, or if he has unexplained lesions, it could indicate either marginal care by the present owner or nagging health problems. I once owned a gelding who had recurring ringworm. It didn't affect his usefulness, but it did require treatment each time. Furthermore, if one horse has ringworm, others are likely to contract it.

Beginning horse owners rightly want to know about problems such as bucking or kicking. While these traits are dangerous, they aren't nearly as common as the minor problems already mentioned. True kickers are so dangerous that few reputable owners would sell you one, particularly since the potential for litigation looms over any transaction. A bucker is not only dangerous, he's usually very obvious. You have every right to ask sellers about bucking and kicking and to see the horse in action in order to learn about its behavior.

Runaway horses, like kickers and buckers, are relatively rare but very dangerous. Runaway horses have learned to "take the bit" and run blindly. Actually, they aren't "taking the bit" at all; they're just not responding to it. This is a learned behavior and there are solutions, but in the meantime these horses are so dangerous that purchasing one should be avoided.

Horse shoppers can't be shy when it comes to inquiring about dangerous traits. But once you're satisfied with the answers, you need to keep digging. Minor problems can become significant enough to ruin your experience.

Finding a Horse

Start your horse search by reading classified ads in the local newspaper, as well as Web sites such as Horsetopia.com, Horsetrader.com, and Equinenow.com, to check prices and available animals. There are also Web sites for specific breeds and associations, and others run by individual brokers. Listed prices may be wishful thinking on the part of the sellers, but they are informative nevertheless.

Go to a sales barn and watch an entire auction; it's a good way to learn about conformation, performance, and sellers' lingo, while sitting on your hands during the bidding. Don't be in a rush to buy the first animal you see, even if it seems like a screaming deal. Believe me, there are more horses out there, and good ones.

Breed auctions are a step up from regular monthly horse auctions. Here there will be some very nice representatives of the breed, but there may also be inflated prices, even if it appears to be an open auction. For instance, you might see something like this: Breeder A sells a beautiful mare at a final bid of $12,000. "Wow!" you might think. "These horses must really be something." A little later, Breeder B sells a beautiful mare for $14,000. Wow again! But what you don't see is that B bought A's mare, and A bought B's mare. The only money exchanged was the $2,000 difference. Of course, when this kind of thing goes along quietly between insiders, sooner or later some starry-eyed outsider is going to lay out $12,000 or $14,000 for a horse probably worth far less.

Skepticism about advertised qualities is always wise. Breeders love to advertise their young horses as "ready to start" as if this were a valuable attribute. If you read between the lines, what the breeder is really saying is something like: "This seems to be a nice young horse, but I really don't know because we haven't done a whole lot with him. I can't afford to put $1,000 worth of training into him the way the market is right now. But so far he's a nice horse." Technically, a twenty-year-old, sway-backed, one-eyed, man-killing, mongrel feral stallion is also "ready to start." We probably shouldn't buy him, however.

Breeders also love to list bloodlines in detail. They're like football fans in this respect, rattling off names and winnings from years back. Obviously, breeding does affect a horse's potential, but the bottom line is that you will be left dealing with the horse that is standing in front of you, regardless of his lineage.

A dealer or breeder might be honest and knowledgeable, or he or she could be dishonest or ignorant or accidentally wrong. Where does that leave the buyer? Who can you trust?

No matter who you buy from, it's a gamble. But you can hedge your bet to some extent by arranging for a money-back guarantee and/or a trial period. A couple of weeks' careful use will teach you more about the horse than all the talk in the world. Understand, however, that the owner's risks may be even greater than the buyer's if the buyer's skills or facilities are marginal. A fair solution might be to pay a small fee to ride the horse at the seller's place several times before buying.

If you buy through the sales ring, you can't expect a return guarantee, but you can still consider it a provisional purchase. Promise yourself you will give the horse thirty days of good care and steady use, and then, if there's anything wrong, take him back to the sale barn and sell him. You might lose money, but at least you won't be pouring a winter's worth of feed through an animal you hate, fear, or can't ride. This is not a good choice, however, if you've paid an inflated price for the horse.

Though it also carries no guarantees, possibly the best method of making a purchase is to get help from a professional trainer or someone who has bought enough horses (successfully or not) to know the pitfalls. That person can evaluate horses with you or even go horse hunting for you. This may cost money, but if it gets you the right horse, it's money well spent. After you purchase a horse, you might also consider paying a professional for several weeks of lessons for both you and the horse. It will be worth it in the long run.

The pitfalls of horse buying are pretty much the same for everyone, regardless of experience, because unless you've seen the horse in action many times, you don't really know him.

Case in point: I went horse shopping with a retired friend who was looking for a quiet horse that would renew his interest after many years out of the game. Both of us were reasonably experienced with horses. We began by following up on ads from backyard owners like ourselves. The plan was to take whatever he purchased to a trainer for a tune-up as needed.

We first found a sixteen-year-old Arab gelding, big and strong, supposedly well schooled, certainly priced right. Kept in isolation, he did appear friendly enough, and when ridden in a short demonstration, he appeared useable. Once at his new home, however, the horse gradually showed himself to be flighty, resentful, oddly and unpredictably aggressive, and unable to adapt to other horses. I rode him for an hour or so one morning and found him to be jiggy, unwilling to settle down, and fearful of everything we encountered. The new owner rode him on mountain roads and he found the same goofy results. Ground work over several months didn't improve the horse's performance. We came to the realization that the horse had so many problems he simply wasn't worth working on. Strike one.

We also found a quiet young quarter horse mare who was very strong, easy to be around, and supposedly started under saddle. But the lady who had first told us about the mare rode it several times and began to get suspicious. A trusted professional trainer entered the picture and within two weeks revealed the truth about the mare: she was a dirty, unpredictable bucker. Strike two.

A few months later my friend and I visited a breeder. This time the purchase was an eighteen-year-old Tennessee walking horse mare. She turned out to be great—a quiet but ambitious and experienced pleasure horse. Home run.

The reality of horse shopping is that it's very rare to find the perfect horse. Even professionals ride flawed horses, though the flaws may be invisible to the rest of us. Horses are complex individuals placed in a human environment, which for them is an artificial world. The inevitable result is quirks. The horse, if he is capable of thinking about the situation, probably doesn't think of his actions as quirks, but rather as what he has to do to get through the day under his own terms. But while some quirks we can tolerate, others may be dangerous, or may at least drive us bananas.

Part of horsemanship then, is learning to live with what we can't fix, and learning to fix what we can't live with. This may simply mean being more patient. It may mean significant time learning training or rehabilitation techniques. It may mean selling the animal. But it should never mean that we neglect the animal, or that we give up on horses.

CHAPTER 7
Health and Feeding

Equine health can be a complex subject, but it is often made more complex than necessary by people who have a vested interest in doing so. We can take good care of our horse's health without obtaining a degree in nutritional science.

General Health

In feeding and caring for your horse, the goal is to maintain a level of physical condition that allows the horse to feel good and tolerate his normal workload without undue physical or mental stress. That seems simple enough, but it's subject to many variables.

While stories of starvation and abuse are enough to make us want to bring back stocks and public floggings, they actually originate from only a tiny proportion of the horse-owning population. Most people have sense enough to put out more hay when ribs begin to show. In fact, many horse owners go to the opposite extreme—overfeeding—believing that overfeeding is a form of affection. They're wrong.

The idea that fat is desirable comes not only from a misguided sense of kindness, but from images promoted by show judges and commercial feed producers. "Fat is the prettiest color," they say. That's permissible only if the horse is getting regular, strenuous exercise to stay in top shape for competition. Television shows constantly decry the problems of obesity in Americans. If we're smart enough to see those problems in humans, we should be able to see them in horses, too.

In horses, as in people, physical build reflects inherited characteristics. Ponies, grade horses with some pony or draft background, quarter horses, paints, appaloosas, and Morgans commonly have a rounder build than thoroughbreds, walkers, or Arabs. But any horse that seems to be built only in round chunks is probably too fat. Withers should show some slope. Haunches should show some muscle delineation. Necks should not have an arched fat deposit. Shoulders between the withers and the elbow should not have a roll that becomes pronounced when the saddle is cinched up.

On the other hand, if the horse is built only of angles, he's probably too thin. On a thin horse, the hip bones and ribs are plainly visible. Withers are bony and concave. The neck appears to be wasting away at the base.

Somewhere between these extremes is the ideal to shoot for, with muscle delineation visible, but flesh still there in quantity. A healthy horse doesn't look either fat or bony. His hips are rounded but the big pelvic bone is palpable. There should be a shallow channel between the hips from the tail up over the croup, but not a deep crease. Ribs may show if the light hits them just right, yet they are under a good layer of flesh.

Coat condition is also an indicator of health. A coarse coat in summer, or belated shedding of winter hair, particularly under the belly, could reflect poor diet, extreme age, internal or external parasites, or undiagnosed illness.

In winter, coats vary from a 3-inch eyes-to-hooves mat on a hardy Shetland to a velvety fuzz on a grain-fed hotblood. In some cases genetics dictate a shorter coat, and on cold days the horse suffers because of it. For fine-coated horses, it is especially important to have a roof, a windbreak, and a proper diet. Judging coat condition is not an exact science, of course. One quick clue is simply to decide whether this horse's coat is in similar condition to that of other horses getting the same feed and shelter.

General health also encompasses care of the endless string of little dings horses get from bugs,

This mare's broad back, cresty neck, and fleshy shoulders demonstrate what good feed and no work can come to. She's healthy, but a sudden dose of hard work would be rough on her system, and maybe fatal.

fences, other horses, and sometimes, it seems, just from the air they breathe. Pride in horsemanship includes ensuring that our horses are well cared for when they head out to work.

Working Condition

Working condition is part of a horse's general health, but it also includes stamina. Buyers aren't likely to get a clear picture of working condition in most buying situations. In most cases a buyer has to assume that working condition can be developed if the horse's general health is good. Once you own the animal, you become aware of his ability to build stamina, and you can begin to improve it with conditioning.

Conditioning should occur gradually; otherwise you risk overworking the horse to the point of stress. We wouldn't expect a person who is 30 percent overweight to withstand a twenty-mile hike or a three-mile run, and we shouldn't expect similar feats from a horse. I once invited a young visitor, an experienced rider from Australia, to ride Daisy, a horse in need of some exercise. The young lady walked Daisy out into a five-acre pasture, trotted around a bit, and moved into a quiet lope. Fifteen minutes later I checked on them, and they were still at that lope. After another fifteen minutes I saw they were still loping, and I went out and stopped the show. The young lady was beaming. Daisy's nostrils were as big as the air intake on my truck and her sweat was a-pourin'. Daisy hadn't had thirty minutes of loping in the last three months, just some two-hour walks out over some mild hills. The rider fell all over herself apologizing; she was accustomed to horses that were exercised strenuously almost daily. She'd been having so much fun, and Daisy just wouldn't quit.

Horses can be expected to lope for miles—but only if they've been properly conditioned. Horses in a soft-surfaced arena can be expected to spend a half-hour running hard, stopping hard, spinning, and breaking out at full speed—if they've been properly conditioned. Horses can be expected to carry packs in the backcountry for multiple twenty-mile days—if they've been properly conditioned.

Horses are tough, but their owners need to be sensible about that, especially with those horses that are willing to work until they drop. Any horse will begin puffing and sweating almost immediately under hard work. It's the recovery rate that tells the tale of conditioning. Recovery rate can be checked by taking the horse's resting heartbeat with a stethoscope right behind the elbow, or by counting the breathing rate at the flanks, and after fifteen minutes of vigorous exercise taking the readings again. Even in unworked condition, recovery to resting heartbeat should be nearly complete in less than ten minutes. Horses in working condition recover in two or three minutes.

Any healthy horse should be able to shuffle right along over eight or ten miles of easy terrain, even on the first spring ride. If he can't, he could be ill, older than we think, or developing muscle or skeletal problems that aren't visible. Or he might have been penned up so close that his natural stamina has been seriously compromised.

How much riding time does it take to keep a horse in good working condition? This depends on a variety of factors. Generally speaking, horses build stamina faster and keep it longer than humans do. That doesn't mean horses can be expected to perform once-a-year miracles, however. And some horses can take much harder work with less preparation than others. Such toughness varies more between individuals than between breeds or sizes.

A good schedule for us backyard types to shoot for might be six or eight hours of light work spread over three or four days per week. Light work would entail walking and jogging for the first couple of weeks of spring; after that it should include hills, running, or pulling weight to build wind and muscle tone. If you continue this same regimen through the riding season, your horse will gradually build greater stamina—not enough for endurance competition, but enough that the long days you work him on occasion won't hurt him at all. In fact, after the first few weeks it's good to put in some long days for variety and further conditioning. Late in the season, the number of rides per week could be reduced by half without seriously compromising the conditioning you've attained.

Yet even this much work is minor compared to what truly conditioned horses can do. During a two-day cow-working episode, I watched ranch horses work six or seven hours straight, much of it at a steady trot, including two or three trips up and down some long, steep inclines. Even late in the day, those ranch horses had more energy every time they were asked, unlike my willing-but-tired backyard horse. The difference was that the ranch horses had been working several of these strenuous days every week all summer and fall.

Wilderness outfitter Smoke Elser, in his book *Packin' In on Mules and Horses* (Mountain Press, 1980), describes a simple conditioning routine: four two-hour days, and two four-hour days with a day or two off between sessions, carrying full loads. He used this to prepare his animals for twenty-mile days of mountainous backcountry.

How you develop the working condition of your horses will certainly depend upon your time availability and facilities. But even when you don't feel like riding, even if "going riding" for a particular day only means a jog around a few miles of subdivision roads, it's time that needs to be spent. The alternative is a lazy, rider-splitting horse suffering from poor saddle fit, burning lungs, and weak muscles, expressing his suffering at best with bad manners or an inability to keep up, and at worst, by permanent physical damage.

Feeding

Basic health depends more upon quantity and quality of feed than upon any other aspect of care. Yet, as important as it is, the horse's diet can be pretty simple. The right quantities of clean forage and grain, clean water, mineralized salt, and clean feeding facilities can be easily managed.

On pasture that's in good condition and well managed, horses stay healthy with almost no supplementing, assuming they're kept off the feed enough hours daily to prevent obesity. A diet of primarily pasture grass maintains adequate energy for considerable exercise. But if the pasture is never fertilized and never given a chance to regenerate itself, a horse gradually removes the best, most nutritious grasses. If the pasture is allowed to deteriorate to marginal grasses and barely edible weeds, that's not adequate. If needed nutrients aren't in the grass and soil, they won't get into your horse, and his condition will show it. Even good pasture can lack essential minerals. A county extension agent can help you decide how to improve soil quality, or you can purchase feed supplements mixed specifically for your area. Supplements won't help the soil, but they will help the horse maintain necessary biochemical balances.

Hay can be a real problem for backyard horse owners. We feed it at least all winter and in many cases year-round. But like pasture grasses, hay quality reflects the nutritional values of the soil it grows from and of the plant itself, not to mention the care with which it was harvested and stored.

Buying hay is a bit tricky, because it's easy to pay as much for low quality as for high.

Buy the best hay raised in your area. You can avoid poor hay by checking for good green color on the inside of the bale. The outside of the bale can be misleading, since even a few days of sunlight will bleach out the color. But whatever species of hay, and whatever the size of the bale, the inside of the bale should be clean, green, and smelling of hay rather than of mildew. Obviously, the seller isn't going to be happy if the buyer breaks a dozen bales to check quality. But you can dig into the bale somewhat with your fingers, leaving it intact yet pulling some inside material out. On big, round bales that were recently baled, I've had some success checking for heat by hammering a pointed steel bar four or five inches into the center. If there's heat or moisture inside, the bar comes out warm and damp. Needless to say, when I find that situation, I don't buy.

Over the years I've drifted back and forth on the subject of alfalfa. My Minnesota ancestors didn't use it for horses, saying it was too "hot." While it's true that a sudden, complete change from feed of low nutritive value to top-quality alfalfa can cause kidney problems, when eased into alfalfa a horse does just fine. Compared to most other common hay species, alfalfa can be the best hay for horses. As my vet once said, "The only alfalfa that hurt him is the alfalfa he didn't get."

In northern states, alfalfa is cut two or three times a year, with the first cutting having the highest protein content, but the second and third having fewer weeds, fewer thick stems, and more fine leaves. Horses will rummage around and leave the heavier stems if they can get all the quantity they want from the leaves. Also, if the field has weed problems, the first cutting is where those weeds will be in the harvest. Horses pass weed seeds through their systems intact, ready to spring up in unwanted places. Given these factors, second and third cuttings are the best buy.

High-quality alfalfa has multiple advantages: excellent nutrition, minimal waste, and cost similar to inferior hay. Less of it—10 or 20 percent in weight—can be fed to a horse because of its superior nutritional qualities, and consequently there's less likelihood of the rounded "hay belly" that

Long-stemmed orchard grass in big, round bales (left) and fine-stemmed grass in small bales (right)

results when horses stuff themselves with larger quantities of lower quality hay.

That said, there are also some good reasons not to feed your horse alfalfa. If all you can get is a late first cutting, you'll be buying a lot of heavy stems. A second drawback, particularly with the large, round bales now common, is that alfalfa harvested with the least bit of dampness will mold quickly, and moldy hay is a major health hazard for horses. It simply cannot be fed. I've read that when Napoleon was invading Russia, he had to cross hundreds of miles of country that the retreating Russians had burned black. Napoleon's starving cavalry horses were reduced to eating the wet, moldy thatched roofs of peasants' huts. The immediate result was miles and miles of roadways littered with Europe's finest war horses dying in the quivering agony of colic. But at least those horses didn't have to live another five years gasping for air with a lung disease called "heaves," something like equine asthma, which would have been the case if they'd ingested the moldy thatch over a greater length of time.

Another drawback of alfalfa is that it can make your horses fat. A certain amount of roughage is necessary in an equine diet. With alfalfa, if that roughage quantity is adequate to keep the horse happy, it's probably going to add pounds.

My own solution to the alfalfa question? If I can find it, I feed it, but not as much as I once did. I buy alfalfa/grass mixes, or I feed one flake of alfalfa to two flakes of grass. If I can't find alfalfa, I don't worry. I feed grass hay and supplement it with grain.

Grass hays will serve well, particularly if supplemented. Orchard grass is a common irrigated hay with good protein content. I have had problems with orchard grass souring if put up with any moisture content. It isn't moldy and appears clean, yet horses will avoid the soured piece if they can. Horses really like grass hays such as crested wheat, timothy, or blue grass, as well as grass hays with some clover mix.

Any moldy hay absolutely must be discarded, but hay that is rained on several times before baling can still be dry enough to be fed to horses and may not have any mold content. It will be bleached out and of negligible protein value, but the most serious problem is that it is likely to be dirty, since rain splashes mud onto the windrows. This dirt is nearly as hazardous to equine lungs as is mold. (During the summer, when chaff, airborne dust, and low humidity can combine to cause lung problems even with quality hay, soak the hay in a tub of water for several hours before feeding.)

One reason old-timers got by feeding their horses only grass hay was that their work teams were being fed plenty of grain at the same time, since they were being used winter and summer. On that type of diet, the hay itself is more for roughage than for nutrition. The proper diet for horses in training for strenuous events such as endurance riding will lean toward this same ratio of less hay and more grain. Cavalry horses received almost as many pounds of grain as of hay.

Storing hay carefully is nearly as important as its original quality. Successful storage depends first upon a harvest with minimal moisture content, and second upon weatherproof but not airtight storage. A careful job of covering hay saves waste, and it eliminates the temptation to feed hay that was spoiled by careless covering. If you suspect the least bit of moisture in the hay you're stacking, sprinkle each layer liberally with rock salt to prevent molding.

Throwing a sheet of plastic over the stack is a common practice, but hay will mold this way as its own moisture content condenses under the sheet. Also, thin plastic is so flimsy as to be troublesome. Hay will poke holes in it, and any moisture that leaks in will stay in, starting the molding process.

A heavy tarp is better than a plastic sheet. Build a tight stack with the bales, tapering it toward the top, and place a row of old tires or some planks on the top bales. This will help keep the tarp from being abraded, and it will allow for airflow. Buy tarps big enough to extend 5 or 6 feet down the sides of the stack. Punch grommets every 24 inches and use all of them to tie the tarp down snug. Although this method will serve you well, your enemy will be the wind. Wind will whip a tarp to shreds overnight if it can get the least bit of purchase, and even if the tarp survives the wind, it may balloon up and allow rain to blow underneath. You can get by with a good tarping job, but you're better off with the right kind of building.

I have a 12-by-16-foot open hay shed, with about a 10-foot clearance. It holds up to two hundred small bales. It eliminates waste, allows for air circulation, and looks presentable. However, my hay shed is almost useless for the large-sized bales (800–1,200 pounds) round or square; 4 feet longer and 4 feet wider would make a better size hay shed for the number of small bales I need, but it still would be useless for big bales. Big rounds have the advantage of shedding a lot of weather without being covered. The outside layer may be wasted while the inside remains perfect. Still, if possible these should be covered, too. Waste is still waste.

Whether you buy big bales or small depends in part on your equipment. Big bales need to be handled with machinery. In order to make them more manageable for measuring out individual feedings, big rounds can be unraveled, working around the outside edges with the bale sitting on the flat end. If the bale is on its round side, it can be split down to the core with an axe, chainsaw, or old-fashioned hay knife (also called a stack knife). The bale then lays out flat and can easily be pitched out with a fork. Big squares can be chain sawed between twines before opening, in order to get a more manageable size for measuring individual feedings. (Gas chain saws must have a spark-arrest muffler.) Twines must always be removed before feeding since they are real safety and health hazards, sometimes ingested, sometimes entangling feet or legs.

Given free access to large bales, horses will waste hay by trampling and by overeating. If possible, give access only at night, or for three-hour sessions morning and evening. When big rounds are left whole, horses can get sore noses from continuously grasping at the tightly wound strands of hay, especially with thick-stemmed hay. Also, much eating is done head-up instead of head-down, and eating head-up is unhealthy for the horse. Finally, big bales are expensively wasteful if moldy, since there's so much that must be discarded.

A rule of thumb for feeding hay is 2 pounds of hay per 100 pounds of animal. That's 20 pounds per day for a 1,000-pound animal, divided between two or three feedings per day, 7 to 10 pounds per feeding. After a month or so you'll know if the horse is gaining, losing, or maintaining weight. Longer, leaner horses generally need proportionately more feed than short, round horses. Only experience will show what an individual animal needs.

Horses get their body heat from digestion more than from stored fat. In the worst weather, they really want more groceries. Once, during a rare, three-day blast of twenty below and north wind, I deliberately doubled my feedings, stuffing the feed bunks and throwing more out on the snow. While the blast was on, the horses cleaned up every stem.

Big, round bales are more difficult to maneuver and store, which can be problematic for small operations.

As soon as the weather broke, the horses started wasting hay, using the excess more for bedding than for food.

It's common practice to just throw hay on the ground at feeding time. If the feeding spot is continually moved, if the ground is well drained, if there's no accumulation of manure, and if we don't mind paying for waste, this method is adequate. And, since horses need gravity-fed sinus flow to assist in keeping dust out of their lungs, feeding on the ground is the most natural. However, feeding on the ground in the same areas for a whole winter creates unsightly and unhealthy messes. Some form of manger or hay bunk improves cleanliness and appearance, and it also saves a lot of waste. Any feeding method should take into account the nose-down necessity, as well as proximity to hay storage.

Even feeding in bunks can get messy, however. In summer, the ground around hay bunks gets pounded to fine dust, which sifts onto the hay and into horses' eyes and nostrils. In wet weather, that same dust turns to muck, which is not only unhealthy for hooves but also uncomfortable in cold weather. Horses hate standing in mud or icy water. The problem occurs whether we're using small square bales in a small bunk, or big rounds in a feeder built specifically for such bales.

This is where a barn or even an open feeding shed is a real improvement. I don't have such a building, but I have largely solved the problem by laying a 4-by-8-foot platform of railroad ties in front of my feed bunks. These stay relatively clean in summer, and keep horses out of mud and icy water in wet weather. The only drawback is that they are slippery when wet or covered with compacted snow.

In addition to hay, in winter I feed grain, but only enough to keep the horses coming to the corrals

Feed bunks prevent waste and provide clean feed. The horse should always eat head-down to help keep nasal passages clean.

This feed bunk for multiple horses is 5 by 8 feet and 32 inches high. It will feed two horses who don't like each other, or up to four who do. Made of treated lumber and with air space beneath it, it will last for many years.

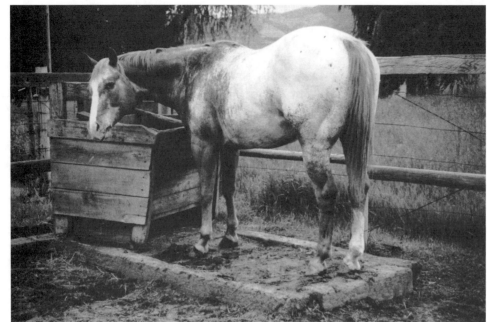

A 4-by-8-foot deck made of railroad ties keeps horses out of winter muck.

Commercially built round-bale feeder designed for horses

every day. Assuming they have access to shelter and treatment for any parasites, hay-fed horses maintain their coat condition, weight, and alert attitude. They also shed out on schedule in spring, and they pick up working condition rapidly with use. I have, however, seen horses wintering on hay alone grow thin, shaggy, and apathetic. Hay quality is critical, and when it is questionable at all you should supplement hay with grain.

For naturally lean horses, for horses working steadily, for pregnant mares, for immature horses, and anytime there's a doubt as to quality of hay or pasture, regular graining is necessary.

Oats are the traditional favorite. Horses love it, and a quart a day or more will affect condition. Crimped or rolled oats are somewhat more digestible than whole oats. For horses getting regular and significant exercise (an hour or more a day, several days a week, for instance), start with a couple of quarts on working days. After a few weeks, adjust the amount according to the horse's weight, energy, and attitude. Grain can be fed on nonworking days, too, but not in large quantity. When a day's grain feedings aren't worked off on a regular basis, horses are vulnerable to a crippling illness called azoturia, or "Monday-morning sickness."

Barley is a "hotter," or higher energy grain than oats. It's also excellent for horses, most commonly in crimped or rolled form, but you'll need to take care not to feed too much. Corn is even higher in energy. It's usually found in combination with other grains and supplements. "Three-way," or COB (rolled corn, oats, and barley), is a common high-energy mix, often with molasses added for flavoring. It is excellent feed in terms of quality, taste, and digestibility, but too much of it will have a horse dancing on the ragged edge of frenzy all the time.

There's a host of supplements, mixes, and specialty feeds all purported to give dazzling health results. And if we have horses in serious training, learning about and using these specialty feeds is a worthwhile goal. When conditioning a horse for extreme stress—endurance riding, for example—we might feed a horse ten pounds or more a day of such hot feeds, plus supplements so potent they are fed in increments of tablespoons. However, feeding these without a specific purpose is neither scientific nor kind nor smart. A sedentary horse pumped full of hot feed is not necessarily either happy or healthy.

My own favorite amongst the simple grains is a two-way, a combination of plain rolled oats and barley. It's one step "hotter" than plain oats, though not much, and no more expensive. When my horses are working, I can increase portions dramatically without worrying about side effects.

Grain must be stored dry in a mouse-proof and horse-proof location. Heavy plastic garbage cans kept in your tack room do nicely. An old chest freezer works well, though you may not like the looks of it. A main consideration is security, because horses will literally eat themselves to death if they get into the grain.

Since horses are so aggressive about their grain feedings, they may push or nip at humans and squabble with each other at feeding time. This is not only bad manners but dangerous for everyone. One way to avoid this problem is to dump grain into feed boxes in an empty pen and let the horses in only when you're ready for them. Horses also like to put a front foot in any grain container on the ground. This can be avoided by building boxes up about 3 feet

off the ground, or by using any of the hanging feed buckets available at farm supply stores.

Hoof Care

The "no hoof, no horse" maxim has been with us since ancient times, and it remains as true today as whenever it was coined. Here I offer some common day-to-day tips on hoof care, but I suggest you read more widely on this subject. If you don't do your own hoof work, you should know enough about it not only to understand your horse better, but also to understand and evaluate what your horseshoer is doing. I like Robert F. Wiseman's *The Complete Horseshoeing Guide* (University of Oklahoma Press, 1968) for its completeness and succinct style. More recent is *Well Shod* by Don Baskins, available from the *Western Horseman* magazine's book collection.

In the late 1980s, professional farrier Gene Ovnicek did a controlled study of hooves on captured wild horses, and he found that the break-over point on wild horses' hooves (the point where the hoof finishes rolling forward and actually lifts off the ground) is shorter than that on horses conventionally trimmed and shod. Additionally, wild horses' hooves were much tougher than those of domesticated horses. Similar findings are beautifully explained in *Making Natural Hoof Care Work for You*, by Pete Ramey (Star Ridge Publishing, 2003). While Ovnicek applied his findings to shoeing, Ramey took the idea a step further, arguing believably that iron shoes may not be necessary at all on a naturally shaped hoof. Natural hoof care, according to principles devised by natural hoof care practitioners, relies on trimming alone to preserve the hoof's shape and toughness.

Despite Ramey's work, many owners and farriers continue to argue that shoeing is, in many man-made situations, necessary to prevent or correct problems. But even skillfully done, it is not "natural," and most horsemen do agree that it's good to leave the hoof bare as much as possible.

Whether or not natural hoof care revolutionizes hoof care methods, the work of Ovnicek, Ramey, and others deserves serious consideration, and owners should know that farriers may be working from many different perspectives.

Like a hiker in poor shoes, a horse with sore feet may survive, but he won't be happy or comfortable, and he can easily be damaged. If nothing else, hooves need careful trimming a couple of times a year. Anyone in reasonable shape can trim up a

Even horse owners who never do their own shoeing need to know how to lift a horse's hind leg safely.

1. Picking up a hind hoof safely is done by keeping your near hand on the hip and running the other hand from the hip to the leg. Keep your body close to the horse.

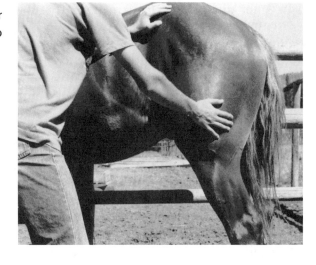

2. Keeping the near hand at the hip, grasp the lower leg and pull forward. Once the hoof is off the ground, give the horse a moment to agree that this is okay. A horse can kick you at this point, but not with any force. He has to come forward to reach you, and you'll have time to move. If he kicks straight back, you are clear.

3. Step ahead, past the horse's tail. Get a firm grip on the lower leg. You will be safer by being assertive rather than timid. With your near arm, lock his hock against your ribs. Don't pull the leg out to the side as that impairs the horse's balance. The horse will be more comfortable if you hold the foot as low as possible. The average person can out-muscle the average horse in this position, since the horse's muscles are made for pushing back, not pulling forward. To release, step sideways and set the foot down—don't just drop it if you can help it.

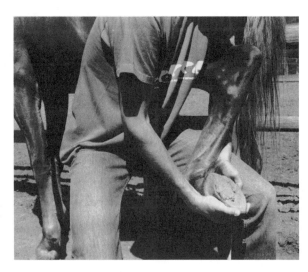

cooperative horse in twenty minutes, so there's no excuse for not doing so.

If you keep your pens and pastures free of debris, your horse isn't likely to pick up foreign objects in his feet. Yet it's still a good idea to make a quick inspection frequently. A quick dig with a hoof pick will clear out enough muck to get a good look. Any large objects such as stones or sticks will pop right out, too. A side benefit of this practice is that the horse stays accustomed to having his feet handled, something the shoer will appreciate.

Injuries of the foot can be insidious. What appears to be a minor ding in the flesh just above the hoof can be the outside evidence of more serious problems within. Twice I've had horses laid up for weeks to heal from a twig that jammed itself into the coronet band and then snapped off, out of sight. A prolonged, inexplicable lameness can come from a piece of gravel that works its way from the sole up through the entire hoof, eventually oozing out an infected spot at the coronet band. Since the hoof stands all day in conditions that make infectious little bugs wriggle with delight, no hoof injury should be ignored.

Shoeing itself can be complicated and difficult work, but it isn't magic. If you want to stretch your budget, one significant way to do so is to learn trimming and shoeing. You can glean informa-tion from watching a shoer, from textbooks, from short courses for owners, and from Web sites such as www.horseshoes.com and www.aanhcp.org; the latter is the official Web site of American Association of Natural Hoof Care Practitioners.

Of course, at some point you have to put down the book and pick up the hoof. It's probably not good timing to make the first try just before dark on a Friday night and expect to be on a trail at 8:00 a.m. Saturday. You need to study and learn over time, starting with removing old shoes and trimming the feet. It is possible to seriously injure a horse with poor shoeing, so it isn't wise to practice on performance horses. Start with a horse that will put up with the handling, and be sure you know what you're doing when you drive that first nail. Don't leave your novice shoeing efforts on a horse for more than six weeks, and pull any shoeing job after eight weeks.

Dental Care

Horses' teeth don't need constant care, but they do need occasional checking. Tooth problems can lead to other general health problems and to mis-behavior.

A wolf tooth is a small, purposeless tooth in the upper gum, in a position likely to come into contact

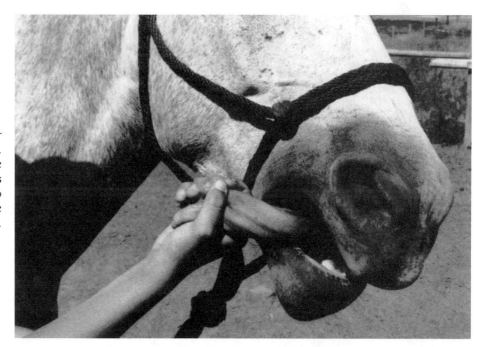

To check your horse's teeth, stand to the side and hold his tongue next to your finger so he won't bite it.

with the bit. It can lead to a lot of head throwing or rearing, since any contact on the bit is painful. A vet can easily pop these out and the horse won't miss them.

In mature horses, a common problem comes from jagged edges that develop as teeth wear down. These can become so abrasive on the inside of the cheeks that chewing is painful and, consequently, digestion is compromised. They can also cause sores to develop inside the cheeks. A horse that slobbers excessively and lets a lot of food fall out of his mouth may have bad teeth. You can check for such problems by running your finger along the outside edges of the chewing teeth. Hold the horse's mouth open by pulling his tongue out to one side. He won't bite his own tongue, so if you have hold of it he won't bite your finger.

A veterinarian will "float" bad teeth, using a long-handled specialized file to flatten the tooth surfaces so the teeth fit together. It's painless for the horse, but while it's happening you can almost feel the grinding noises on your own teeth.

Common Illnesses

Colic is a common gastrointestinal disorder that can come from a sudden change of diet, parasite damage, or eating too much grain. The colicky horse has a bellyache severe enough to be potentially fatal, because he cannot pass feces. Symptoms include lack of appetite, kicking or biting at his own flanks, alternating between listlessness and almost panicked behavior, pacing restlessly for no apparent reason, whinnying, and lying down and rolling repeatedly.

Sometimes colic subsides on its own, but the risks are so high that waiting to see what happens just isn't a good choice. Colic is a reason to call a veterinarian. It is usually treated with a combination of mineral oil, administered through a nose tube, and an injection of a pain killer such as Banamine. In the meantime, the horse should be kept up and walking, and blanketed if the weather is cold. If the colicky horse twists an intestine while writhing on the ground in pain, it blocks all intestinal action. Without quick, risky, and expensive surgery, this horse will die, painfully.

Founder, or laminitis, is another diet-related illness. Oddly enough, its symptoms appear in the horse's feet, though it takes different forms. A horse suffering an attack of founder appears lame in all four feet, though somewhat more so in the front. The hooves may feel fevered. A standing horse attempts to find relief by resting on his diagonals rather than on the more usual three legs with one hip cocked. Often, he is simply reluctant to stand at all.

Founder commonly comes from overeating, and it is the reason owners keep grain secure. But founder can also come as an aftereffect of giving birth, from running on hard surfaces, from overuse in soft physical condition, or even from unexplained micronutrient combinations in the diet. Whatever its cause, it is painful and debilitating, and while a recovered horse might be useable, he will always have some residual effects of the attack.

"Grass founder" is laminitis caused by overeating in lush pastures. It's chronic because it comes a second time more easily. It's a vicious cycle. I've seen foundering ponies in so much pain they couldn't stand up, yet squirming around to eat every blade of grass they could reach.

Even in remission, chronic laminitis shows up as long, curled hooves and/or a neck crested with a thick deposit of fat. This is true for both horses and ponies.

Early treatment is the best hope of forestalling permanent damage and repeated episodes of founder. Of course, prevention is far better. Most founder is preventable simply by storing grain securely. Grass founder is preventable by curtailing the horse's uncontrollable urge to consume vast quantities of grass.

Horses are also subject to minor colds and allergies. As in humans, these are characterized by listlessness, poor appetite, coughing, and runny nose. "Summer cold" may not be a cold at all, but rather symptoms of prolonged standing in dusty conditions. For colds, an intramuscular injection of equine penicillin is a common treatment, though it carries some risk because some horses are allergic to penicillin. (Any injections should be done under veterinary oversight.) Any coldlike illness that lingers more than a few days should get a vet's diagnosis; it might be the beginning of distemper or strangles, serious contagious illnesses, or the horse's living conditions or diet might need rearranging.

Worms

Internal parasites, or "worms" in everyday terms, are a fact of equine life. In a backyard operation they're even more problematic than in large-pasture situations, since confined horses have the unsanitary and unromantic habit of picking through their own manure for tasty leftovers of yesterday's meals. Worms and their eggs live in the manure.

Fortunately, there are plenty of effective dewormers on the market. Considering the benefits of more efficient use of feed, improved health and stamina, and the reduced likelihood of vet bills, deworming easily pays for itself.

Powdered dewormers are simply poured onto grain rations. These work for horses that wolf down the groceries no matter what, but many horses are suspicious about new tastes and smells. Paste medicines in large plastic syringes seem to be the most commonly used form of dewormer. Some horses will fight these, too, because they're afraid when you place the plastic tube in their mouth. Use a syringe to inject applesauce or molasses occasionally, and the recalcitrant horse will change his mind about the process.

Following is a list of dewormers and their target populations (from "The Parasite Battlefield" by April Fingerlos, *Western Horseman*, June 2004):

•Fenbendazol, oxifendazole, oxbendizole: all except tapeworms and bots

•Ivermectin, moxidectin: almost all worms, including bots, but not tapeworms

•Pyrantel pamoate, pryrantel tartrate: some effectiveness against tapeworms, effective against others except bots

•Praziquantel: tapeworms

These are not brand names, but regardless of brand, the chemical name, percentage of effectiveness, and dosage should be listed in product literature.

Your vet can analyze a stool sample to learn what kind of infestation a horse might have. At minimum, pastured animals should be dewormed twice a year. For confined animals, four or even six times a year is advisable. Change brands and types to avoid developing a local strain of resistant worms. Retailers have handy charts that detail types and times for deworming.

Tapeworms, bots, roundworms (ascarids), pinworms, and a couple of types of bloodworms are common in the United States and Canada. Some can be deadly because they cause so much intestinal damage. Colic is believed to be at least partially caused by such damage. Unfortunately, there aren't always external signs of worms, though poor coat condition is one general clue, and continual itching of the tail may indicate pinworms. The annoying little beelike, curve-tailed flies of autumn—the ones that make your horses stamp and run like crazy—are bot flies. They lay their yellow eggs on the horse's hair, from where they'll be licked up and transferred inside. A sharp blade scraped sideways on the hair will remove these eggs and help keep down the bot population.

Vaccinations

Many equine illnesses are transmitted by shared feed bunks or watering troughs, or simply by nose-to-nose contact. Horses that never have any contact with others might not have trouble with influenzas, distemper, strangles, rhino-pneumonitis, or tetanus, but if horses are likely to travel to any shows, trail rides, or training facilities, or if they are likely to greet even one unfamiliar horse at home, vaccinations are necessary. They're also effective and inexpensive. A veterinarian can do the job for you or, in the case of common vaccines such as four-way or five-way, you can do the job yourself. However, it's best at least to consult a veterinarian to determine what vaccines are needed and when to administer them in your area.

Vaccinations keep your individual horse healthy, but they also help keep illnesses from becoming epidemics in the horse world. In the early 2000s, we horse owners were dealing with West Nile virus, which leaves a considerable percentage of infected horses dying a gruesome death. It is also fatal to some humans. West Nile virus quickly became an epidemic, marching across the map from the East to the West. Fortunately, effective vaccines quickly became available and were widely used to keep individual animals immune.

Common Injuries

Several types of minor injuries commonly occur. One of the most common is a sore back. After a long ride, a simple check for a sore back (on the horse, not the rider) is to run your fingers and thumb firmly along the spine from withers to rump. Soreness is usually indicated by flinching.

A rider flopping around in the saddle or bumping down hard in a trot causes muscle soreness beneath the horse's skin, and can abrade the skin badly enough to cause open sores. A heavily loaded saddlebag over the kidneys can also cause problems. A common error is to place the saddle too far forward, causing the saddle to ride on the rotating tips of the horse's shoulder blades rather than sitting in the "pocket" behind them.

Minor sores can arise from ill-fitting equipment, sloppy riding, equine obesity, or a combination of the three. Woolskin or soft leather pads can be purchased to wrap cinch rings. A longer cinch might be the answer. You could try a ¾-rigged saddle instead of a full rig, or positioning the saddle more carefully and keeping it in place better by tightening the rear cinch or using a crupper. In unusual cases (for instance, if withers are so round that the saddle will not stay in one place), a breeching with an extra strap holding the cinch rings back might help. Sores at the corners of the mouth come from heavy-handed riding or from incorrectly mounted bits and curb straps pinching.

Possible leg and hoof injuries are many, and they are often hard to diagnose. While the horse may appear "off" or lame, visible symptoms may not be immediately apparent. It helps to learn the "feel" of sound legs in order to feel leg injuries when they do occur. Uneven "bobbing," meaning that the horse's head doesn't rise and fall in the rhythm of his gait, is easy to watch for at all times as an indication of lameness. Odd swellings are another sign of problems.

Small cuts and scratches are not matters for serious concern and usually don't need wrapping or specific medicines, since they heal faster when open to the air, but it is necessary to keep them clean and as dry as possible. Mild salves help with healing and keeping the flies away. Of course, any injury that causes lameness, infection, or significant skin loss requires full-blown veterinary care.

At minimum, three types of medicine should be kept on hand:

• A mild salve to apply topically on minor exterior injuries

• Equine penicillin to use against infections under veterinary consultation

• Bute (phenylbutazone), either in paste or pill form, for reducing pain and inflammation in muscle or bone injuries. It is available from veterinarians and used under their advice. Banamine is the updated replacement for Bute.

Use and Abuse

Some people think that every time a horse breaks into a sweat he's being abused, and others think that anytime a horse survives the day he is being pampered. Somewhere between these extremes is a gray area where it's necessary to consider how human horse handling is affecting the horse's health and safety. Are we asking for so little that the horse has no incentive to perform well at all, or are we asking for so much that it borders on or is abuse?

Abuse can take the form of improper care, neglect, overuse, or outright violence. I'll offer some scenarios and explain why I think each is abuse or use. You may not agree with all of them, but they should stimulate your thinking.

Keeping a horse in relatively clean, dry pens with enough room to romp a little certainly is not abusive, even though the horse isn't getting the wide-open spaces he may think he deserves. But if he's in a tiny space year-round with negligible shelter and only enough room to walk a few steps each way, and if he is constantly standing in his own filth and gets sporadic exercise, if any at all, that is abuse. Even if the horse is well fed and well loved, his minimum needs are not being met.

An owner who feeds a lot of grain to build condition for strenuous events or to sustain a milking mare is doing what is right. But if an owner simply likes to feed grain and the horse develops health problems as a result, that's abuse just as surely as if the horse goes hungry.

If an owner is careless about the quality of winter feeding arrangements and the horse becomes thin, that is neglect. Even if the horse is wintered on distant pastures, an owner is obligated to check him frequently and to supplement the pasture at the first hint of trouble.

•Work is good for a horse. So is judicious fatigue. Exhaustion is abusive.

•Preventable suffering, illness, and injuries are abusive.

•Cramped or filthy facilities and those littered with dangerous obstacles are abusive.

•Failing to meet basic standards of feeding and other health care is abusive.

•Inflicting severe pain is abusive (but mild pain inflicted to maintain respect or stop bad behavior is not).

•Punishment that results from a human's inadequate knowledge is abusive.

•Pain or severe discomfort inflicted to attain artificial ends is abusive.

If an owner spends the night at the local watering hole and forgets to feed until noon the next day, the horse will survive, but his owner is neglecting him. The horse shouldn't have to suffer for a momentary lapse of human attention. But if an owner is backcountry camping and, despite reasonable care and planning, gets in a tight spot where there's no feed, he or she can tie up and quit for the night anyway. That constitutes use, as does any situation in which comfort and safety of the animals must be sacrificed for the safety of humans. But if an owner rides into that tight spot with no plan for feed and no knowledge of terrain—in other words, with no thought for the horse's welfare—that's abuse. The horse doesn't know the difference between the accidental and the avoidable, but his owner should.

If an owner has been riding a horse for five or ten hours per week and then spends a day or two of long, hard trail hours, requiring of the horse more in a day than he's previously worked in a week, the horse is being used hard, but he's not being abused. He's constitutionally built for this kind of thing, just as are humans. But if that long day's work is the first ride of the spring after a winter of no work, that's abuse. The horse may survive, but there is no excuse for not building him up to it.

If an owner pickets a horse in a well-thought-out place with shade and water, if the horse is accustomed to being picketed, and if the owner is available to get the horse out of trouble, picketing falls within reasonable care. But if an owner pickets a partially trained horse in a poorly planned location and steps away for a day or night, that is abuse.

If a horse nips, one reaction might be to swat him on the nose with a hand, a loose glove, reins, or the halter rope. That's discipline. But repeated bashing with a fist, riding bat, or any other solid object is abuse. This is true even if the horse bit badly. Brutality accomplishes nothing except to prove that the human has lost control of the situation as well as self-control. The severity of the punishment will not be any more useful than milder punishment; in fact, it may do more harm than good as the horse learns exaggerated reactions to apply to new situations.

Competition can breed abusiveness, too—not only the momentary abuses when tempers flare, but deliberate practices that are awfully hard to justify, such as extremely harsh bits used for "tuning up" right before an event, then switched for something mild and legal in the show ring; deliberate soring (sometimes with acid) on the fetlocks to make the horse pick up her feet in an exaggerated, artificial gait; heavily weighted shoes hanging from unnaturally angled hooves, again, just to produce an artificially high step; cutting tail muscles for a cosmetic effect; or bloodletting to calm a horse before a show. All of these practices are abusive, if not downright macabre.

People who are abusive to horses do not understand true horsemanship, and I really wonder why they bother to own horses.

CHAPTER 8

Horse Psychology

For both beginning and experienced horse owners, equine psychology is a significant part of life. Understanding our horses is as satisfying to us as our more visible accomplishments. As with other aspects of horsemanship, horse psychology takes a long time to learn, and none of us will ever understand it completely. Beginners may feel lost sometimes because there's so much to learn and only limited experiences to learn from, but advanced horsemen are in a similar boat. Yes, they know more, but they also know how much more there is to learn, and as the years tick away, they realize the task is infinite.

This chapter touches briefly on some of the principles of horse psychology, but you should read a great deal more than this chapter in order to understand it well. I suggest you start with Robert W. Miller's *Western Horse Behavior and Training* (Dolphin Books, 1974). Other books listed in the bibliography at the end of this book will also be helpful. Most importantly, observe your horses carefully to see the principles of horse psychology at work.

Soft Horsemanship

Over the last thirty years or so, a profound shift in the philosophical foundations of horsemanship has occurred. (For a readable and encyclopedic look at this shift, see The *Revolution in Horsemanship* by Robert M. Miller and Richard Lamb (Lyons Press, 2005). The result of this shift is "soft" or "natural" horsemanship, which, simply put, means approaching horse handling from the horse's point of view. The related term "horse whispering" has at times been overly idealized, but in its useful form it means communicating by the quietest possible means in the horse's own language, which is almost all nonverbal.

When we humans take the time to understand how horses think and communicate, our relationship with them becomes deeper, more satisfying, less troublesome, and simultaneously more emotional and more rational. But humans are perhaps slower to learn than are horses, and so for centuries we have largely based relationships with horses upon techniques involving force rather than upon communication. Somewhere around age forty, I made the philosophical change described here, and having done so opened my eyes to what horses are really doing, as well as to what I'm doing to them. It's also made me realize how much I don't know.

The fact is, a horse already knows how to do every single thing I think I'm "training" him to do. What he doesn't know is when it's appropriate to do these things, or how to set aside his instinctive fears or reflexive actions to accomplish these things on command. So, instead of trying to force knowledge into his head, I must try to communicate what I want from his vast repertoire of existing capabilities.

This philosophical shift can also be described as a change from physical pressure to mental pressure. Here's one example of that change, something I learned years ago by watching a video of master horseman Ray Hunt.

Since 2005 I've had the opportunity to do the initial groundwork on numerous ranch-raised, performance-bred yearling quarter horses, most of them relatively high strung. While these kids wouldn't qualify as wild horses, they'd never been handled except for being chased into a trailer, and they'd never been kept in confinement. In their view, humans were pretty scary.

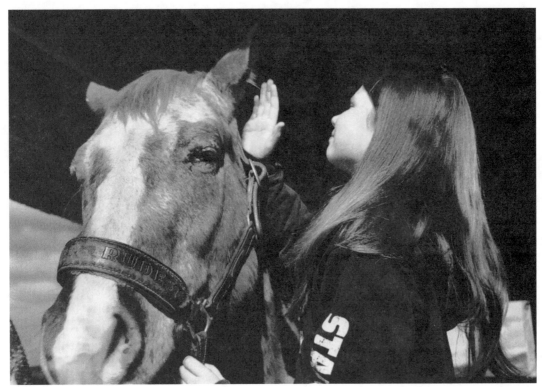

The author's granddaughter practices horse whispering.

At one time I would have started by roping each of the colts and teaching them to give to the tightening noose, not choking them down, but certainly roughhousing them until they respected the rope. (That's not as rough as roping them by the front feet and jumping on their head when they're down, a common trick from the cowboy past.) Instead, I just moved toward the young horse close enough that he was ready to climb out over the top of the corral, and at that point I backed off. I repeated this over and over and over.

Typically, the first session took an hour. The horses were looking for escape from my closing in on them, and eventually they figured out that if they turned toward me, I quit the pressuring. Once they had that response figured out, they were able to generalize it into something like, "Oh. If I stand and face him, he won't hurt me, even if he's really close." That first session, my goal was simply to get them to allow me to scratch their forehead.

The truly fascinating part of this process was that in the second session it took less than ten minutes to get to the forehead scratching, and before that second session was over, the colt would stand still while I scratched his withers, and then put on the halter. By the tenth session, most could be tied, groomed, and rubbed with a blanket. They let me handle their feet, they led at a walk and a trot, and they worked on a longe line. They loaded into a stock trailer and backed out quietly. Their progress varied only as their personalities varied. They wanted to feel secure. When they felt secure, they learned fast.

I was feeling smug after about a dozen successes. Then Big Bay Filly came along. She was snuffy enough to threaten with both front and rear ends. For two days, the best I could do was get an arm's length away. I gave up, roped her and shut off her wind enough to make her face me. Within ten minutes she respected that rope enough to stand for me rubbing her neck and putting on a halter, though she was still rigid and volatile.

Thus, a logical question might be: Why not rope 'em all at the get-go, and save all the monkey business? The answer is that the colts that had learned to come to me for security were doing what the experts call "hooking on," which essentially means focusing their attention on the handler as a way of getting relief from mental pressure. A horse that doesn't "hook on" will progress but seems to stay a lot more wary, a lot more reactive, at least for a much longer time. Big Bay Filly needed a lot more reassurance than those that hooked on, and I had to be very careful not to make any moves that might set back her progress.

Along with Big Bay Filly came Dirty Black Stud Colt. Despite my most patient efforts (at times I was gritting my teeth trying to control myself), he wouldn't hook on, remaining fearful and explosive. He'd run right over the top of me and slam into corral walls. I had to catch him by sneakiness, snapping on a lead line when he was reaching for the oats bucket. He did learn to lead and stand tied, pick up his feet, and more or less tolerate grooming, but he threw back frequently, and even when standing still he was quivering and touchy. I told the owner this colt was going to be borderline dangerous. Then, three days before he went home, he suddenly melted after forty minutes of circling while I approached and backed off. Two weeks behind the others, he hooked on. He stood docile while I haltered and unhaltered him several times. The next day took perhaps fifteen minutes of circling, but once again he melted. He went home on the fifteenth day trusting and submissive, and four months later a veterinarian told me the colt was still "very respectful." I learned more from Dirty Black Stud Colt than from any of the others.

There's no doubt in my mind that the soft-horsemanship methods made a far better start for these hot-blooded youngsters than would have been possible using force. And the proof came when, having spent the next two years once again running untouched in ranch pastures, two of the original

yearlings came back to me for a tune-up before going to a trainer for starting. Both remembered every single thing I had done with them.

Yet, what works on some won't work on all. That's why horse psychology can be so fascinating. I hope it is clear that throughout this book, my suggestions for working with horses are based on a belief that soft horsemanship methods, which rely on understanding and communication rather than force, are so superior to older forceful methods that there is no reason for any owner to refuse to study and practice them.

Herding

In the wild, horses don't feel secure very long without other horses in sight, because the herding impulse is so closely tied to survival. Knowing this makes it easier to understand that growing up without the herd can result in a kind of equine neurosis. Without those first several months of life in a herd, horses just don't know how to behave to achieve the mental security they crave. This doesn't mean such a horse is eternally hopeless when it comes to relationships with humans, but there are more likely to be issues, because what is learned as "herd manners" transfers to behavior when humans are involved.

One way the herd instinct manifests is simply as the need for company. Some horses go crazy when you take away other horses. They whinny, charge up and down the fences, and ignore human commands, sometimes for days. (It's one more reason

Half-wild range horses string out behind a wise gray mare.

97

to have a good corral and proper fencing.) Others overcome this need. If you find a horse that seems comfortable living alone, that's a real plus for the backyard owner who can have only one. But even with this horse, it's reasonable to expect some silly behavior when other horses show up, or when you travel to horse activities.

Some horses need the security of the herd so badly that they will never work well alone. These are called "herd sour," or "herd bound." A related term is "barn sour," which refers to a horse who feels secure only in his stall or pasture and refuses to leave. Almost any backyard horse will exhibit some symptoms of these two problems simply because so much of our riding is localized. Being "home safe with buddy" is an image of security for the horse, while anything else is stressful.

For either a herd-bound or barn-sour horse, there are methods of reprogramming. One way is to trailer to distant locations and do a lot of riding alone on routes that have nothing to do with home or other horses. Initially, some of these rides won't be much fun. The herd-bound horse can also be reprogrammed to some extent by deliberately riding away from other horses in increasingly larger loops.

Dr. Robert M. Miller, a nationally known veterinarian and trainer/clinician, explains in one of his videos that he works out this barn-sour problem by going for a short ride from home (however annoying that ride might be) and, upon returning, working the horse hard in the arena, then tying him up. Gradually, the horse's association with home changes from "safe with buddy" to "that's the place I have to bust my fanny and then stand tied, saddled, and hungry for four hours."

Being herd bound is actually an advantage when a horse is used for backcountry camping. As long as other horses are in camp, the herd-bound horse won't leave. As long as the other horses are traveling, he'll keep up.

Natural herd behaviors will be demonstrated by as few as two horses on a small acreage. When a horse tries to walk away rather than being caught, that's partly a hint of the wild herd's wariness. About the only difference between a domestic herd and a

Buddies in a herd of two

wild herd is that, in the former, the horses don't panic at the sight of humans, and a gelding may be boss.

Horses in a herd develop a pecking order based upon dominant and submissive personalities and upon reproductive roles. While that order is being established, punishments for infractions can be brutal. But once the horses learn it, this order is so ingrained that it operates with a minimum of punishments, at least until somebody forgets his place. The rules are communicated with visible signals: a look directly into the other's eyes, a pinned-back ear or switching tail, a slight shift of the hips toward the other horse, a feigned kick, or an assertive move into the other horse's space.

If there is a herd stallion, his jobs are to guard the herd from predators and, of course, to ward off other stallions. When the herd travels, a dominant older mare leads, having an almost foolproof memory of routes to food, water, shelter, and safety. She knows how to hide and when to run. She depends upon the stallion for news about danger, but she also maintains wariness for her own and the herd's security. She has at least one perk: she gets to be first at the table. She doesn't share voluntarily, except with her most recent offspring. She may let others paw away snow, then steal what they have uncovered. She has established her position with teeth and hooves, but most of the time she maintains it fairly calmly, with a flick of an ear, a swish of the tail, or a kick. The others on down the order will use the same signals to assert their position.

Larger numbers of horses break into smaller clans, and the pecking order can occur between clans as well as between individuals. It works its way down from most dominant to most timid. However, the order isn't always strictly linear. A truly dominant horse may choose a timid horse for a partner, and the two may live in relative harmony. Breeding farms have learned that even stallions can live together harmoniously if there are no mares within sensing distance. Stallions kept together break into smaller clans of two or three.

In the herd, trouble commonly occurs when an individual or two get an urge to better themselves, thus forcing the next horse up or down the hierarchy to defend himself. The little tensions that occur become much more complicated if reproductive urges are involved. (People who study the dynamics of wild horse herds say that breeding season resembles a soap opera.) Consequently, horses

in a herd wear some scars, despite the eons their ancestors spent living together in the same patterns. This is the reason owners must be so cautious about putting unfamiliar horses together, especially in confined places.

Even a three-acre pasture becomes defended territory. Put a new horse in that space with two or three that have established herd dynamics, and those three are likely to brutalize the newcomer. More than once I've seen resident horses drive a newcomer into a barbwire fence corner and not only beat him bloody but put him through the fence, cutting him to ribbons. Of course, in those situations horses probably aren't really trying to kill the newcomer. They intend to run him off as they would in the wild, but fences prevent the escape. Since he doesn't leave, they read him as a challenger who has to be put in his place.

Herd psychology dictates that even two old buddy horses must have room to keep away from each other, because one is likely to be quite dominant. I've had a lot of different horses, usually between two and four at a time, and in every arrangement I can remember, one of those horses (some geldings, some mares) insisted upon maintaining the right to launch unannounced, full-scale attacks on a buddy horse's ribs. I've never seen the more submissive buddies do anything to deserve this. Once the bruising is done, things quiet down again, often for days at a time.

Pecking order problems also show up at feeding time. If hay is crowded into one small feeding spot, newcomers or submissive horses will have to wait until the dominants are done, and those dominants aren't going to voluntarily leave feed. In fact, they'll literally let the submissives starve to death.

Experts agree that individual horses fit their handler into the pecking order. In other words, each horse, rather than figuring out how to fit himself into your plans, first figures out how you and he fit into the herd order. If you handle him with calm assertiveness, he submits to it because he accepts you as being at least one rung up the ladder. He also comes to trust you, just as in the wild he would trust the boss mare. If you are too timid around him, he sees this as a chance to advance in rank, and he gets hard to handle.

Herd dynamics demonstrate the kind of trouble you can have if you insist upon staying in the fog of romanticized images of the relationship between humans and horses. You might stand in misty-eyed wonder while your horses gallop about the pasture greeting a new horse, but you'll be heartbroken and confused when that greeting turns to blood and vet bills. The reality is that for the horse/human relationship to work, we need to acknowledge that, while horses can indeed be all flowing manes and quivering velvety nostrils, they are also devious, selfish street-brawlers.

Gender Behavior

The reproductive urges of horses will affect your working relationship with them. Mares are famous for being unpredictable just before and during their heat periods, which means about a week out of every month, at least from early spring through late fall. I'm not convinced that reputation is entirely fair, however. Some mares certainly can be cranky, but others cycle with almost no behavioral changes, and a well-schooled mare will work for you in spite of her moods. And I've had mares that would squeal and tease in the corral, but would be all business under the saddle.

Younger unschooled mares are likely to be moodier than geldings, and any mare has the potential to cause trouble in a herd (even a herd of two) because she excites the geldings. Some geldings will repeatedly mount a mare, while others may just fight each other for the chance to be the mare's best friend. Mares get blamed, but it's the geldings that are misbehaving. If there's reproductive horseplay, pawing over the fences is a common form of it. This is one more good reason to get rid of barbed wire.

Despite mares' idiosyncrasies, they're hard to beat as saddle horses. The bias against them means that a lot of good horses don't have their potentials developed, and a lot of riders miss out on some very nice horses. Within a few months of being neutered, male horses lose the raging excitement of the unaltered state and from then on are generally the most stable personalities. But as far as endurance or intelligence is concerned, there's less difference between geldings and mares than there is between individuals of the same gender.

Stallions are just about out of the question for backyard horse owners. They are capable of causing more trouble on a regular basis than any gelding or mare. Although some are peaceful most of the time, more are not, and when a stallion's hormones are humming, even the most peaceful can become a powerful and unmanageable dynamo.

A big stallion owned by an acquaintance showed up in my family's yard early one morning, shrieking for mares. Dad and I jumped in our old truck and went after him, catching him just as he was about to tear through a barbwire fence after a mixed bunch of geldings and mares. By the time the dust settled, we learned he had torn up fences, geldings, and himself in an eight-mile spree. Most days this stallion could be trusted to carry the grandkids around the yard, but this was June, and his libido had the best of him.

The potential for such troubles isn't the only reason backyard owners should avoid stallions, however. We generally have neither the space nor the extra-secure fences and pens to keep a stallion. We don't have the work for a stallion either, unless we happen to be on a performance circuit full time. It takes a lot of work to keep a stallion from accumulating excess energy. We also aren't likely to have a long clientele list for breeding—the other activity that keeps a stallion even-tempered. Unless we're committed full-bore to a specific breeding program, we just don't have a reason to own a stallion.

I've seen more than one example of questionable care of stallions. The extra care required gets to be too much of a chore, so a typical solution is to build one small pen with a shelter at the end of it. The horse spends his entire life there, with the exception of being brought out for breeding. He's lonely, overenergetic, noisy, and neurotic. This scenario subjects the horse to real torment just for the sake of saying we own a stallion.

Hunger

Hunger is a powerful motivator of horse behavior, though until it reaches the critical stages, it doesn't compete with the need for company. Equine metabolism is geared for frequent small meals (a heavy meal is hard to carry when running from predators), converting marginal forage to adequate energy storage. On unlimited lush pastures, supplemented by grains, horses' natural eating habits mean they balloon up fast. And the more they get the more they want. Nowadays, horses suffer many health problems because of the ease with which they get fat.

For the backyard owner, hunger can become a behavior problem as well as a health problem. A horse's attention to human wishes isn't nearly as focused as his attention to a flake of hay. A regular feeding schedule, usually early in the morning

If there's one thing all horses understand . . .

and late in the evening, will accustom the horse to forgetting about food most of the day, and it helps command his attention when you want it. The night-pasture routine mentioned earlier does the same, because the horse has learned he can survive some time without grazing.

However, there is never a complete deprogramming of a horse's built-in need to feed. Even the nicest horse exploits any chance he gets to grab a mouthful of grass when being ridden. If the rider is weak or meek, the horse quickly learns the habit of eating more than moving. This problem needs firm and consistent correction.

If pasture gets short, horses don't suffer it long before they hunt food elsewhere. They lean over fences until the wires or rails fall down. They pick locks on gates, and they paw and chew gates, feed boxes, water tanks, and corral rails. If they get loose, they gorge themselves on your lawn or the neighbor's corn patch. Of course, if they get loose once, they get more aggressive about it.

Hunger (which in a lot of situations seems more like gastrointestinal greed) can be used in the owner's favor. A small portion of grain every time

the horse is caught can cure a lot of silliness about being cagey to catch. When you bring home a new horse, he'll notice the fact that we visibly provide him with feed, and that will help develop the dependency that eases into a good relationship. But frequent hand-feeding from a pocket full of goodies works against the owner. The human becomes the candy man, and if the horse is disappointed, he gets disrespectful.

Flight Response

The flight response—the immediate urge to run in the face of a perceived threat—is instinctual with horses just as with other prey animals. For a long time I assumed that any flight was motivated by terror, and I always felt pity for animals on the run. But perhaps flight doesn't always indicate fear. Often there's a quick burst of speed for a short distance, then a sharp circle to see what the problem was, perhaps accompanied by a brave blast from the nostrils and some prancing around as if to say, "Hey, Fangs. Whaddya think of that first hundred yards? Kind of impressive, huh?"

Of course, if a predator or other source of danger keeps on coming, flight resumes. When the danger goes on long enough, (and in true danger, "long enough" might be a matter of a few seconds) I'm sure terror does become part of that flight.

Most horses aren't fighters. Their motto is: run first, ask questions later. This running reaction makes horses dangerous to humans. Once they are past the initial burst of speed and into terror-stricken flight, they become incredibly strong, stupid, and pain resistant.

Within the herd, the flight response is easily triggered. Just the sound of the pounding hooves of one individual can set the other horses running. Thus, at a trail ride on which most horses are well behaved, one runaway can wreak havoc amongst the rest.

Personalities

While it isn't realistic to pigeonhole every member of the entire horse species, there are several common personality types you might encounter: nervous performers, chargers, deadheads, knotheads, and the good ones. (These are strictly my own homegrown terms.) Some of these personalities and their attendant behaviors are genetic, and some arise when heredity and environment collide.

There are variations and combinations of the categories, as well as varying degrees of intelligence within them.

The nervous performer type is, as you might guess, nervous and quirky. You might hear such a horse described as "wound a little tight." They are usually lesser powers within the herd and, in my experience, are more often mares than males. They watch for horse-eaters constantly, and they flee from anything new. Tied up at home, they never quite relax, and while you're riding they're tense and sometimes volatile, at least until they're well seasoned.

I like nervous performers, not for their nervousness but because they are performers. Carefully handled, they work their hearts out. It almost seems as if, along with all their other fears, they're afraid of doing something wrong. They seem to have a lot of stamina. Some melt submissively when they do feel safe, though others don't seem to relax under any circumstances.

One nervous performer I remember was a quarter horse mare who never did become the least bit friendly. She was grouchy while being caught, shod, groomed, or saddled. But under a rider she was all business, a quick study, and very sensible. Another was a gaited mare of unknown ancestry. When I knew her, she was in her mid-twenties and was still too nervous for small children, and still hard to catch. Her training had been amateurish; however, she knew a bovinal escape was a crime and she'd breach any obstacle to bring a cow to justice. The last time I saw her at work she was twenty-six years old, and that day she put in a twenty-mile cattle drive.

For beginning riders, the nervous performer is a challenge, and perhaps even a danger. This personality is certainly not for the beginning rider, and especially not for kids; a wrong move on the part of a human can elicit explosive flight reactions. Luckily, you can recognize this personality fairly easily when horse shopping. Watch for a quickness of movement, a poised alertness even in familiar surroundings, a suspicion of strangers, and an "aura" of being charged with electricity.

Handled quietly, the nervous performer is a nice enough horse and a good learner. A confident rider with competitive performance goals can excel with a horse of this type if conformation is right for the event. Just remember that even after developing a good working relationship, you can never be careless around him. He won't attack you, but he may hurt you.

The second major personality type is the charger. Chargers are aggressive workers that can become seriously unlikable if their worst characteristics win out. The chargey horse is well known to experienced riders: it's the horse that insists on being at the head of the group, even if he can't walk fast enough to get there. Chargers may become hotheaded if they don't get to the front, prancing and looking for excuses to bite or kick nearby horses, or pretending to be afraid of tree stumps or automobiles. They're likely to be aggressive in a herd.

Chargers are also hot tempered when working at speed or in close quarters—for instance, a jumper refuses to check his speed on the course. The charger can develop a hard mouth, because if you push him at all during training, he wants to run madly. You spend a lot of time hauling him in to start over again. The charger tests not only your patience but your nerve. He pays little attention to the ground and simply bulls his way through whatever shows up—trees, rocks, rivers, or brush.

But charginess can be an asset. While it seems to stem from an aggressive personality, it only becomes unmanageable if training is too fast or too rough. Unlike the more timid horse, the charger doesn't hesitate to resist you. But if his tendencies are outwitted by careful handling, and then channeled in the right direction, he's a brave, dependable, versatile saddle horse. As he gets older, hard use and good schooling push much of the charginess under the surface. There's nothing wrong with a chargey horse if your skill and patience are adequate. Ironically, a charger might be a quiet, friendly pet when not being ridden.

A charger whose aggressiveness either is unbendable or is worsened by premature handling can become what I call a prancer-dancer. Prancer-dancers wear themselves out performing a variety of pawings, floppings, foamings, poundings, and sidelings while being ridden. Some are unsafe as saddle horses, because they may ignore their footing while doing their dance.

I won't keep one of these myself, though when I was younger I thought it pretty heroic to travel sideways and up-and-down more than forward. I confess to having created one of these monsters during my college years. I had a palomino quarter horse and American saddlebred gelding (yes, an odd cross, but that's a different story). Sparkey was hot and chargey, though nice to handle from the ground. Early along in my amateur training, I discovered that he had a talent for trotting miles and miles fearlessly and effortlessly. I wished later that I had known then about endurance riding, because Sparky was a natural. And wouldn't he have made a spectacular finish, cruising in at that smooth trot, his golden coat darkened with sweat and his flaxen mane and tail flowing in a breeze of his own making.

Unfortunately, I also discovered—purely by accident—that if I collected him up tight and legged him on at the same time, he would start prancing, and pretty soon we could gallop for minutes at a time without moving ahead even 50 feet. By the time Sparky was five or six, I couldn't stand riding him. He absolutely would not walk. Every ride quickly became the pounding nightmare I've described above. When I left for the Army, he went to the sale barn.

A type I like much better than a charger or a prancer-dancer is a deadhead. Deadheads are sometimes referred to as "born broke," which rather loosely means they don't mind anything you do to them as long as you don't disturb their slumber. These are the horses that kids can break to ride and that make good packhorses or guest-ranch horses. They may not be very bright, but they aren't mean or flighty either. The lower intelligence and mellow attitude of the deadhead are a good combination for novice horsemen, for families that share riding time, and for unsupervised children.

For trail work or slow cattle work, the deadhead is ideal because his flight reaction is subdued. I had a big, young gelding once that fit the deadhead type. Five minutes into his first session as a packhorse, I crossed a creek. Instead of dallying the lead rope around my saddle horn, I held the rope in my right hand. The horse pulled the rope out of my hand and, realizing he was free, trotted off. Now, a nervous performer or a charger in that situation would likely have bolted through the fences at thirty miles an hour, packs bouncing and dragging. But the deadhead couldn't be troubled that much, so he just jogged about fifty yards and stopped.

Deadheads do have some drawbacks, however. One is that no matter how much time you invest in them, they may not get much beyond the "broke and rideable" stage. As starter horses they're great, but as competitive horses they may fall short of what, for instance, the nervous performer can accomplish.

They don't have what ropers call "sting," the fire or intensity needed for high performance. Another drawback is that on the rare occasions when the deadhead does get pushed to the point of serious reaction, his reaction is unexpected.

The deadhead may also be sullen, a trait frustrating to deal with in horses. If he ever does get a whole idea in his head, there's no talking him out of it. And if he's strongly opposed to something, there's no talking him into it. It's as if he locks up his muscles, grits his teeth, and, like the caricature of the ornery mule, defies you to make him do anything. Overall, however, a deadhead handled with some understanding of his personality is a darn nice horse.

The knothead is the horse that is both sullen and bad mannered. A knothead may not be dangerous, but he may disobey angrily one day and ignore you the next. And some knotheads are aggressive, especially within the herd, but towards humans, too, if they can get away with it. In general, a knothead is no fun to work with. I once started a gelding that loved to buck; and what's worse, as he bucked around the corral, he'd reach out and kick the corral posts with deadly accuracy. I never dared get on him, because I figured if he bucked me off he'd kick my brains out in midair. This horse refused to be hand fed, didn't like grooming, and couldn't be approached safely. Had he been abused? No. He had been raised on a small acreage and was accustomed to humans, traffic, and other horses.

One type of horse that seems prone to knotheadedness is the horse raised apart from other horses and in a small area. Knotheadedness in this case may have to do with the horse never having learned herd manners. I'm sure there are exceptions to this, but I've seen it enough times to believe it is a pattern. It may not be the fault of the horse, but I won't let sympathy for his past lead me into wasting my time or endangering people by keeping a knothead around.

If you end up with a horse you think may be a knothead, your first step should be to visit a professional trainer. Trainers are familiar with this personality (you might hear them use the derogatory term "registered dink horse"), and once they recognize it, they often don't like wasting their time with it. But a month or two of training might straighten out the knothead's behavior, because knotheadedness may be learned rather then genetic. You won't know until you've given the horse a fair trial. If training doesn't stop the bad behavior, step two is to get rid of the horse as soon as you can without hurting someone else.

And that, finally, brings us to the subject of good horses. These are the horses we all want, and, despite the space devoted to describing the negative types, the good ones are the majority.

Good horses vary widely in personality, but in general are alert and calm. The good ones may be nervous or troublesome when facing new situations for the first time, and may present the same risks as others if handled poorly, but they are willing to be talked or trained out of unwanted behaviors. They don't have the explosive reactions of the nervous performers, or the aggressiveness of the chargers, or the dull stubbornness of the deadhead on his bad-hair days. While good horses can, with patience and skill, be made out of the other personality types (except, perhaps, the knothead), good ones are more naturally "good" in human terms.

Good ones respond well even to amateur training. They're willing workers, limited only by their conformation and the rider's skills. With practice they become steady performers, and you can count on them to keep learning throughout their lives. Good ones are often praised as "honest," meaning they'll give a good effort. A ranch family I once worked for had a pet term reserved for the good ones. "She's a good a-horse," they'd say. Silly, maybe, but in this family that extra little syllable conveyed the affection and respect a good a-horse deserves.

When professionals are interviewed about their career successes, almost inevitably they come around to telling their own "good horse" stories. Amateur horsemen do the same. Good ones might be rope horses, for example, that know the difference between the roper and the roper's kids. Chip was such a horse. I watched him quietly carry children around the turmoil of a rodeo arena while still puffing from heading steers.

Daisy was another, a grade Walker mare I owned for twelve years. She was a powerful, fearless mountain-trail horse. She'd willingly shoulder right into a cow to turn it—if she could catch it. She was a quiet, tireless rope horse in a branding pen. Ponying a green horse's bucking spree, she'd yank him off his feet. My grandson at age seven tried running barrels on her and fell partially off, hanging there in midair (just as my heart was doing). Daisy stood rock solid while he monkeyed his way back aboard.

I watched a heavy adult hang off her too, unable to pull himself into the saddle. Gradually the saddle pulled over and hung on Daisy's side as the would-be rider fell under Daisy's feet. Daisy didn't move. Maybe I heard her sigh.

Not that these horses were perfect. But, quirks aside, they were a joy to work with, and that's what we're looking for. Those horses are out there waiting for us, though we might have to work our way through a few others to get there.

If you already own a horse or two and you've begun to suspect they're not in the "good one" category, don't despair yet. While some personality traits are genetic, and while some of these traits aren't exactly what humans want, with enough work negative characteristics fade away while good characteristics blossom. If I had to state what I think is

What's between these ears will decide a lot of things for an owner: Deadhead? Knothead? Or sweetheart?

the single most important cause of equine behavior problems in small-scale horse ownership in America, I'd have to say it's just lack of use.

I've seen nervous performers that, with copious and consistent use, became "kid horses" in their later years. Deadheads worked frequently and regularly can become so reliable that they are priceless. Chargers generally have plenty of potential for many uses by confident riders.

Many horses lean toward one type of personality when you're handling them on the ground, another type when being ridden. Your horse might be so flighty one day that you start thinking, "Oh, she's a nervous performer. I don't know what to do with that. I just want a deadhead." But the horse may not be a nervous performer at all. She might be showing a symptom occasionally, but chances are that overall she's a good one, *if she gets consistent use*.

If you suspect a nervous performer, go slowly. Set up situations to build confidence. Studiously avoid mistakes that might cause unforgettable emergencies. Work the horse hard within the situations he's comfortable with, but don't fatigue him until he's really comfortable with what you're doing, because you don't want to make him mad. You need to build him up mentally more than physically. Gradually, the number and severity of his fears diminish.

If you suspect a charger, go slowly. Don't ask for big, new things all at once. He may need wearing down, so work him hard in long, uncomplicated sessions. Ten miles of walking and trotting on trails might be just what's needed before twenty minutes of close training in the arena. Gradually, his patience expands and his angers fade.

If you suspect a deadhead, you might push a bit harder, testing the situation, but you still don't ask for big, new things all at once. Work the horse, but

First Time Home

When bringing a new horse home for the first time, knowledge of horse psychology and of the range of horse personalities and behaviors can greatly ease the transition. Keep these general guidelines in mind:

•You can't turn any horse loose in a new environment and expect him to be perfectly sensible about it. The younger and less experienced a horse is, the sillier he will be at first. Even old campaigners may fret about all the reasons the new environment is uncomfortable. Personality type can't be judged during the first couple of weeks. When the horse is under the stress of change, he may seem to be a different horse than the one observed at the previous owner's place.

•In a new environment with changes in feeding, some horses tend to colic. Short intervals on grass, or light feedings of grass hay rather than alfalfa, and very little grain, will help him adjust to a changed environment and changed diet. Also, it is normal for him to be "off his feed" for a few days, even dehydrating a bit. Initially, the need for familiar surroundings and familiar companions will be more important to him than food.

•Spend time these first few days getting acquainted. That doesn't mean immediate training sessions or long rides. Rather, it means repeated catching, grooming, handling the feet, some longeing, an occasional treat, and visible delivery of small rations of hay. I like to just stand around the loose horse, perhaps leaning on him, finding body parts that like to be scratched, demanding nothing except that he stand with me, even if this is a horse that's already well schooled. I want him to trust me somewhat before I get into anything stressful.

•After a few days, the work must start. If you procrastinate, previous training and previous good attitudes might fade. We're obligated to treat him right physically and psychologically, and part of that means he's got to go to work.

not so hard that resentment or sullenness results. Appreciate that he's useable with little training, but still gradually pursue further training so you're not stuck with a plug.

If you suspect a knothead, move cautiously. Ask repeatedly for simple things. If the horse shows progress, you can eventually give a sigh of relief and keep doing what brought that progress. If not, go for help.

If you suspect a good one, still go slowly, enjoying each increment of progress as it happens. Work the horse hard because you don't want him becoming spoiled, but not so hard as to cause injury or exhaustion. Study the masters so you can get the best out of your good horse, neither limiting nor damaging him.

If you can't categorize your horse's personality, go slowly. Probe for the limits of his patience and temper. Capitalize upon what works and gradually push the edges of that. Vary your approach, keeping notes on what works and what causes problems. When you hit problems, look for sophisticated solutions that can be incorporated into familiar work. Stay patient, willing to go back to basics and start over. Work, work, work.

Jack Brainard, a writer, rodeo producer, and reining-horse trainer, described an experienced reining horse that was becoming more fractious with each use. The young man working her for Brainard was at his wit's end. One day Brainard told him to saddle her up and ride her to a distant town, twenty miles away. The rider sputtered something about the long distance, then rode the horse as instructed. The next day, Brainard repeated the instructions. After just a few days of this, the rider realized the mare was a changed horse. In reality this mare wasn't a knothead at all. She was a good a-horse, just sick and tired of short, fast work in that danged cramped indoor arena.

Learning

Psychological conditioning is the foundation of behavioral science and a practical tool for schooling horses. If the rider gives a stimulus (signal), and if the horse follows with the right response, the horse is rewarded with something tangible, such as a treat or a release of physical pressure. This is conditioning using reinforcement. To increase a desired behavior, the behavior is followed by a

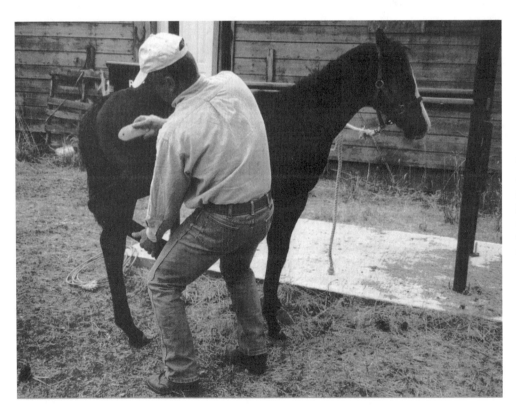

This weanling likes having his fanny scratched. Here his first lesson in lifting his hind feet is associated with the pleasure of a scratching.

106

reward, which can be either something good (positive) or something bad taken away (negative). An example of positive reinforcement:

1. Rider's right leg presses horse's ribs (stimulus)
2. Horse moves away from that pressure by turning left (response)
3. Pressure is released (reward/reinforcement).

Horses must be rewarded immediately in order to understand the connection between a stimulus and the reward that follows an appropriate response.

A punishment is either something the horse does not like, or the removal of something he does like. If the horse nips, an immediate slap on the nose is a clear consequence of his behavior. It doesn't need to be severe for learning to occur. Horses cannot connect the severity of a punishment to the seriousness of the offense, nor can they make an association between events separated by too much time. So, if you dance around nursing your pain, then go looking for a stick, then come back and give the horse a half dozen sound whacks, the horse has already forgotten the nipping incident. You have now given him a new stimulus (pain) to which he will respond with fear, and he will use his fear reaction against you in some way.

Look for ways to use positive reinforcement— rewarding good behavior—because it is more effective than punishment. Rewards teach more quickly, more directly, and more permanently. An edible treat can be a good reward, but if you reward the horse's every little correct behavior with a handful of grain cubes, instead of connecting his behavior with the reward, he connects you with goodies, and when you don't produce, he gets pushy. In other words, you've conditioned him to be obnoxious. More practical awards are a brief massage on the neck or withers, a pat on the neck, a scratch on the chest, or an immediate release of pressure on the rope or bit. Situations in which the horse is able to reward himself are even more effective than those wherein we provide the reinforcements artificially.

Conditioning starts with simple associations, so training needs to be broken down into its smallest parts. Eventually, you want increasingly complex responses from the same simple stimuli. If a spin to the right is the goal, the first tiny steps strive simply to place the horse's head and feet with the reins. Tug lightly, and if his head moves to the right, relax the pressure. Later, a light tug on the rein together with a bump of the left leg result in one step to the right, followed by a release of pressure. But some months down the road, the same stimuli should result in a 360-degree spin followed by release of pressure.

Psychological conditioning is the mental muscle behind the "knowing where you're going" principle and the sequences professional trainers use. There's no reason backyard horsemen shouldn't use it, too.

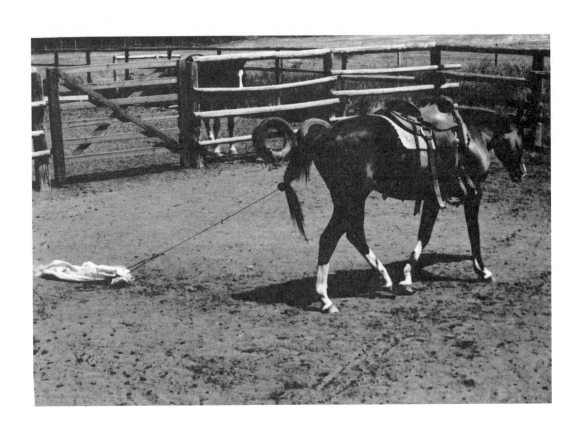

CHAPTER 9

Going to School

Once while horse shopping, I looked at two beautiful half-sibling colts. From what I could gather, the owner had adequate time and money to spend on horses. I was therefore curious about why the colts were for sale. It turned out that the owner was a pretty good trainer of bird dogs, and he'd thought that if he could train dogs, he could train horses. But, he'd quickly learned that wasn't true. He was getting nowhere with these colts and was worried about ruining them. At least he was wise enough to recognize his limitations.

Showing a two-year-old stallion in a local Western plea-sure class. Competence in fundamentals is more impor-tant than a blue ribbon.

Training horses isn't as easy as the professionals make it seem. Even for experienced riders, unaided first-time success is about as likely as making a good showing in the Indy 500 the first time we ever slide down into one of those funny cars. But whether out of vanity or ignorance or economic constraints, we backyard horsemen seem particularly prone to overlooking the gap between ourselves and the professionals. Although not all our efforts turn out to be fruitless, we do produce a lot of dead-end horses that never progress past the "sort-of-rideable" stage: horses that tolerate our bumbling enough to allow us to ride them, but with so many bad habits that further training is nearly impossible.

This chapter deals with the fundamentals that any saddle horse, Western or English, should know. These basic skills apply to mature horses that need some tuning up as well as to young horses that are just getting started. Even if you're one of the lucky few who happens to buy a horse so well trained he's "push-button," you still need to work with the horse to learn what he knows. Training, or schooling, is a necessary a part of any horse owner's life.

Professional Trainers

Doing our own nonprofessional training, whether with young or mature horses, we backyard owners can easily strike out on a half-dozen horses before finally schooling one well enough for him to be useful. You will learn from each encounter, but if the first or second horse of that half-dozen was, in retrospect, a perfectly good prospect, then you're already way behind in time and money.

Consequently, training is one aspect of ownership that requires caution about getting into do-it-yourself projects. The rationale is the same as for taking your car to a mechanic. Yes, it costs you money; but if you aren't a professional, the money you spend on tools and misused parts, and the time you spend doing the job several times over, may end up costing you more. And your results may be less than professional.

A good trainer can make more progress with your horse in a month than you might make in a year. A trainer knows the best sequence of lessons to use, as well as the theory and the practical aspects behind the sequence. A trainer puts in the daily hours of training that you may not be able to, and it is those well-planned steady hours that make a good horse.

It's true there are some trainers who don't do much of a job, and there are trainers who will only do careful work on the most able horses. There are trainers who are very good at starting young horses but not so savvy with specialized training, and vice versa. You can avoid problems by requesting a list of the trainer's clients and doing some phone work. You can also ask questions of other local horsemen. The effort required isn't nearly as troublesome as the problems you could have with a spoiled horse.

Be aware, though, that sometimes trainers get into trouble in ways they can't avoid. Some trainers can't afford to be selective about which horses they accept. Owners sometimes don't tell the whole story, which might be that the horse needs a lot of work just to correct the owner's mistakes. We can't judge trainers only on the basis of one or two situations that, according to the local rumor mill, turned out badly.

When you do send your horse out for training, it's a good idea to ride at the trainer's establishment under his or her tutelage several times before bringing the horse home. No matter how well you ride, you ride differently than the trainer. It helps you and the horse if you both understand the same cues. The trainer's directions should be followed to the letter, at least until you and your horse have made the lengthy transition to each other, and a trainer's advice is easier to follow if you're working together. The need to follow instructions is true not only for owners getting young horses started, but also for experienced horsemen who send a horse out for extensive specialty training.

When you ride with a trainer, both you and your horse progress. A good trainer will correct your mistakes immediately; have you practice and reinforce efficient, safe ways to ride; and spot your horse's quirks and tell you how to handle them. I've felt good about helping others make progress this way, and I've experienced such progress myself with the help of others. Some clinicians emphasize this "ride-with-the-trainer" portion of training, knowing full well that training the rider is often as important as training the horse.

There are also a host of clinicians offering educational opportunities that were simply unavailable prior to the popularity of the "soft horsemanship" trend. Of course, unless we're made of money, eventually the professional training must end. At that point the owner must be ready to apply, continue, or reinforce schooling at home. That's what the rest of this chapter is about.

Fundamentals

Some people think there are shortcuts to training—that if they just get on and rough the horse around enough he'll eventually hit on what they want, or that they can pet and feed and love the horse into doing what they want him to do. Forget both approaches. Training horses is a complex process of communication, presented in tiny pieces arranged in patterns the horse can assimilate without anger or fear.

Schooling a horse is science with a heart, and when accomplished well it is an art. Whether it's a quiet, safe ride through the woods or a high-speed steeplechase you're after, a solid foundation makes the difference.

The first thing you need to do is to picture the kind of behavior you want from your horse. For most horse owners without a great deal of experience, the image should be that of a quiet, well-mannered, seasoned pleasure horse. This ideal horse should have a light mouth, good ground manners, and a good attitude. He'll go wherever asked, keep going until asked to stop, and stop no matter how frantic the situation. He isn't perfect, but his quirks are such that you can live with them. Picture a horse that doesn't need to know the specific skills of any event but is quite capable of going on to more specific training. No matter what your ultimate goals are, this pleasure horse is where it all starts.

If your image of horsemanship is a wild gallop into the sunset, training your horse in the basics may not seem very important. But if you wish to have a quiet, well-mannered horse that will neither hurt nor embarrass you—and you should be wishing this—the training techniques that follow will be very helpful. Besides, they're fun to try, and simple enough that the novice will gain some confidence for later training. They're also free, and they'll give you a clearer understanding of what personality type your horse has—something well worth knowing.

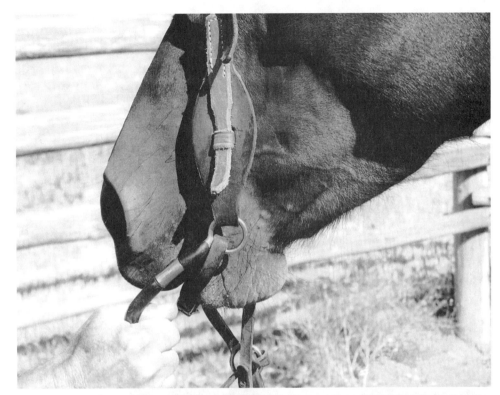

The simplest actions can demonstrate the difference between force and communication. We don't push (force) the horse into accepting the bit, possibly setting up a showdown.

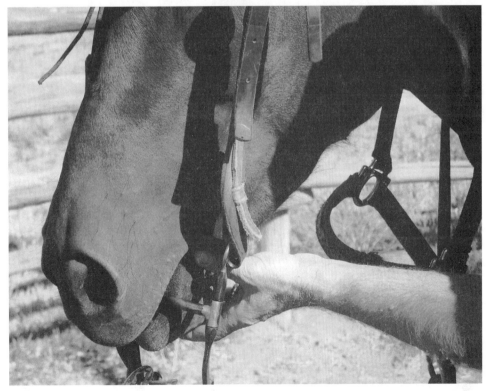

Instead, we ask (communicate), and soon the horse picks up the bit on his own.

Tying

Any horse should be trained to stand tied quietly for hours, and he should allow you to do any number of reasonable things to him while he is tied. He shouldn't pull back against the rope. He shouldn't prance, paw, nip, or kick. Teaching a horse to stand tied is the most basic of the basics—a good item with which to begin schooling both horse and rider.

When teaching your horse to stand tied, tie at a strong post or wall, using a halter knot with roughly 2 feet of slack, 4 to 5 feet above the ground. The halter, snap, and rope must be bull-strong. Two wraps around the post before tying the knot, or a half hitch around the halter knot's finished loop, ensures that, if the horse pulls back, he won't jam the knot. Tying is never done with light equipment, with bridle and reins, or with long slack, and never at a wire fence or at rails that could be pulled off the post if the horse jerks back.

While the horse is tied, pick up his feet, touch his ears, scratch his belly and private zones, bump against him, lean on him, and pull and brush his

Tying the halter knot. 1) The lead rope goes around the post from right to left and crosses under, forming the shape of the number 4. The free end is in the right hand.

2) A half-twist of the left hand forms a loop. The right hand forms a sharp bend (bight) and runs the bight through the loop.

112

3) The loop is tightened around the bight. Pulling on the dangling free end unties the knot.

4) The rope was double wrapped around the post before this halter knot was tied.

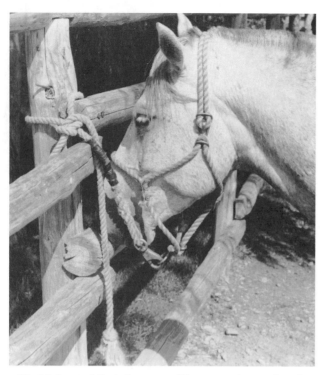

Tie high, and that rhymes with eye, *as in eye level. Also tie short, meaning without excess slack. Tie to posts rather than rails.*

This horse is tied long, and that rhymes with wrong.

tail—all while standing beside, never behind, the horse.

Some horses will tolerate all of this, and others won't. When you discover what your horse doesn't tolerate, do it until he does tolerate it. You might need to start out near the sensitive area and work toward it incrementally. Don't do anything to hurt him. Don't punish any misbehavior except nipping or kicking, and then only with one immediate slap. Don't surprise him, and don't assume he won't kick, bite, pull back, or smack you with his head. No matter how well you know him, safety comes first. Gradually increase tying time until he will stand quietly for two or three hours. This might take days of repetition in short sessions, but it works.

Two benefits happen here: one is that the horse learns to behave when tied, or you learn what he already knows; the other is that you discover whether you have one of those horses that really will never like being groomed. In the second instance, assuming other characteristics are workable, you just have to work around it.

A common fault in horses is the habit of pulling back violently against the halter rope. Several gimmicks can help break this habit, but as far as I know, none is foolproof. Don't leave the horse unattended during the first few sessions with any of these techniques.

The Be Nice Halter is a commercially made product that, as the horse pulls back, applies pressure to nerve areas on the head, threatening to squeeze his brains out his ears. It doesn't cut or bruise, but it hurts. The instant he quits, it loosens, immediately rewarding him for doing the right thing. In my experience, this halter is not a cure-all for a confirmed puller, but it is a good tool for a mature horse toying with the idea. One precaution: until a horse respects this halter enough to move forward when it squeezes him, he may react by rearing.

Homemade variations of the Be Nice Halter include a variety of war bridles fashioned from rope, applying pressure to nose, chin, and poll. If you can get the job done another way, however, don't use these devices. They are very severe, and they don't

114

One way to get a horse over his skitishness about ropes under the tail is to get him used to one. Allow him a couple of hours of this one day, a couple of hours the next day with the rope raised, and on the next day raise it up to the private zone.

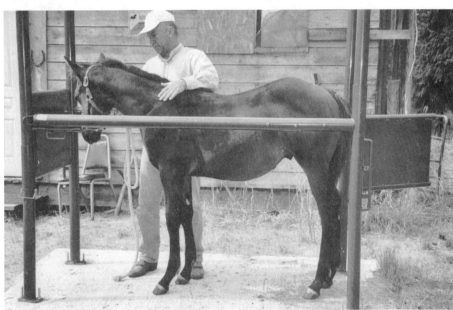

A pasture-raised weanling. This is his first time out of his weaning pen and his third actual contact with human touch. He's being rewarded for stepping onto the concrete floor of a "stock."

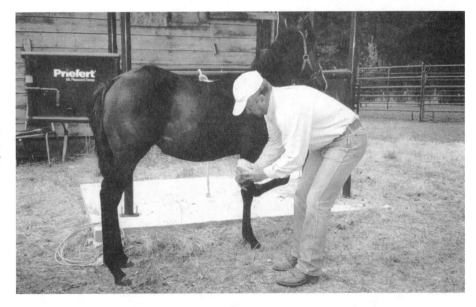

Same weanling, same session. He is still wary but is standing tied and picking up his feet.

115

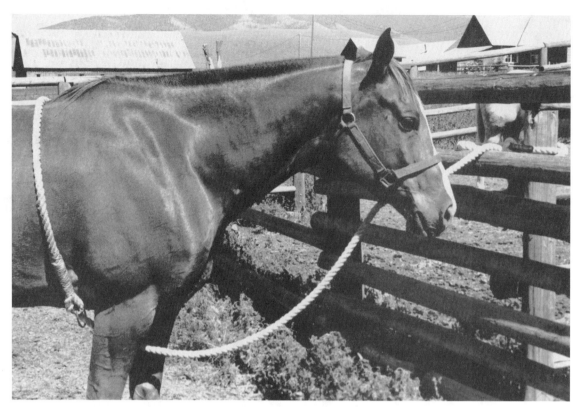

Ol' Gus models the way a good horse wears the belly loop.

loosen as easily as the Be Nice Halter. Never use a war bridle on a young or unschooled horse. Those horses need education, not punishment.

A second type of gimmick is a belly loop. Tie a stout lariat (I use my 1-inch cotton scotch-hobble rope) around the belly just behind the withers, using a honda or a bowline knot to prevent jamming. Run the free end between the front legs and through the tie ring of the halter, and tie to a stout post or wall at eye level, with about 3 feet of slack—a bit more than with normal tying in order to give room for some action. When the horse pulls against this, the rope around his belly gets uncomfortable. He may come forward in a rush, so be sure to stand back. Some horses may simply sit sullenly against it, in which case it is not the right tool for that horse. The one drawback I've seen with this item is that, even when it does work for a particular horse, the pulling problem is only cured while this gimmick is applied.

Though I've used these gimmicks, I prefer techniques that may prevent the problem from occurring in the first place. One preventative measure is to use flexible tie stations. This can be as inex-

pensive as a heavy inner tube hung over a stout post. Tie the halter to the inner tube rather than to the post, and when the horse pulls back, two things happen: one, he doesn't get that solid hit he's accustomed to fighting (and breaking); and two, the inner tube keeps pulling back at him. If he relents even the slightest degree, he gets that much relief.

There are also commercially built specialty tie rings that allow the halter rope to slip, but with considerable drag. These accomplish the same thing as a flexible tie station.

Using a heavy bungee cord instead of an inner tube works the same way, with emphasis on "heavy" because a horse will break the lighter bungees, and when they break, they become projectiles. I also like bungee halter ropes, which work according to the same principle as the flexible tie stations. I've used a bungee halter rope for tying a second horse to one I'm leading on trails, and I've had some success with it preventing pulling back.

The flexible gimmicks are intended for prevention, and thus they are especially useful for babies getting a first try at being tied, for two- or

Flexible tie station made with a heavy inner tube

three-year-olds just being started, and for older horses that haven't been handled in a long time. Moving to relieve pressure instead of pushing (pulling) against it is critically important for any training.

A variation of the flexible tie station is to teach tying with blind tie stations. This requires a barn or garage wall with a hole through it at tying height. Run a halter rope through the hole and tie it to a tire on the floor inside, leaving the usual 2 to 2½ feet of slack outside. When the horse steps back, he pulls the tire off the ground. Until the tire hits the wall, this arrangement won't stop him from pulling, but he will get tired (pardon the pun) of pulling against it, and he will learn that stepping ahead releases pressure.

Useful for both cure and prevention is the buddy system. When horses are tied with a buddy in a tie stall, they rarely become pullers. If you can arrange such a situation, tie two horses in a two-horse stall and feed them there, gradually increasing the length of time until the horses can be left tied overnight.

Finally, if we should be unfortunate enough to own a confirmed puller and the gimmickry isn't helping, there's one last hope. Don't tie at all. Instead, teach hobbling. It won't work for every situation, but it will help for many.

Hobbling

There's a good possibility that, if your horse has been worked by a professional, he has been hobbled during initial schooling. Unless you've seen that demonstrated, however, it's best to begin as if starting from scratch. As with any other new training, start in a strong corral. Be sure nothing in the corral dirt will injure the horse's knees. It's a good idea not to hobble horses under three years old, since hobbles can injure growing bones.

Soft latigo twist hobbles or cotton-rope hobbles are best for training. Anything of firm leather, synthetics, or buckled hobbles can bruise or burn. Horses might throw a fit at the first hobbling or two, but they seldom hurt themselves. To avoid too much trouble, put the hobbles on for only a few minutes the first several lessons. Do this two or three times a day for a couple of days, and soon your horse won't fight them at all. He might learn to gallop away in them, though, so remember they aren't foolproof.

The quick-and-dirty method is to just go for it while the horse is confined in a small corral with a soft surface. This method is used often, though I'm not recommending it. While the quick-and-dirty method generally works just fine for older or spoiled horses, there are better ways even for those. A horse standing quietly hobbled is one of those images which even inexperienced owners can and should break down into component parts.

Using a soft rope, first get the horse accustomed to rope being draped and dragged around his legs. Gradually start giving a tug-and-release action on the rope, first on one front foot and then on the other, first forward, then to the side. As soon as he gives, you release. Within a few minutes, this method can have a skittish horse relaxing or a quiet horse being led by the foot. Repeated sessions of this rope work are good warm-ups for hobbling. The horse will probably still struggle during the first round, but with enough warm-ups, he begins to understand: Don't fight the pressure.

You can do similar warm-ups on the rear legs. First get him accustomed to a rope draped over his back, then sliding softly back and forth around belly and flanks, then slithering down and around the back legs at the hock. He can kick, so you need to be positioned safely. With patience, in a few short sessions you can lead him backwards with tugs and releases, along with the verbal command "Back!"

An additional benefit is that familiarity with the rope around his legs can help forestall panic should the horse become entangled in rope or wire.

After the horse is accustomed to these warm-ups, introduce hobbling gradually. For the first few sessions, put the hobbles on (front legs, of course) just for a minute or two. Keep some control by maintaining a hold on the halter rope. The moment he tries to move, calm him and remove the hobbles. Wait a few minutes and do it again, repeatedly. In this way, the horse learns to tolerate longer and longer periods with the hobbles on.

The scotch hobble starts with a nonslip loop around the base of the neck. The rope then runs back around the rear pastern and back to the neck loop, where it is tied off with a quick-release halter

Twist hobbles are good for teaching your horse to stand for anything. Place them up on the legs as shown, and they usually settle just above the hooves. These could have been one twist tighter.

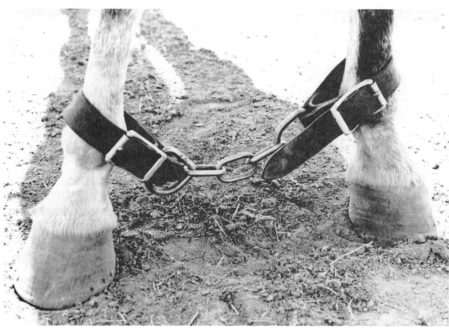

Chain hobbles, or grazing hobbles, are good for the hobble-broke horse. These allow tiny steps and thus allow quiet grazing in your backyard or out in the wilderness. The pair shown is too big for the pony and should be pulled a couple of holes tighter.

118

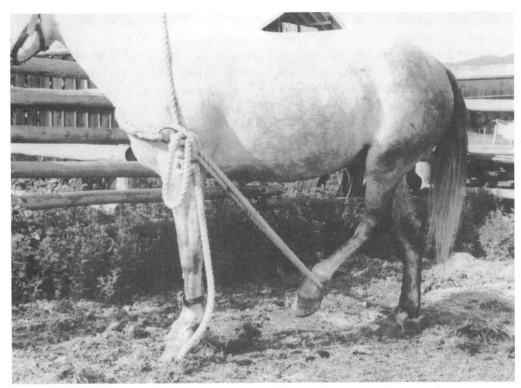

The ancient and honorable scotch hobble

knot. Use a cinch around the pastern if you don't have a thick cotton rope. Scotch hobbling is almost guaranteed to cause a fight at first, because horses fear anything that might prevent flight, so the more gradually you introduce it, the better. Start with a lot of warm-ups, including just lifting the hoof with the rope.

No matter how many warm-ups you do, most horses have to figure this thing out with some kicking. Don't get overwhelmed with pity; let your horse learn. If you do bail him out, hold off until he's quit kicking for a moment so that the lesson they learn is plain: stand still, and the rope comes off.

When a horse tolerates both regular and scotch hobbles, you can take it one step further and accustom him to a sideline hobble, front to rear. This is handy in backcountry. A regular hobble might make a horse travel slowly, but he can still travel miles. In a sideline hobble, he might still travel, but the distance will measure in yards.

Restraining a horse with hobbles and halters is sound psychology because it teaches the horse to control his flight response. When he can't run, he thinks, and sooner or later it dawns on him that there is a connection between the rope in your

hands and his helplessness. You are communicating that you are the boss hoss.

While hobbles and scotch hobbles are often used only on green horses, they are also good for well-broke horses. Hobbling is a great aid for doctoring minor wounds. Hobble the front and scotch hobble one rear, and you can cleanse and medicate all you want, if the horse is accustomed to restraint. (For wounds that really hurt, of course, we need a vet to sedate the horse. The last thing we need is further wounding caused by pain-driven struggles.) When you want to put on a load the horse doesn't like, or when he's restless during shoeing or grooming or saddling, scotch hobble him. Out in the backcountry, a hobbled horse can be tied to a tree without the problem of pawing around the tree roots.

Longeing and Driving

Longeing is the technique of working a horse in circles on the end of a line, or in a round corral with no line at all. There are many levels of schooling that can be accomplished with longeing, but backyard horsemen most frequently use it as a tool to calm a nervous horse. It's also a tool to teach a

119

reluctant horse to obey while we avoid the dangers that come from being mounted, though when overused it can just make a horse mad. It's often used as part of starting young horses and then dropped, but it can be useful later on and for that reason should be repeated from time to time.

To really learn how useful longeing can be, study the work of clinician Pat Parelli. In my opinion, he has thought it through and applied it better than almost anyone else.

For the first session or two of longeing on a line, start with a regular halter rope and a stock whip (or just an old fishing rod). Step back toward the horse's rump and away from his body perhaps 3 feet. The cue for the horse to begin moving in circles is the command "Walk" and a tap on the rump from the whip. Success is mainly a matter of where you stand in relation to the horse's body. If you step into what he perceives as his line of travel, he tries to stop, or turn toward you, or turn away. If you maintain a position more toward his rear end, he thinks he's getting away and continues to move ahead into what he perceives as free space. The same is true with free-longeing in a round corral. Move just slightly into his travel and he stops. Move toward his rear end, and he goes forward.

Some horses start right out, while others step away from you or turn to face you. Patience is key. Keep at the job from both sides until the horse circles freely at the end of the halter rope. With most horses, a rough longeing job can be accomplished in the first five minutes. After two or three times a day for a couple of days, you'll get beyond the accidental stage and into the learned stage. As soon as longeing is working at all, increase the line length to 20 or 25 feet.

Horses are incredibly perceptive about body language. When you're standing in the center of his circle, he's eyeing you, and your every move has him wondering, "What does that mean? What should I do now?" If you make the right moves, within just a few sessions you can stop and start him simply by raising a hand in conjunction with verbal commands. A hand in his line of travel, along with the verbal command "Whoa," means stop. A hand toward his rear means go. At first these motions are exaggerated, but soon they get to be subdued, even subtle. It isn't magic, and it isn't romantic, soul-to-soul horse whispering. It's an animal tuned to his environment and reacting to signals he understands.

I teach a green horse "Walk," "Trot," and "Whoa" while longeing. I like to have the horse understanding enough that I can get him started and then just stand there while he continues moving until the next command. With yearlings or weanlings, however, I don't push it for more than a few minutes. Repeated circling, especially at speed, could cause injuries. Besides, it's boring. Why make a baby hate his first serious lessons?

One practical use of longeing is teaching a horse to travel through obstacles, such as parallel rows of small logs (cavaletti work), sheets of plastic or tarp, rows of tires, narrow spaces between obstacles, and low jumps. As with other training, start longeing over obstacles in a strong, safe corral; use communication rather than force; and gradually introduce new expectations in small increments. After one or two quick taps in the early lessons, you seldom need to do more with the whip than wave it or slap the ground with it. If you teach the horse to fear the whip by smacking him with it, you're forcing, not communicating. You're also being abusive. You want him brave, smart, and willing, not fearful or angry.

You can use longeing with a saddled horse to help make him "bomb-proof" (unperturbed by noises, unfamiliar objects, or scary situations). Start by putting a couple of small stones in two plastic milk jugs. Tie the jugs together with about 5 feet of baler twine, with a 6-inch loop in the middle of the twine. Hang one jug on either side of the horse and the loop over the saddle horn, then longe him. When he can stand this rattling, he's a better horse. Do the same with empty feed sacks hanging from the twine instead of, or in addition to, the milk jugs. Put a slicker or sheet of plastic over the horse and longe him some more. This will save trouble when you need to ride wearing a slicker. Again, all of these training sessions must introduce your intentions incrementally; never just lash it all together and step back to see what happens.

You can take longeing even further by dragging a rope from the saddle horn, eventually adding an empty feed sack, a stick of wood, an old tire—again, moving incrementally and repeatedly over the course of a week or more in a strong corral. There's no guarantee that a horse with this training will never spook out on a trail or in an unfamiliar arena, of course, but he'll be more bomb-proof than the horse that has had no such work.

No self-respecting horse would voluntarily walk through old truck tires, but if a longe line is involved, one has to do what one has to do.

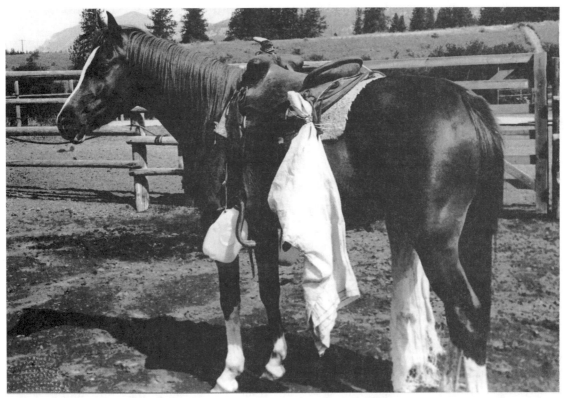

Stones rattle in the milk jugs, and sacks rustle in the breeze, but after a few hours it's all old hat.

The ol' tire-packin' trick. Do this in a good corral, and only after plenty of other bomb-proofing work.

Once the horse has been longeing for a while and has become somewhat bomb-proof, you can teach him to drive. After a few minutes of longeing, stop and clip long lines to the halter; run these back through the stirrups, one on each side. Tie the stirrups down to the cinch with a short string for this training, but don't forget that you've done so. For horses accustomed to the bit, you can tie a piece of bicycle inner tube between bit and lines to absorb shock until driving gets more refined.

Step back and begin longeing again, using the inside line as your longe line. While the horse is circling, begin tightening the circle by pulling the inside rein with light tugs, never long, steady pulls. When the horse moves at a walk, tug the opposite line and turn him in the other direction. Stop him with a voice command and alternating tugs on both lines. Teach him to back up with the voice command "Back" and alternating tugs. Expect only a step or two for the first few tries. Be patient, calm, and gentle. Once you are confident that the horse is responding more out of understanding than luck, take him into a bigger arena or pasture and drive some more.

Driving teaches control, and it can have uses in later training. If you ever decide to have the horse pull a buggy, he's already accomplished the driving basics. For pulling practice, driving is more practi-

cal than longeing because the object being pulled is in the correct position relative to the horse. After a long winter off, you can start with longeing and driving to tune the horse a little before that first ride of the season. And a young horse trained to drive has learned to turn left, turn right, stop, back, and obey voice commands, all before you climb into the saddle.

Loading

It's nearly impossible nowadays to do any amount of riding without also doing some trailering, and it's nearly impossible to find an owner who hasn't had trailering troubles with at least one horse.

Let's take Elmo, for example. When I lead Elmo, a 12-year-old gelding, into my stock trailer, he doesn't hesitate, because he learned long ago that the trailer means taking a rest. However, if I haul him alone, he paws and weaves frantically the whole time we're moving. And when I loan him to others, he's a loading disaster. In his mind, there's only one trailer in the world that is safe, and that's a 16-foot, surface-rusted, 1984 slat-sided Chapparal trailer from Quitman, Arkansas, inhabited by at least one other horse.

The fact that any horse will ever load into a trailer is testimony to equine adaptability, because it's noisy, unstable, and cramped; he can't adequately scan his environment; and he sure as heck can't flee. The smaller the trailer, the more likelihood there is of trouble both loading and traveling. A trailer big enough to allow a horse to turn around and walk out, instead of backing out, eliminates one major source of fear for the horse. To understand that fear, stand at the top of a flight of stairs and back yourself down, looking straight ahead, imagining that you don't know how many steps there are, or whether the bottom step actually touches Mother Earth.

But horses are adaptable, and they can, like humans, learn to overcome their fears. The main reason Elmo doesn't load for other people is that I haven't taken the time to work him at it. Unlike Elmo, your horse should load and unload easily from any vehicle. If you bought an older horse, he probably already does. But if he doesn't load easily, there are some training techniques you can try.

Too often, horse owners skip all the small, sequential steps of training and instead leap immediately to the ultimate goal of the horse inside the trailer, calmly enjoying the ride. A better method is

to train the horse to load long before you're desperate. Don't be fooled by the fact that somebody got the horse to your home. There may have been a battle, or even a handful of tranquilizers.

If you check around with other owners, you are likely to find gimmicks that involve force. I don't recommend them, not because they don't work, but because they are dangerous, and they tend to be applied too quickly. I strongly urge readers to pick up Pat Parelli's videos or CDs on trailer loading. One of the most important things Parelli highlights is that you don't coax, trick, or force the horse to load; you train him. And if you've done the right groundwork with tying, leading, and longeing, they are all applicable to teaching the horse to load.

During loading, trouble often begins with a hesitation right at the point of entry. The owner mistakes this for the beginning of a refusal, and smacks the horse on the rump. In the horse's mind, that sequence goes something like this: "Yo! Dark in there. I'm going to hold up right here and check this out . . . Ouch! I knew there was a reason to be afraid!"

Horses should load so easily that all you have to do is step out of their way.

123

That hesitation often isn't a refusal at all. It's what the horse needs to do to figure out the next step. If he paws the rack, if he sniffs the floor, or if he makes false starts but doesn't quite jump in, he probably will cooperate, but he just has to worry for a while yet. Give the horse time to figure it out, and most of the time, he will. That might take time, but nothing like the time we spend if you have to fight the horse every time you want to load him.

Sometimes a hesitant horse just needs you to pick up a front foot and place it on the trailer floor for him. Once he holds it there, coax him with a clucking or kissing sound and he'll probably put the other front foot in for himself. That's big progress by itself. If he backs out, let him. There's no sense getting him scared at this point. Start him again. This might take twenty tries. Let it happen. Loading a horse into the trailer is as much a matter of human self-control as it is of controlling the horse's actions.

A hesitant horse that has his front half inside will often finish the task if you have a lariat loop around his hindquarters. Give a tug and up he goes.

Or watch what racetrack attendants do to horses that hesitate at the starting gate. Once the head is in, two attendants lock hands under the rump and give a pull. It's the same idea, though for obvious reasons dangerous to you. Still, it's a handy idea, at least for weanlings or yearlings who just haven't figured out the second step.

Once it becomes obvious that a hesitation is an actual refusal, another technique that works at the hesitation point is to place a rope around the back of the front legs, keeping an end in each hand, and from a position up in the trailer, alternately tug left and right, releasing at any sign of compliance. This works better, of course, if you've done some of the rope work mentioned in the section on hobbling. Being prompted to move his front legs rather than being provoked from behind seems to break the pattern of refusal. Be careful, because some horses might jump on top of you when they feel the rope.

When you find a technique that works and finally get your horse into the trailer, don't hit the road immediately. Give the horse a minute to settle, reward him with a handful of grain or a brief massage. Then take him out, give a breather, put him back in, take him out, repeating a half-dozen times, praising the heck out of him when he does it right. Ideally, you would do this routine three or four days in a row before actually driving with the horse.

Another thing to avoid, once you get the horse inside, is immediately tying him. So often an inexperienced horse tries to get back out and, unaware that he has been tied, panics. Another possible problem is that when you whip that knot into place and step away, the horse, unaware that he has been tied, thinks he's supposed to step back with you. Either way, terrible thrashings result, dangerous to both owner and horse. I learned this the hard way

Trailering Safety

- Never be inside a trailer in a position you can't escape from.

- Never position yourself where you might be kicked.

- Always check trailers for protruding objects.

- Always fully trailer-train the horse before traveling any significant distance from home. (Corollary: you can't get home if the horse won't load.)

- Always drive defensively, more slowly than normal, braking and cornering more slowly, too.

- On long trips, give the horse a break every three hours, at least by stopping, and if possible by unloading him and walking him around.

A safe and gentle way to teach your horse to load: Position the trailer securely in a small corral and leave it open. Put the food and water inside, and sooner or later the horse loads himself.

A filly learns to cross a "bridge." Early one morning a bridge appears between the pen with water and the pen with hay. By the next morning, the filly will have crossed it a dozen times.

125

while trapped in a narrow trailer with a quiet mare who didn't know I had tied her. She beat me black and blue with her head as she tried to fall out backwards, and the only reason I got away was that this was an old topless trailer. I finally squirted up, over, and out.

In standard two-horse trailers, *always* snap the butt chains *before* tying the head. For unloading, release the head *before* releasing the butt chains. In a wider slant-load or stock trailer, the horse's fanny is against the sidewall. That usually prevents

backing motion, but even so it's wise to put up a hand, command "Whoa!" and pause long enough to make sure the horse is settled in his position.

One way to ease a horse into loading is to let the horse train himself. Park your vehicle where the horse can get in it by himself, and leave it there for a few days. Then put the horse's only food and water supply in plain sight inside the vehicle. It takes patience, and the horse might grow pretty hungry before he cooperates, but when he does the training is painless and permanent. (This technique can

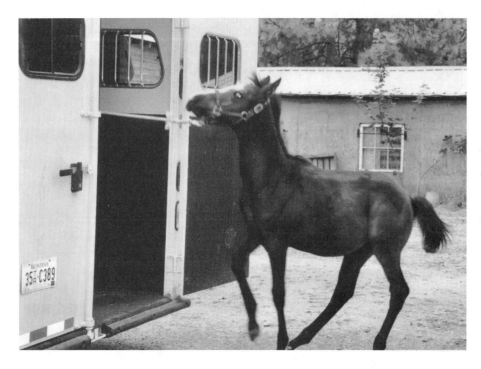

The stiff neck and the whites of the eyes signal fear at being introduced to a trailer, but introduction is a lot easier with a 400-pound youngster than with a 1,200-pound adult.

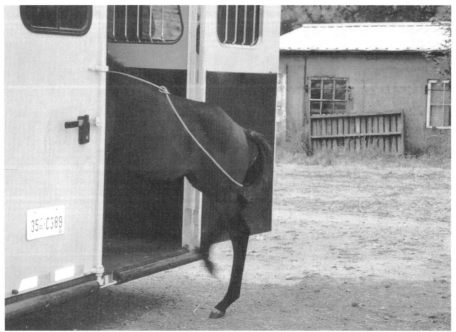

Patience, repetition, reward, and a "butt rope" combine to teach calm loading and unloading. After an entire year of no handling, this youngster, having grown many hundred pounds and reaching 15 hands tall, loaded quietly into a different trailer and rode calmly from Montana to Michigan.

be adapted to training your horse to negotiate all sorts of obstacles.)

However, this doesn't work with long, narrow trailers. The big stock trailers work because the horse can turn around inside, and a short, two-horse trailer works because long before the horse is fully inside, he'll have backed out many times. This method still requires some transition work: the horse loading himself isn't the same as being loaded by a human on command. But it is a good start.

An acquaintance of mine bought an older mare who loaded well but was really agitated once inside his new, two-horse slant-load trailer. The only thing we could figure out was that the angled front position against the full-height wall was just too confining for her; she was accustomed only to large stock trailers. In this case, we made progress by removing the dividers. With more space, she settled down nicely.

If you are patient, if you think far enough ahead to prevent injury, and if you reinforce good behavior, most horses will soon load cheerfully when you lead them to the opening and toss the halter rope over their shoulders as they step in. Most will soon back out carefully if you tug on their tails (in a narrow two-horse trailer) or will turn and step out cautiously (in a wider trailer).

Even with well-trained horses, however, accidents can happen while loading or unloading. An experienced horseman who lives near me, unloading a well-broke cow horse, stood helpless when the horse put one hind leg under the trailer too far, then sat down, flipped over backwards, and smashed his head on the ground. The horse died in a matter of minutes. The owner had done everything correctly. The gentlest horses sometimes panic, and they can kick, strike, stomp on you, or beat you senseless with their thrashing heads. Never be inside a vehicle in a position you can't easily escape from. If you're in a dangerous situation, don't hesitate; get out any way you can.

Mounting

Mounting is a moment of vulnerability for any rider, and when it's done badly, that vulnerability multiplies. It's further compounded by a perverse law: the shorter the rider, the shorter (and therefore higher up) the stirrups. Two things make mounting safer: the horse's behavior, and the rider's methods.

The well-schooled horse stands still while you mount and adjust yourself in the saddle. After you're mounted, he waits for a signal before moving. Teaching a horse to stand for mounting requires patience and repetition, and it is much easier if he already knows how to stand restrained. It also helps to be sneaky—for instance, mounting in a corral corner where the horse can't move away.

Each time you mount, give the verbal command "Whoa," and demand absolute stillness from the horse. Demanding doesn't mean violence; it means a firm voice and a light tug-and-release on the bit (never a steady pull) if he moves. It requires being patient enough not to mount until the horse is still. Step aboard only when the horse is stationary. You can apply an unpleasant pressure by bringing the horse around in a tight circle a couple of times and attempt the mount again when the horse is allowed to stop. If he moves, circle him. If he stands, remove that pressure.

Mounting also takes some skill and coordination on the part of the rider. I've seen people so clumsy in mounting that they're pulling the horse off balance, pulling the saddle down, or hanging backwards from the reins—even yanking the horse into a half rear, and then punishing him for it. Especially for shorter people on taller horses, mounting

Safety Tips for Mounting

•Hold the reins in your left hand so you can manipulate them any time, even mid-mount. This means that your left hand grasps the mane rather than part of the saddle.

•Keep enough slack in the reins so that the horse doesn't get signaled to back up (or worse, rear).

•Bounce from your ground foot to move quickly into the saddle, rather than depending upon arm strength to pull yourself up.

•Catch the free stirrup with a toe instead of leaning over to adjust it by hand.

Suicide mount. The rider is off balance, has no rein control, and will pull the saddle off the horse by dragging on the cantle.

Preparing to make a controlled mount (the look of concentration is optional) using one acceptable Western method of mounting. Rider is balanced, can pick up the reins for control mid-mount, and, with a bit of bounce from the ground foot, pulls almost weightlessly into the saddle.

should be practiced until it is quick and confident. A saddle lashed to a dummy or a 5-foot corral rail can be used for practice. Given my own five-and-a-half-foot stature, I've taken to using a 12-inch block for the first mountings on young horses, just so I don't make any mistakes at that critical time.

Riding

The well-broke horse is, for the purposes of this book, one that is a pleasure to ride on trails and in the training arena, but is not necessarily ready for competition in pleasure classes. The well-broke horse stands while you mount and doesn't move until you ask. When you do ask, the lightest of signals—a bump with your leg or just a touch of the spur—brings a response. He walks willingly and energetically and he doesn't jig or prance, at least after he's limbered up.

The well-broke horse doesn't necessarily neck rein, though he may be starting to learn this at slower gaits. However, his mouth responds to direct reining even at a gallop. While standing still, he'll follow the slightest touches, even just the weight of a pinky finger. His reining foundations are solid,

and he may still be unspecialized in either English or Western.

The well-broke horse will hold a slow jog or an extended trot, whichever the rider asks, without trying to break away at a run or drop down to a walk. He'll also gallop (lope) quietly on a loose rein. He won't get excited while loping; he will hold his speed. He may not know flying lead changes, but he can be moved into correct leads most of the time. Turned loose to really run, he can be brought back to the lope, the trot, and then the walk without heavy-handed pulling. He doesn't have an instant stop, but he definitely understands coming to a halt from any speed.

The well-broke horse has some understanding of the leg aids. He can be backed and side-passed smoothly. While turning, he crosses his front feet rather than simply pivoting in the middle with the hind quarters doing all the moving.

The well-broke horse has enough experience not to panic at traffic, dogs, hay bales in the distance, the sound of noisy rain gear, or the feel of rope around his feet or under his tail. He won't forget his manners every time he sees an unfamiliar horse, or

128

when he's asked to pony an unfamiliar horse. Even when he is frightened or suspicious, he's willing to pay attention to the rider's commands. (Some horses, even well-broke and experienced, always protect themselves first in an emergency. These may never become good horses for beginners or children.)

The well-broke horse will try new things without fighting them, assuming the rider isn't jumping too far ahead of the horse's level of experience. He may stumble over the cavalettis and hesitate at the first jump, but he won't shy off, buck, or run away. In activities where he has to put in long days, he resigns himself to the task and takes his rest breaks quietly. He can trailer to a backcountry ride one day and a pleasure-horse clinic the next, work in his own home pens the third day, and herd cattle the fourth day, and he will perform sensibly, though not necessarily skillfully, all four days.

How does a horse attain these skills? Through experience, of course. Trouble and frustration are guaranteed before you can call your horse well broke. And even well-mannered pleasure horses annoy their riders at times. This is normal. Humans can't control all the variables of horse psychology and environment that might interact to cause prob-

lems. But, as much as possible, experience must be gained under controlled circumstances. This can make the difference between annoyance and disaster.

Take your horse frequently to unfamiliar horses or new surroundings. Set up minor obstacles for him at home and change his surroundings often— if nothing else, hang a tarp near his water, or set a cardboard box near his grain. Ride him to, through, and around things he doesn't like. Find out where he is silly and approach that point over and over, incrementally pushing the limits. These may not be enjoyable rides, but they don't have to be long. They will certainly be valuable.

All of this takes time, slowly adding the new and repeating the old over dozens of sessions, experiencing results and setbacks, and going at it again. The younger your horse, the more of this kind of riding he'll need. Don't resent this time; it's part of what you volunteered for when you decided to get a horse.

You may have to "ride through the troubles," says an acquaintance of mine, a skilled team roper and cutter. He told me of a soured rope horse brought to him who would charge back to the starting box after finishing a run. The habit had become an

The author rides an inexperienced five-year-old while leading an older, seasoned pack-and-saddle horse, which is leading an inexperienced packhorse. The older horse is a calming influence on the other two.

129

unpredictable, blind dash, so dangerous that when the horse did it he scared his riders into quitting for the day. The horse had learned how to get out of work. My acquaintance approached the problem with persistence and patience. Instead of jerking back, getting a harsher bit, whipping the horse's face, or yanking the horse into wild circling—the usual desperate measures for this kind of behavior—he just spurred the horse on to top speed back to the start box whether the horse had tried to bolt or not. By the sixty-third steer, the horse was walking quietly back to the box, and the lesson was permanent. For that horse, the fun had come in taking control of the situation. The learning came when the horse was fatigued physically enough to dread the return run, at which time he figured out that walking to the box could be a moment of relief from the pressure of working.

While there may be times you have to ride through the troubles, experienced horsemen know there are other times when you have to just get off the horse's back, perhaps literally, certainly figuratively. I received a letter once from a young lady seeking advice. She was getting frustrated with her two-year-old stallion's unruly responses to her care. She wasn't riding him yet, but she did take him out of his stall and longe-line him daily for an hour or so, then worked him as a competitive halter prospect (perfect manners, perfect posing), disciplining him any time he was out of line. And yet he was becoming more and more unruly. My feeling was that this cooped-up young horse, probably well fed and certainly beginning to feel his hormones, was just plain sick of being dinged with for hours every day. Since he wasn't old enough to be ridden enough miles to calm him physically and mentally, my advice was simple: geld him and turn him out to pasture until next year. In other words, get off his back. Just let him be a horse for a while.

Between these two extreme examples fall most of the troubles encountered at the foundational, pleasure-horse level. For example, there might be a spot in an arena that seems to spook your horse. Riding past that spot, particularly at a canter, you are vulnerable. A fast sashay sideways can unseat almost any rider. But in this case you need to ride through the trouble, not avoid it, taking the horse to the spooky spot slowly, gradually coming closer to it over several attempts if necessary. Don't punish him for spooking, since that only reinforces his fear. Once he's going there at a walk (however

floppy that walk might be) work him hard somewhere else, then walk him back to the spot for a rest. Gradually move your cantering circles closer to the bad spot. If he spooks off, ride it out and start over. Even if a horse needs sixty-three repetitions to lose his fear, the rider does it, and doesn't get mad. It's training, not trouble.

Time and time again, I've heard people say things such as, "I'd love to go along, but I've never loaded my horses," or "He won't stand tied, so I can't bring him," or "She won't leave other horses, so I can't use her." If an owner can't get the most basic performance out of a horse, why have a horse at all? Such dilemmas illustrate the difference between an owner and a horseman. An owner might leave the horse unused, or dump a horse into events he isn't ready for. A horseman builds a horse's skills and confidence piece by piece, starting with sound foundations. Even when the work isn't completely polished, the horseman and his horse perform with class.

The Well-Broke Rider

The master rider uses hands, legs, and seat position in complex and subtle combinations to communicate complex and subtle performance expectations. Reaching this level of ability is an admirable goal for any rider.

A primitive idea in horse training is that it takes strength to hold a horse, and while this might be true in the occasional rough-and-tumble moment, in most cases strength can actually work against communication with the horse. Men more than women tend to want to power on through. A good rider uses light hands, avoiding the temptation to apply any more than the slightest force necessary to signal. Too much strength at a horse's mouth teaches him to fight. The biggest, meanest bit in the world won't stop the horse that hasn't been schooled to stop. Jerking the horse's head around at every turn won't teach a fast or controlled turn. A light hand is especially necessary with young horses to avoid bad habits and tough mouths. Learn to hint with the reins, not demand.

Somewhere I've read that as a test of feel on the reins, old-time California horsemen would attach reins to bit with a horsehair. If the hair broke, the pull was too hard. That may be an extreme practice (it was practiced on highly schooled horses), but it illustrates the subtlety that can be expected of skilled hands.

Related to the need for light hands is the need to use light bits—not necessarily light in weight, but light in terms of severity. The plain snaffle mouthpiece, perhaps with the addition of a running martingale, will serve for most training purposes—if the rider stays light handed. There is no need to start horses in harsh bits out of some misguided fear of runaways or buckers. A horse can be started in a snaffle, or a hackamore bosal, or a caveson, or a side-pull, or even just a rope halter in order to keep the mouth light. Teach him what you can without any metal-to-mouth pressure, and he'll be a better horse for it.

The more situations in which snaffles or hackamore/caveson variations are used, the more likely it is that the rider will develop educated hands. That is because these tools are designed for two-handed reining, and using both hands is essential for educating the horse's mouth. As the rider becomes adept at using both hands, he or she should also become adept at hinting or suggesting with a tug-and-release motion rather than with steady pulls. Tug-and-release communicates, while steady pulling just gives the horse something to pull back against, both physically and mentally.

The legs are the second major method of communication in riding. The well-broke rider learns to use the leg aids, meaning that the rider's lower leg controls the rear half of the horse. A bump from the rider's lower leg on the horse's right side says the rear half of the horse must move left, and vice versa. Bumping with both legs signals the horse to tuck his hind legs up under him, giving him balance to move in any direction. Eventually, the bumping becomes so light that it's an almost imperceptible squeeze. While the leg aids are something taught to the horse, they must first be mastered by the rider. When they become automatic, the rider has made a significant step up in skill.

The skilled rider remembers that complex tasks must be broken into simpler parts, and then gradually recombined into a whole. When you learn to lightly coordinate hands and legs to put the horse exactly where you want him, you move into a whole new dimension of riding. If you can't work directly with clinicians or trainers, you must rely on books and videos, studying them over and over until you know through the feel of the saddle and reins, "That's what that writer is talking about!"

With hands low, the pinky finger suggests a turn.

While I am firmly committed to the wisdom of purchasing well-broke horses for owners with even considerable horse experience, the reality is that many people will buy younger or partially trained horses simply because the well-broke ones aren't available or affordable.

Every horse is different, but there are some common behavioral characteristics and reasonable training expectations for young horses in the process of becoming well broke. Professionals may move training along at a faster pace than suggested here; they have money involved, and if a horse cannot take the mental pressure of high-powered training, he is simply rejected. We backyard owners have the luxury of allowing young horses the time they need to become mentally and physically mature.

THE TWO-YEAR-OLD

Characteristics: The two-year-old exhibits much silly behavior, is unpredictable, curious, and moody. Flight responses are immediate and thoughtless. Under heavy work the two-year-old gives up quickly, and if overworked may respond by becoming sullen or angry. With short lessons, long rest periods, and occasional reinforcement sessions, the two-year-old can learn a great deal. Physical and mental fatigue should be strictly avoided.

Training Expectations:

• Trailer loading

• Standing quietly while tied alone

• Standing quietly while tied for grooming, hoof care, and first set of shoes

• Longeing at walk and trot; learning voice commands *Walk*, *Trot*, *Whoa*, *Back*

• Trailing quietly (with or without saddle) behind a seasoned horse for outside experience

• Carrying lightweight riders

• Approximately thirty nonconsecutive days of riding, including:

  • walking and trotting on voice command with unsophisticated leg aids

  • some light cantering in an arena or open fields—just enough to be comfortable at speed

  • standing still for mounting and for up to two minutes while mounted

  • willing response to direct rein

  • backing four or five steps willingly

  • quiet but aggressive walking on mild trails, up to two hours

  • familiarity with traffic, bridges, dogs, etc., under controlled situations

THE THREE-YEAR-OLD

Characteristics: The three-year-old is somewhat more stable than a two-year-old, but is still flighty. The three-year-old is still quite easily overtaxed mentally, though stronger physically. Some three-year-olds are filling out significantly, others are still spindly. Mares are maturing sexually and might be moodier to work with at this age than at four or older. Because a three-year-old can take more physical exertion than a two-year-old, some trainers prefer not to start until the third year, at which time steady schooling can proceed without having to back up and review previous training.

Training Expectations:

•Review of previous training if horse was started as a two-year-old

•Manners are still more important than event training

•Hobbles and scotch hobbles

•Full season of light work: occasional travel to shows or trails, showing in amateur classes, and similar activities that do not stress the horse physically

•Cantering on correct leads

•Beginning of neck reining, but emphasis is on soft, direct reining

•Practice at packing light loads or driving in a buggy

THE FOUR-YEAR-OLD

Characteristics: The four-year-old is beginning to understand his strength and may be practicing some assertiveness in the herd. Handled incorrectly, the four-year-old may offer less flight and more fight than younger horses. In either flight or fight, the four-year-old is more dangerous because of attitude and strength. Reactions are becoming predictable and patterned. The four-year-old is much stronger mentally, and thus less affected by strenuous exercise. Handled correctly, the four-year-old becomes a relatively reliable picture of what the rest of his life will be, although the four-year-old is still not to be treated as a mature horse, either physically or mentally.

Training Expectations:

•Review of previous training

•Basic training in specialties:

♦Roping: could include box training, running stock, roping small calves, all on soft surfaces, avoiding hard stops and turns

♦Jumping: could include cavalettis, low jumps

♦Events where slow work can go on for extended times; strenuous events such as endurance riding should be avoided

•Plenty of trail rides and other pleasure rides

•Could be campaigned on show circuit for events requiring mild exertion

THE FIVE-YEAR-OLD

Characteristics: The five-year-old is at the front edge of about ten prime years. If the five-year-old has been treated right, he is mature physically and mentally, lacking only the repeated experiences which finally mean "seasoned." The five-year-old may still grow in strength and bulk for a year or two, though imperceptibly. A five-year-old is predictable, for better or worse.

Training Expectations:

•Review of previous training

•Serious competition training, but with extended rest periods, plus sessions of slow work interspersed with any "hot" work

•Still should not be seriously campaigned in the most strenuous events, such as endurance riding, rodeo, polo, jumping, or three-day eventing

CHAPTER 10

Getting In on the Action

An old adage says there's something about the outside of a horse that's good for the inside of a human. But that adage doesn't hold true if you just throw horses their hay and watch them age. If you don't use them, they don't progress, and neither do you. If you set goals, get involved, and make progress, you'll have a better horse, and you'll be a better horseman. So saddle up and get going. Horses aren't supposed to be yard candy.

Many activities, some informal and some organized and competitive, are available to horse owners. This chapter briefly introduces some of the ones more popular among backyard horsemen.

Pleasure Riding

Moving about forty pairs of range cows, I happened to be riding beside the owner and his roping buddy, both much younger than I, both the latest in several generations of ranch folks. We'd been at it for several hours and the cattle had figured out they were headed home, so they traveled almost independently. We humans were just riding and jawing on a mild October afternoon. We were talking about how so many ranches have switched to ATVs, which, of course, are more efficient than horses in a lot of situations. "But they miss out on this," said the cattle owner. He was referring to the pleasure riding we were doing at the moment. We were virtual strangers, from different generations, in different professions, who happened to be together for one day, with no real purpose except to follow these cows, and with nothing really in common except enjoyment of the outdoors and the horses.

Pleasure riding is touted as the single biggest reason people own horses, not only because it is enjoyable, but because it is simple. Pleasure riding attracts all sorts of riders: young and old, rich and poor, lazy and ambitious. It's the activity most

beginners start with. But it isn't just a matter of climbing aboard any available horse. The horse's behavior will make or break "pleasure," and good behavior must be learned piece by piece. I hope I've covered that ground adequately.

Good pleasure horses provide enjoyable trail riding. For readers who haven't seen them elsewhere, here are some simple trail rules, rooted in human and equine psychology:

1. Stay behind the leader.

2. Stay at a walk, but keep up. Don't speed uphill or down.

3. Single-file riding will calm horses; doubling, tripling, passing others, or dropping back all risk agitating your horse or others.

4. Keep one horse-length between horses.

5. No dogs, stallions, or unattended children.

6. At trailheads and rest stops, take care of horses before humans.

7. No horse and no rider gets left alone, even if that means holding up the whole ride for one person's toilet needs. Usually, it just means one or two others staying back with the person who needs to stop.

Pleasure horses offer an additional intriguing possibility for many of us: pack trips into some serious backcountry. Backcountry travel isn't as simple as it appears. Safe backcountry packing requires planning, practice, and considerable horse expertise. Joe Back's *Horses, Hitches, and Rocky Trails* (Johnson Books, 1994) is a minor classic on the subject, and fun to read. Smoke Elser's *Packin' In on Mules and Horses* (Mountain Press, 1980) is more practical and comprehensive for the small-party packers. Excellent for basics is *The Packer's Field Manual* by Bob Hoverson (Stoneydale Press,

Pleasure riding gives an opportunity for some serious male bonding.

Retired veterinarian Norm Lazor and his friend Jake take five on a hot afternoon in western Montana.

2005). The U.S. Forest Service and the Back Country Horsemen of America organization also offer good information.

The only drawback I've found with this activity is that, at least when the weather's good, packing is addictive. It offers the great outdoors and a simple, physically demanding existence that gets us beyond our perceived need for comforts and conveniences. Plus, we get a real education about what our horses can do.

There's also something about full days ahorseback in backcountry that brings on maturity for kids. Over the years I've had several opportunities to put my sons or teenaged family friends on a quiet horse out front of a string. Each time, I watched those kids grow daily in horse knowledge and riding ability, but more importantly in self-confidence.

Pleasure Classes

Of course, many people sooner or later feel motivated to test themselves and their horses in competition. Pleasure classes provide an excellent way to do this because there are so many levels of competition—everything from the amateurish local show to finely tuned nationals. Everybody from elementary school children to retirees can take part. Understandably, the top levels are dominated by professionals. But a dedicated backyarder, given time, motivation, and the right horse, can compete at top levels in pleasure classes more readily than in many other events.

Unfortunately, there's a bizarre sidenote on the subject of competitive pleasure classes, at least within the quarter horse breed. I've read for many years how the excesses of quarter horse pleasure-training have been corrected, but I and others can attest that the problems are still alive and well at some shows. Pleasure class quarter horses are bred for spindly legs and tiny hooves supporting tall, powerful bodies. In competition they move at a dejected, plodding walk; shift up to a painfully slow shuffling jog (billed as a trot); then notch it up to a canter so slow and measured that it really isn't a canter at all. These horses are trained to keep their head well below the level of their withers. That—coupled with a stiff, lean-back rider position that looks as if it should require chiropractic treatment on site—makes an artificial wedge-shaped profile.

I suppose the sequined Ken-and-Barbie costumes and rigid seat are forgivable, since they have nothing to do with the horses or, ironically, with the pleasure of riding them. The horses are the real problem. In quarter horse pleasure classes, the artificiality and anemic performance are rewarded with ribbons. Make no mistake: these horses are pampered and highly trained. My criticism comes because the image these horses are trained to project is a caricature of what a true pleasure horse does. Thank goodness it is partly redeemed by the many other events for which quarter horses are bred for sturdiness and allowed to exhibit their superior athletic capabilities.

Roping

Roping is fast, rugged, and complex, an adrenaline rush each run, and a real test of horseflesh. Good ropers and good roping horses are made over a long period of time. Ropers spend hundreds of hours practicing on the ground and in the saddle. They spend months training horses to stand in the box, run up on a steer or calf, hold position, turn and stop hard, and work the rope on command. Since the event is so strenuous, ropers who don't learn how to care for their horses soon find themselves staying home and paying vet bills.

Calf roping is one of five traditional events at rodeos, while team roping occurs both at rodeos and at independent events. In the late 1900s interest in team roping mushroomed, and numbers have become so huge that events sometimes go on all night. There is a national organization with annual championships, big-name commercial endorsements for winners, and suppliers specializing in roping gear.

Local gatherings are still available in many areas for backyard horsemen to break into the game. Almost anywhere there are horses and cattle, there is roping.

Any reasonably willing horse can learn roping, and even if he's not truly competition quality, both he and his owner will benefit from the training. Because roping is so strenuous, fine-boned horses or those with old injuries or serious conformational faults will break down rapidly. Serious competition requires stout, sound, fast horses.

It's possible to make some serious money as a roper. Rich Skelton, the 2002 World Team Roping Champion, had logged earnings over $1.4 million by that point in his career. However, most ropers don't profit at all after accounting for the investment in the horse, training, equipment, transportation, and practice and entry fees. The joke about ropers is that their most important equipment is a spouse with a good job and a credit card. The payoff comes in that moment when the horse is working well and the loop lands right.

Cutting

Cutting is one of the fastest, most complex, most strenuous, and most beautiful events in the horse world. Cutting—wherein a single horse and rider remove, or cut, a cow from a herd and prevent her from returning to it—is less accessible to the backyard owner because cutting horses are among the most expensive performance horses in the world, ranking up there with race horses. Training facilities needed aren't any more extensive than for roping, but because cutting is so specialized it doesn't generate the quantity of informal neighborhood get-togethers that roping still does in many places. Consequently, opportunities for practice are fewer.

That is not to say cutting is an event closed to nonprofessionals. As with roping, cutting only takes one good horse, a facility within reasonable distance, and perseverance. If those needs can be met, backyard horsemen can participate in this classic cow-horse event. But they will be playing with the big boys and girls right from the get-go.

A good overview of this event can be found in *Cutting: Training the Horse and Rider*, by Bill Freeman (EquiMedia Corporation, 1994). Freeman competed and won at national levels throughout the 1970s, 1980s, and early 1990s. His book is both broad and deep, and its sometimes specialized language demonstrates that this event is a world of its own.

Reining

Competitive reining includes high-speed sliding stops, spins, rollbacks, circles, and flying lead-changes. In competition these are performed according to a mandatory pattern. These maneuvers originated in cow-horse work but have been refined and adapted to solo performances.

Reining is as complex as any equine event with the possible exception of dressage, and while the competition is fierce, the event is accessible to the backyard horseman in at least one respect: much training can be done at home with a minimal facility. However, even experienced riders will have trouble

Young ropers enjoy the thrills as much as the skills.

138

progressing without specialized professional help, because the necessary training is so advanced. The good news is that at least some of that professional help can come through books, CDs, and videos produced by some of the top competitors.

Reined training is worthwhile at whatever level the rider can pursue because it leads to a light, responsive Western horse. And nearly any Western horse can benefit from it, but for serious competition the horse needs the right conformation and temperament. A horse prone to blow up in anger at every new move—the types I call knotheads and chargers—will be difficult to work with. The good horse and the nervous performer, with considerable muscle, good coordination, and good legs, are more likely candidates. While quarter horses dominate the event (and should, since it is the kind of thing they are bred for), there are open classes, plus Morgan, Arab, paint, and appaloosa events up to national levels.

Serious reined training is not for young horses. While professional reiners are often caught in a time-and-money vice that makes them train three-year-old horses heavily, you don't want to do this because the risks of lasting injury are high. Also, the backyard horseman will likely want to continue other types of uses, such as pleasure riding. Owners who want a horse that can perform for many years can set some foundations on three-year-olds, but should wait a couple of years longer before training or showing heavily in reining.

Team Sorting and Penning

Team penning and team sorting are separate but similar events that incorporate the skills of working cow horses into team sports. In a nutshell, teams of riders cut specified animals out of a herd and drive them to specified locations or in specified patterns in the arena. There is also a related event for individuals, called simply working cow horse.

These three events continue to grow in popularity and are accessible to backyard owners. Necessary equipment is a horse, a saddle, and access to cattle, and the main ongoing investment is in travel and arena fees. These events are fast and fun, excellent experience for the horse, and strenuous without having a high risk of injury. To be really competitive, the rider needs to know how to "read" cows (predict a cow's reactions), yet practice in these events will teach that skill.

Basic training in these team events can proceed almost anywhere, beginning with the foundational skills of a well-mannered pleasure horse and progressing into some finesse as a reining horse. At that point, however, training without cattle becomes fruitless. The transition must be made, and for most people that transition comes in the competitive arena. These are excellent events for people who want to start informally but move ahead steadily in Western training. Local amateur events are numerous, but as with other events, there are national circuits that require top levels of skill and competitiveness.

Cowboy Polo

Polo is almost a foreign concept in Montana. Whether it is accessible to the backyard rider in states where it is more common, I don't know. Cowboy polo, however, is open to anyone who doesn't mind a few bruises. The rules are somewhat different from those in regular polo, but the concept is essentially the same: opposing teams of riders attempt to put a ball into a goal. The crowd is probably different as well, with cowboy polo being to polo what a six-pack of beer is to a five-hundred-dollar bottle of La Pinky Finger 1952.

For the horse, this event is loaded with suspicious things: swinging mallets, a scary ball scooting across the ground or flying in airborne-attack mode, plus unfamiliar horses approaching at a gallop. Any polo horse has to be fearless. This might be a good event for a chargey horse. But he'll also have to be well schooled, since polo maneuvers are fast and intricate.

With this kind of event, you won't know what your horse's reactions will be until you're out there in the actual melee. An acquaintance who filled me in on this sport had a mature, aggressive gelding with which the owner started the sport. It didn't work out; the gelding wanted only to protect himself. So the owner switched to a younger, less-aggressive mare who surprisingly took to it immediately.

Some states have a cowboy polo organization or have combined this sport with other horseback games organizations. There's also an annual national event.

Jumping

Here in western Montana, a common notion of a good horse is one that will pack an elk out of the

A short, stocky appy mare learns the discipline of jumping while her rider learns the techniques.

mountains in the fall. Up a step is the horse that understands digging cattle out of brush holes and steep hillsides. Higher still in this hierarchy is a well-trained rope horse. Thus, I take it as a measure of the popularity of jumping events, which smack of something eastern or English, that there are many jumping horses, facilities, and events right here among the "real" Montana horses.

Jumping, for the purposes of this discussion, is an umbrella term that includes hunt-seat equitation, hunter-jumper classes, and any other event in which horses jump over obstacles. Jumping is quite accessible to the backyard horseman. One reason is that many kinds of horses make good jumpers. The horse must be strong, willing, and sensible—a pleasure horse, in other words. Height is an obvious advantage, but at the local levels of competition the horse doesn't need height or exceptional athleticism, nor must he tolerate extreme physical stress. Of course, at higher levels of competition,

horses that win are superior specimens specially bred for the event, and they are priced accordingly. Tall thoroughbreds are common, and there are increasing numbers of other breeds of big horses. At the national level, the sport is so competitive as to become a full-time occupation. There's even the possibility of Olympics for the elite.

To the uninitiated, jumping looks simple: run the horse at an obstacle fast enough so that he can't help but leap over. In reality, jumping requires complex riding skills and complex training. It requires both finesse and raw guts. While it is associated with spotless formal costumes and pampered horses, to me it appears to rival bronc-riding in the potential for injury, since those smooth wooden bars can be rib breakers when you're free-falling toward them from about twelve feet up.

For equipment you need a good jumping saddle, a helmet, and a pair of tall, English-style riding boots. The helmet is common sense, and the boots will keep English stirrup leathers from bruising your calves. In competition you'll also need the correct costume. While this last requirement may seem impractical, there are many other events, both Western and English, in which incorrect attire can mean disqualification.

Jump training under qualified instructors is excellent training for any horse. There is disciplined practice in trotting, cantering, changing leads, collecting up, rating speed, and cavaletti work, in addition to the jumping itself. I took a few lessons years ago, and I saw immediate improvement in my horse's arena manners.

Unless you are experienced both in training and showing, jumping practice at home may not be very productive. But you can take lessons on well-schooled horses, build your confidence and skills,

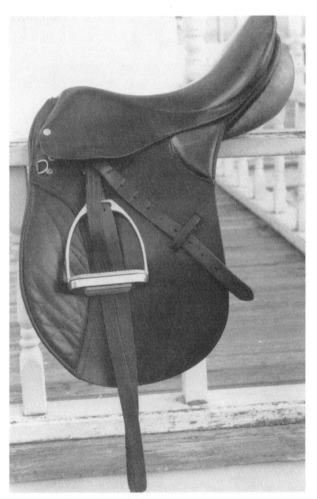

A jumping saddle is a requirement for jumping events, but it's also a versatile piece of equipment for schooling and for other events.

and eventually practice at home with your own horse. A jumping course can be set up at home on as little as an acre. This makes jumping ideal for riders who have just an hour or two of available time after work.

Three-Day Eventing

Since all competitive riding takes place in events, the word "eventing" is a bit confusing. "Three-day eventing" is a special term used for a specific event: a show spanning three days in which each horse competes in dressage, stadium jumping, and cross-country jumping. Three-day eventing embodies two distinct elements of the European cultures in which it originated (British, French, German, Italian, and perhaps others): on the one hand the classic elegance of dressage, on the other the hard-driving dangers of steeplechase. Sally O'Connor's *The USCTA Book of Eventing* (Addison-Wesley, 1982) is a readable and comprehensive book on the subject.

Three-day eventing has to be about the toughest combination of hard work and complex training that any horse and rider can get involved in. The horse that excels at it is exceptionally tall, powerful, fearless, and durable; endlessly willing; athletic and fast; intelligent and independent yet mentally disciplined under extreme stress. I picture eventers as mud-spattered, death-defying, Charge-of-the-Light-Brigade types, the survivors spending the evening in powdered wigs and frilly formals, dancing Strauss waltzes.

The event is, however, accessible to backyard horsemen. At early levels of training, a superhorse isn't mandatory, though it is no place for the timid or delicate. If a horse is at all suited for the training, he will become a better horse for it. Equipment needs are not excessive. While training can be done in many kinds of facilities, actual competition takes place on specially designed, permanent courses.

Driving and Pulling

Driving a horse takes a particular kind of space, and this does limit its popularity. Whether you're driving in a buggy or a sleigh, you can't do it in heavy traffic or on backcountry trails or rough ground. Yet it requires a space much larger than the average arena.

If that space is available, driving has many attractions, including the fact that it is just plain fun. It makes better horses out of good ones because it gives them variety and exercise, particularly in winter, while teaching discipline and manners.

Driving requires some skill and sensitive communication with the horse, but driving for pleasure isn't as complicated as many other activities. As in other training, progress must be slow, methodical, and in a well-planned sequence to avoid trouble. You'll do a lot of groundwork before you actually get to go for a long, quiet drive.

The two basic elements of driving that a horse must acquire are (a) mental comfort about objects dragging behind him, which is commonly a source of panic; and (b) mental comfort about how much weight he can pull. Horses that are overloaded will either balk or panic, and they can be ruined in a couple of sessions.

My dad's method of training driving horses never failed him, although I wouldn't necessarily recommend it. On a winter day Dad would take two of our saddle horses, throw on the harness for the first time, hook up to a bobsled, and slap horse rumps with driving lines. His first pass around the pastures was pretty spectacular, with horses plunging, snow flying in clouds, and Dad standing straight up, handling the lines just enough to keep the horses in big circles. Eventually the horses slowed, and while they were still moving Dad headed them out onto the snow-packed back roads. After those first few minutes in the deep snow, I'm sure the horses thought the roads were a piece of cake. By the time they came home, the horses were broke to drive. Well, at least Dad could drive them.

For some people, pulling can become more of a passion than driving. I often use the words "driving" and "pulling" interchangeably, but pulling actually means driving with heavy loads. For pulling, draft horses or very large saddle horses are necessary, even in the lightweight divisions. Big feet and heavy bones are critical, along with the obvious need for massive muscles. Pulling is exciting to watch or participate in. It shows just how much horses will actually put themselves through for humans. You can almost hear the well-trained pulling horse thinking: "There ain't no way that ton of dead weight can stop me."

A team of Belgians rest after pulling a farm wagon to a local horse event. A relic of the nonmotorized past, they are nevertheless a passion for many people in the present.

142

Under the right circumstances, driving can be recreational and occupational at the same time.

Owning bigger horses means more expense in feed, shoeing, and bigger trailers. Pulling horses usually aren't comfortable saddle horses. Owning these heavy horses in a backyard operation isn't very practical; unless there's some regular work for them, their capabilities are wasted and their training will lag. But they do have the advantage of a relatively steady market value.

A driving harness is less expensive than a new saddle, while heavy pulling harness costs as much as a heavy-duty commercially made saddle. With reasonable care, harnesses outlast their original owners. Harnesses, buggies, and driving gear are all still manufactured by expert craftsmen (some from Amish communities), and catalogs are advertised in most horse magazines.

Barrel Racing

Barrel racing consists of a few seconds of high speed run in a modified cloverleaf pattern around three barrels set at exact distances. The horse must switch leads, rate his speed at the barrels, acceler-

ate instantly between them, and corner so sharply as to almost be spinning, yet without touching the barrel. It's not as tough on horses as roping events, yet it is certainly strenuous.

Though anyone can participate, competition is not for slow or inexperienced first-timers. Even ten-year-olds in this event ride fast and fearlessly. And the horses they ride aren't your average backyard pet; they're highly trained, bred for speed and athleticism, and hot to exhibit their heritage.

Dedicated barrel racers need a top-notch horse, good transportation, a support team (usually parents or husband), and time to pull a lot of road miles. For those few, the event pays in big dollars, but for the rest, it's just satisfaction from competition. Barrel racing is organized in local, state, and national forms and is very accessible to the backyard horseman.

Barrel racing under the rules of the WBRA (Women's Barrel Racing Association) is exclusively a women's sport. At one time it was held mainly in conjunction with full-scale rodeos, but more recently interest has grown exponentially, to the point that there's now a separate national organization, professionally taught training camps, and even specific quarter horse bloodlines producing high-priced prospects for this high-energy sport.

Games on Horseback

Many kinds of games are played on horseback, some organized, some informal. O-Mok-See (a Blackfeet term meaning "riding big") is an organization dedicated to a standardized set of games, including either-sex barrel-racing, pole bending, and the notorious hide race. In pole bending, riders weave at high speed between a series of vertical poles. The hide race is a wild event in which a rider pulls a second person who, for reasons incomprehensible to God or man, has agreed to lay down on a stiff steer hide and have dirt scooped in his or her face at full horse-speed. It is based on a method Indian warriors used to rescue unhorsed comrades.

O-Mok-See events are more family oriented than rodeos, and though competition is fierce, there is room for beginners and kids. Perhaps the tolerance exists because a lot less prize money is involved in these events than in rodeos.

Most pleasure horses will perform adequately at O-Mok-See games, and game horses can be used for other activities, too. There is one real risk with game horses: they get caught up in the speed and excitement as much as the crowds do, and they can become almost unmanageable anywhere near an arena. Serious participants avoid this with a lot of pleasure riding and other calmer activities, and just enough game training to keep the horse sharp.

Endurance Events

For the backyard owner, endurance riding is a natural fit. I can't say enough good things about this event or its less-well-known, somewhat more controlled version, competitive trail riding. These events offer action, significant time in the outdoors, and the opportunity to test the limits of both horse and rider, all without the complex training requirements of many other events.

Endurance riding has a national crown jewel in the form of California's Tevis Cup, which covers one hundred miles of strenuous mountainous terrain in one day, with winning times well under twenty hours. Competitive trail rides are in the forty-mile

range, with minimum and maximum times for qualification. Both events include mandatory rests and vet checks. A third endurance event is called "ride and tie." It involves teams of two runners and one horse, with the runners alternating between riding and running. Like other endurance events, it is held over many miles in rough terrain.

Though many breeds compete in endurance events, they are dominated by Arabians. There's a reason for that. The successful endurance horse must be smooth while traveling primarily at a trot, durable under extreme physical stress, and built with no extra bulk. As a group, Arabs fit the requirements better than any other breed.

For the backyard horseman, one advantage to these events is that endurance training can take place nearly anywhere: roadsides, fields, mountain trails, bike trails, dirt-surfaced racetracks, back roads, and farm roads all do nicely. Another advantage is that no expensive equipment is necessary, although you will invest in a lightweight endurance saddle.

Once the horse begins to harden up, he becomes a real pleasure to use simply because you can put a lot of miles on him in a hurry without doing any harm. During conditioning, you'll learn to monitor your horse's heartbeat, breathing rate, and temperature. You'll work to match speed to respiration, uphill and down. You'll learn to recognize excessive stress and how to alleviate it. While basic health and feeding practices will carry you a long way, serious competition will require additional knowledge, such as exact diet measurements and the chemical makeup of feed supplements. In training for endurance events, you'll really learn what makes your horse tick.

Drill Teams

Mounted drill team action is less physically demanding but more precise than many other events. As far as I know, there is no organized competition, though I'm not sure why. It takes plenty of timing, speed, and control, as well as careful practice and good riding habits to work out the intricate patterns. For teams of riders with varying skills and a variety of types of horses, this event is a natural. Once the routines are polished, everybody involved is bound to be a better rider.

Equipment and costumes for this activity are fancier than for many other events, yet not prohibitively

Drill team practice is excellent training for a wide variety of horses.

expensive, since much of it can be homemade. You won't need an expensive horse either. Horses can be of almost any size or breed but must be well mannered to tolerate all the action and confusion.

Drill team is a good activity for backyard owners and an excellent form of advanced training. It is easily accessible to riders of almost any age, it can involve travel as the team becomes skilled enough to perform publicly, and it's complex enough to challenge you and your horse for many years.

For a fascinating look at the origin of drill team routines, find a copy of *Training the Roman Cavalry* (Alan Sutton, 1993). British writer and horse trainer Ann Hyland has gleaned equipment, routines, arena specifications, and more from the Roman cavalry manual *Ars Tactica*. Hyland analyzed and re-created Roman equipment, and using her own horses she practiced Roman tactics so as to better explain them. Some of the Romans' complex combat maneuvers could be adapted directly (preferably without the weaponry) for some very showy drill team routines.

Dressage

Of all the events for which horses can be trained, dressage (also called high schooling) is perhaps the most technically demanding. At its highest levels, it is an almost mystical combination of communication, focus, and physical control. But dressage does exist apart from this lofty level. It exists any time horse and rider begin to understand each other well, any time there is true progress in schooling. That's because dressage principles are the common denominators of all good training methods, Western or English.

For instance, the side pass, a basic dressage maneuver wherein the rider uses hands and leg aids to move the horse sideways, is commonly applied at the practical level by cowboys and pleasure riders opening gates. Trainers use it to fine-tune leg aids, which can be applied in jumping, reining, drill team work, and other activities. In other words, dressage is everywhere. Thus, even for riders not interested in participation, studying dressage principles can be enlightening.

Like other events, dressage at its top levels is dominated by professionals, yet below that it is not a closed club. Dressage trainers can be found even where Western events dominate, and once you become confident in the principles, training can go on at home with limited space and minimal equipment. Any horse can benefit from the training, and lower-level dressage horses will still be versatile enough to use for other activities. (Perhaps the national-level dressage horses are versatile, too. I've never seen one except on TV, so I wouldn't know.) Furthermore, the dedicated dressage rider can take a horse as far as it can go, learn from it, expect to make money on it at sale time, and move on to another prospect.

If you can find a copy, *Dressage: Begin the Right Way*, by Lockie Richards (David and Charles, 1975), is a concise but complete starter manual on the subject. See also www.artofriding.com for a wealth of up-to-date information.

CHAPTER 11
Staying Out of Trouble

Only one thing is certain in dealing with horses: they will give you trouble, somewhere, somehow. Troubles range from the momentary and humorous to the long-term and even fatal. The paralysis and eventual death of actor and horseman Christopher Reeve is a well-known example of how something routine, in his case jump training, can so suddenly become tragic.

While nothing can eliminate all risks, there are ways to minimize troubles, at least the predictable ones. We can benefit by a mindset that continuously looks for potential disasters that might be lurking.

Let's take, for example, something as simple and commonplace as a gate latch. Say you have a 4-foot gate that you've deliberately constructed and placed for convenience and safety. You lead your horse to it, push it open, and as you step through, it happens to swing back, scaring the horse into pulling backwards. The lead rope burns your fingers and the horse is suddenly freed.

Or perhaps the gate must be pulled instead of pushed. You pull it open and step through, but the horse decides to take one step to the side and rams the gate latch into his ribs. He panics and jumps forward. He gouges his hide, then lunges harder, jams the gate tighter, and in a quick fit of violence tears it apart. You need a new gate, and perhaps a veterinarian.

Or, simpler and more common, the gate latch snags a stirrup. It won't bother the horse's conscience

The deadly, lurking gate latch, waiting for an unsuspecting cinch, stirrup, or rib cage

147

whatsoever to give a big pull and land on your heels, ripping the saddle apart at the same time.

After a few of these episodes, you'll be looking sideways all the time to see what's out to get you and your horse.

Eliminate Obvious Dangers

If you've been looking at horses for a while, you've probably seen scars caused by barbed wire. Common locations are on the chest, legs, and pasterns. Down on the pasterns, the wounds often go deep enough to damage the coronet band. When this happens, the hoof itself will be permanently disfigured. On the legs, wounds are often bad enough to leave gray, flaky, hairless scars. And that's just on the survivors.

I've made my barbed-wire phobia clear in a previous chapter. I mention it here as a reminder that, even in good condition, barbwire fences are an obvious danger. If there's a strand of barbed wire around, horses will get into it, and they often get hurt, perhaps badly enough to cripple them for life.

The solution comes in two stages. The first is to repair any barbed wire on your place. Bottom wires should be knee high, preventing some injuries that occur when horses paw the ground near the fence. All wires should be tight. Four or five strands should be used instead of two or three, thus reducing the temptation for horses to stick their head through the wires. The top wire should be electrified to prevent leaning over it.

Second stage: get rid of all barbed wire. If possible, skip the first stage and go straight to the second. Replace all barbed wire with poles, planks, pipe, or smooth wire and electricity. If you're building horse facilities from scratch, don't use barbed wire at all.

Barbed wire isn't the only common danger. Any kind of trash is a horse magnet. Boards and nails from construction projects can lead to punctured hooves. Scrap lumber and metal, piles of hay twine, fence materials, and any other potential hazard should be removed from pastures and pens. Horses are as curious as monkeys and will

Patched, sagging barbed wire: a sure route to the vet

148

Perhaps you own one of these. Not only is it ugly, but it will sooner or later cost you at least a vet bill.

experiment with anything they can paw or nibble. They'll puncture a hoof, hang up a leg, and swallow unhealthy things.

Anywhere there are objects protruding up to about 7 feet above the ground, horses will bruise or cut themselves. Wherever I stop to tie up in the woods, I skim off all those little branches, even if I'm only stopping for a few minutes. A sweaty horse rubs his face on whatever is handy, and branch stubs pull off bridle and halter, rip skin, or stab eyes. Gate and door latches, nails worked loose from corral rails, slivers in planks, sharp metal corners on trailers, gear hangers in exposed locations—all are candidates for causing injury. If a horse can reach it, he will.

Another place horses get into trouble is in narrow corners or passages where a horse can easily walk in but not so easily back out. A horse might get into one of these places and starve or dehydrate while he waits for you to find him. A neighbor called for help one day, having found her retired gelding upside-down in a low manger. He'd already fought himself to bruised exhaustion, but we still had to hold his head to keep him from thrashing it

into the sawblade with which we hacked at the 2-inch planks in order to free him.

These kinds of traps may cause panic and injury during an escape attempt. Or a more aggressive herd-mate might inflict injury while the submissive one is trapped. A few miles from my home a yearling was killed when an older mare trapped him in a corner and kicked his ribs into his lungs.

Leaving a halter on when the horse is turned out to pasture is another recipe for disaster. This mistake remains common despite plenty of bad publicity. The wreck comes quickly: a faithful packhorse, turned loose after a trip to the mountains, rolls in the sheer delight of being free and home. He stands to scratch himself with a shod hoof, hooks the halter with the hoof, and before the tired campers have the coffee hot, the horse has strangled. Or, the halter catches on a protruding object, and injury follows.

Leaving the halter on just to make it easier to catch the horse is a mistake. Once you know the dangers, doing it is at best laziness, at worst abuse. A cagey horse is a cagey horse, and if he's hard to catch, the halter is no permanent solution. The

149

Big nails are handy for a lot of things—hanging bridles, ripping off ears, gouging out eyes . . .

horse needs training. There are better methods of catching a horse than going out and finding him dead.

Riding time also brings some obvious dangers that arise with careless use of gear. Cinches or girths should be tight. Helmets should be available for children and beginners. (Actually, helmets are a good idea for any rider.)

Ropes, hobbles, martingales, slickers, spare halters, spare clothing, superfluous gear, water-bottle carriers, saddlebags—anything with a loop in it—can catch on protruding objects and cause a wreck, or snag the rider's foot and cause clumsy mounting. On Western saddles, that little strap around the stirrup leathers, just above the stirrup, prevents the stirrup from turning upside down if the rider falls off. Upside down, the stirrup is much more likely to hang up the rider's foot. Yet I frequently see riders who have lost or removed that little strap and don't seem a bit concerned.

Worse yet, many of these loose items can tie the rider to a runaway horse. Even a forty-dollar lariat should be attached to the saddle with a breakable rope latch. It's better to lose the rope than lose your life.

Maintain Equipment

There's no substitute for good tools in any trade. The tools of horsemanship include saddles, headstalls, bits, blankets, pads, halters, trucks, trailers, shelters, gates, feed bunks, watering utensils, and anything else necessary for the care and use of horses.

As a hobby, I do some saddle repair. Sometimes the equipment brought in is in pretty poor condition, to the point of being a safety hazard: cinch or girth attachments are dry, cracked, and thin; rigging attachments are held on by the last couple of nails; safety items are missing. These are disasters waiting to happen—things that should have been repaired or replaced years back. They leave me muttering about death wishes.

Picture a horse's lower leg stepping through rotten floorboards of a trailer and dragging on the asphalt at sixty-five miles an hour, as happened

150

after a 2005 show in my home town. Picture broken reins just as the rider asks for a slow-down. Picture broken stirrup leathers fifteen miles from the trailhead. Picture a horse's sore back and nasty behavior when a saddle blanket has a good-sized wrinkle strapped down tight for a few hours.

Finding time to maintain equipment is part of having enough time to own horses. You can't expect to take proper care of horses if you don't make time for the additional chores that are necessary for keeping equipment in good, safe working order.

Drive Safely

When hauling horses, avoid trouble by driving extra carefully. Turn corners slowly. Tap your brakes a few times before stopping or slowing. Horses can stand well for turns or stops if they are warned, but if surprised they may scramble and fall. And since you can't react nearly as quickly with a load of livestock as you can without, you must drive defensively. The speed limit may be seventy-five miles per hour, but no law says we have to tow that fast.

Keep your trailer in top shape and free of protruding objects that can cause injury. Check the hitch periodically while you're traveling. Even the best trailer hitch can come undone.

Finally, if you need to hoist a few on your way home from horse events, hoist soft drinks. Even a couple of beers can fuzz your judgement. You've invested a lot of time, money, and emotion in your horses; don't take frivolous chances with them. Any accident involving alcohol, while it is tragic, isn't really accidental. It's just plain stupid.

Know Your Horse

Trouble often erupts when riders fail to take into account what their horses don't know and then push them too hard. Yet the rider is in a paradoxical position: If the rider doesn't push a horse to his limits, he can't know for certain what those limits are. Without knowing your horses limits, it's hard to progress in training.

Suppose you are one of the few people who have actually spent a few hours handling and riding a particular horse before purchasing him. Even with this experience, it's still not likely that you know his quirks, and every horse has some quirks. That's why it's important to put your horse through the training routines discussed in chapter 9. The horse

may pass all these tests quietly, in which case your task will be simple and enjoyable, and you'll know what to expect from then on.

It's your responsibility to know your horse's personality and the limits of his knowledge. You need to know where he needs pushing, where he reacts badly, what he knows well. If you haven't tested the horse's reaction to automobile traffic, it isn't his fault when he dumps you the first time a car comes up behind you. If you haven't tested and verified trailer loading, it isn't the horse's fault if he refuses to load into a dark trailer at six in the morning while you rush to meet your travel schedule.

Whenever practical, test your horse's limits in a small, strong corral. Anything new to your horse, or anything you have not personally done with him yourself, should start in the corral. Things can get wooly pretty fast even there, but at least the damage is contained.

When it isn't practical to use the corral, set up an artificial situation that simulates the new experience with an added measure of safety. For instance, when testing your horse's reaction to traffic, choose a safe place along a private lane and have a helper drive an automobile past from both directions, at varying speeds. You can also have a motorcycle, a four-wheeler, and/or a lawn tractor drive by. Through frequent, repeated, planned situations, the horse becomes accustomed to new things. But it takes a lot of riding to make this happen, and to know when he's pushed too far or when he's getting lazy.

You can also learn much about your horse simply by observing his natural tendencies while he's on his own, just being a horse. For instance, horses in the wild become flighty before stormy weather. You can see that tendency in backyard horses as well, and from that tendency you can know that at certain times, such as just before a cold front hits, a horse won't be as calm as on a hot summer afternoon. His reaction to the presence of unfamiliar horses predicts what he will be like the first time he warms up in a show arena.

His attitude at feeding time when other horses are near suggests whether he's submissive to others or more aggressive. That observation can teach us whether to let him finish eating before we groom him, or go ahead with grooming and saddling while he eats. Some horses hate being bothered at chow time, perhaps worrying that the human "herd-member" is in competition for the feed.

Finally, knowing your horse is helpful only if you apply what you know. I owned Elmo for many years, and from time to time I loaned him to teenagers for 4-H projects and clinics. One evening I watched Elmo learning drill team routines with an eighteen-year-old rider. She was not assertive, but she was experienced and had good balance and a very nice light touch on the reins. For over an hour, much of it trotting, she kept Elmo collected up tight, and I stood there thinking, "Wow! My borderline knothead is the best-schooled horse out there." And he was, until he came to the middle of the arena, stopped, and proceeded to crow-hop until the girl fell off.

My fault. Two things were wrong that evening, and I should have anticipated trouble from both. First, Elmo was overweight, and we had the saddle cinched extra tight. I didn't want it slipping around with someone other than me aboard. I knew Elmo was mad at that cinch because he'd grunted and bounced for a couple of steps when we started him. Second, Elmo was accustomed to working on a loose rein. He knew to collect up, but he'd never had to stay that way for more than a few minutes at a time. He was tired of being so contained, and maybe his neck was getting stiff. I should have known how he would react. I knew the horse but didn't apply what I knew. The only bright side was that the girl just smiled and said, "No problem."

Know Yourself

Philosopher Eric Hoffer said that naivete can be charming, but coupled with vanity, it's indistinguishable from stupidity. This philosophy applies as well to horsemanship as to any other field.

If we ignore our own limitations and pretend our weaknesses don't exist, we are headed for trouble. I once was hired to break a classy, black quarter horse colt. He was friendly, smart, and strong, and he thought bucking was the answer to all questions. Since he was very good at it, and since I've never been a good bronc rider, I was faced with a dilemma: I could either swallow my pride and tell

the owner he was too much for me, or I could keep trying and risk being hurt. I took the safer road. If I had chosen to overlook my weakness, I would have had no one to blame but myself for any unpleasant consequences.

Another kind of dilemma can arise when training for a specific event. A rider who refuses to look critically at his or her own abilities might charge right into an event without first laying down the foundation in incremental steps. In jumping, for example, it may be tempting to skip the boring, repetitive basic steps that build a strong foundation but can breed impatience pretty fast. Without learning those basic steps, however, the horse and rider have no fundamentals to fall back on when obstacles appear. Furthermore, those basics are what prevent trouble as the event gets more complex. That's the double risk we run when we overestimate our abilities.

One final precaution: when you have done your homework and know a horse well, and in that process find that his reactions are just too severe or not improving, you can stay out of trouble by giving up on that horse. No horse is worth getting yourself hurt.

Think about Others

When we horse owners are concerned about our impact on other people, we avoid the kind of trouble that could interfere with our enjoyment of horses. If your horse walks through a poorly constructed fence and destroys the neighbor's new lawn, the damage runs beyond dollars. It may begin a permanent dislike of horses and their owners. If you leave trash at a trailhead or a campsite, the fact that there are hoof prints with the trash can turn backpackers against us, and those folks already vastly outnumber horsemen when it comes to deciding who gets access to backcountry. Being likeable, helpful, and responsible as horsemen doesn't mean we're allowing the rest of the world to walk all over us. It's an ethical choice, and it's good public relations.

CHAPTER 12

Saying Goodbye

We horse lovers are a whole lot more active about buying horses than we are about parting with them, even when it becomes obvious that parting ways is just what should happen. Sometimes this doesn't hurt anything. But sometimes good animals are unused, perhaps neglected, and they occasionally suffer physical abuse as a result.

The sad fact is that no matter how much we wish to believe otherwise, the day will come when we must separate ourselves from our horses. There are many reasons this might happen, and each comes with its own special circumstances. There are several possible options for the end, depending on how much health and usefulness the horse has lost. Each situation takes careful thought, and the final decision might be a heartbreaker. But honest horsemanship demands that we think and decide.

Aging Horses

Assuming the horse gets old quicker than does the owner, the time will someday come when you realize the horse is old and his working days are numbered. He may still be healthy, but you have a choice to make. And the choices aren't easy.

You can take him to a sale ring, but it's almost certain he will end up going to the canner, at least at those times when the canner markets are operating. You can sell him to someone else, if you can find someone who wants him, but then you lose control of the horse's future. You can keep him until he dies, but that could be seven days or seven years, some of which is time and expense that could be used on younger horses. You could have him euthanized, but if you guess wrong, you could be shortening his llifespan by years. A "retirement farm" is an expensive solution with no guarantee that such a safe-sounding name provides quality care.

Aging Owners

A breeder once showed me a batch of horses she'd acquired when the original owner's age and ill health had combined to render him incapable of caring for his facilities or his herd, yet he'd still been too bullheaded to sell out when he should have. These horses were thin, wormy, and several had wire cuts, most likely from forcing the fences in search of grass.

In another situation, I saw an eighty-plus-year-old "breeder's" facility, which left me depressed for a week. Horses were picketed to barbwire fences, with no grass and no water. Young horses were stashed in buildings, three feet deep in manure, again with no feed or water. The herd stallion was in a tiny corral, muck to his knees. And a dozen or more horses wandered around in acres of broken machinery, piles of scrap lumber, and tumbled-down shacks.

In my early sixties, I'm facing the senior-citizen situation myself. I'm riding two main horses who will easily last until I'm in my late seventies, at which point I should give it up. Still, I keep eyeing young horses. How smart is that? True horsemanship says prepare for the time we must close out the deal. Don't let sentimentalism, procrastination, apathy, or carelessness take the decision out of your hands.

Injury

During the summer of 2000, Montana was in another of its drought-driven fire seasons, so my wife and I hooked up the travel trailer and headed for the Pacific Coast to get out of the smoke for a few days. When we go, we stay out of contact, so it was a sad surprise to return home to a note on the door: "Dad, your white horse is buried by the arena. He broke a leg."

We never learned the exact cause, but my three-year-old Foxtrotter gelding had shattered a hind leg just above the hock. He'd already been lying there many hours when caretakers found him. The veterinarian said there was little likelihood of recovery, even if the horse could somehow be moved to a proper facility—a move that would have been agonizing, given the nature of the break. The solution was clear. He had to be euthanized.

Even when injuries are not terminal, they may eliminate a horse's usefulness for anything except consuming hay. An injured gelding has no value in private sales. At public sales, he'll surely go to the canner. We can euthanize him, but maybe he doesn't like that idea any better than we do.

A crippled mare is different in that she can reproduce well into her twenties. But if the crippling is a result of poor conformation or other genetic problems (such as navicular disease, a tendency in quarter horses), you shouldn't risk perpetuating those faults through breeding. The same reasoning is true of a mare with a surly disposition—a "crippled" personality. Whether mare or gelding, a crippled horse presents us with that same unhappy list of choices as a horse nearing the end of his years.

Wrong Horse

Another reason for parting with a horse is that he is unsuited to your needs. He may be too big, too small, too well trained (a hot-tempered barrel racer, for instance, that you want as a jumper), or too hard to handle. It's surprising how many unsuitable horses people hold on to. It's often due to affection for the horse, but it can also be a matter of vanity; the owner may not want to admit lack of control over the situation. Even among accomplished horsemen, there are horses that have the "evil eye" on a rider, and the rider admits fear or distaste toward the horse. No one thinks less of the rider for it.

Another possibility is that, as a dedicated backyard horseman, your skills improve rapidly and you outgrow the horse who serves you faithfully for several years. Do you dump him? Or do you continue feeding him along with the new horse you need in order to keep improving?

Happily, an unsuitable horse is likely to be perfectly well suited to someone else, and selling the horse is an obvious solution. It may be hard to say goodbye, but at least it's not a tragedy.

Changing Personal Circumstances

Part of the American Dream seems to be the rule that household expenses must exceed income. Perhaps it's even in the Constitution.

Money troubles can destroy relationships with people as well as reduce our ability to take proper care of horses. The horses may suffer from short feed or short tempers or both. This book isn't about how to have a happy home, but too often income problems are solved by neglecting the animals. Be honest with yourself. If money is a serious problem, do the right thing: sell the horses, the trailer, maybe even your good collection of tack, and get back on your financial feet. Going through this problem is no disgrace. It may be a temporary roadblock on our trip to horse heaven, but even if it is permanent, it's the right sacrifice to make. Hanging on to neglected animals is neither romantic nor reasonable, however we might rationalize. It's just wrong.

Perhaps you need to change homes or jobs. If either one means leaving the horses a day's drive behind, then once again you should do the right thing: put the horse project on hold. Particularly when such moves are for family reasons, the move is more important than the horses. I'm a horse lover, but I'm not a fan of putting horses before people.

Another unhappy but common circumstance is an unpleasant change in your immediate environment. In America's frenzy to cover the entire landscape with shopping malls, cookie-cutter housing developments, parking lots, and golf courses, horse owners are often surrounded and imprisoned by encroaching urbanization or by tightening of zoning regulations, which often means no hoofed animals. I think of this situation whenever I drive by the last couple of apparently unzoned acres in Missoula, Montana, where a half-dozen horses are kept up against a four-lane arterial that's traffic-jammed sixteen hours a day. The other three sides of this tiny acreage are surrounded by miles of housing in all directions. Perhaps these horses are trailered to exercise frequently. But in the meantime, there they stand, a rural anachronism in an urban setting, the noise incessant, the air fouled, the view walled off by buildings. It's a poor place to keep horses, and it's got to be inconvenient for owners.

Fortunately, in some cities horse owners have been able to get involved in community planning and have at least ensured that there are travel corridors or open-space covenants for horse use. But for horse folks who are too late to negotiate those kinds of agreements, or for those who can't handle petty political conflict driven by greed or myopia, there are no miracles. Development interests outnumber horse interests by thousands to one. In many cases, there is little to do other than move or sell the horses.

Selling Your Horse

It's common to sell horses in the same places where we go about buying them, as discussed in chapter 6. But it's always difficult to know what price to ask for your horse. The asking prices for other horses are some indication, though those other owners may be engaged in wishful thinking. You can ask for advice from other horse owners, and it's possible to find trained equine appraisers. Generally, unless a horse is specialty trained or specialty bred, you should be prepared to lose money. It's a buyer's market.

However, unless you are trying to make a living from horses, you should not feel bad about losing

some money. For most owners of useable horses, finding a reliable new owner is more important than profit, and for owners of undesirable horses, simply getting clear of the problems makes a financial loss bearable.

If your reason for selling is that you have just too much horse, honesty will save some trouble. "He's too much for me, but a strong, sound horse for an experienced rider. Price negotiable," is better than a list of qualities that can't be demonstrated.

If the horse is truly bomb-proof you can sell it privately as a beginner's horse or a kid's horse. There's an endless market for these. However, there is the chance that, out of ignorance, kids will run our favorite old horse to death.

AUCTION

A well-broke horse might find a good home through the regular auction ring, where it is possible to show the horse briefly. As a seller you have the option of keeping the horse (for a fee) if it looks as if the slaughter buyers are the only ones bidding. One drawback is that a lot of uncontrollable factors will determine whether the horse brings his

Truly reliable kids' horses are scarce, but those that qualify can be priced similarly to seasoned, well-trained horses for adults.

155

true monetary value, since most buyers at auction are looking for bargain prices. You also lose control of the horse's care.

Particularly in spring and summer, guest ranches, backcountry outfitters, riding stables, and other backyard horsemen are looking for good horses at auction. You can insist the horse sell with saddle stock rather than with the loose animals (those that won't get a serious bid because there is no information about their age, breeding, and training). You can ride your horse in the ring or have a ring attendant do it for a small fee. If you have the horse buffed up and showing well, he may sell just fine. Do your part, and the auctioneer will be an ally.

If your horse is registered with a specific breed, you can consign him at a breed auction. Breed auctions do bring in buyers who intend to spend money, and they don't attract slaughter buyers. Buyers at these sales want real potential either for breeding or performance. The horse that has been thoughtlessly bred, mishandled, neglected, injured, or poorly trained, or who is getting old, has little chance of selling.

PRIVATE SALES

If you don't like the gamble of the sale ring, selling on the open market is a good option, though patience is required on the part of the seller. Advertise in the newspapers, regional horse publications, or fee-charging Web sites, and spend enough money to promote the horse's value. "For sale, one brown horse" isn't good enough. Buyers want to know age, size, color, disposition, breeding, training, prizes won, price and what kind of rider the horse is suitable for, and they want to see photos. At the same time, sellers should never advertise what they can't demonstrate, especially in terms of training and safety. "Buyer beware" has long since become "Seller beware the lawyers."

Harsh Choices Revisited

If a horse is suffering or so old he can't function, most people would agree that euthanasia is the most humane choice. But if a horse is eating, drinking, and pain-free but can't be sold because his condition makes him useless to anyone, then the choices are more difficult.

Most horse owners at one time or another face the dismal task of deciding what to do with a useless horse. Of those owners, some will face the problem objectively. Others won't. Their horses will stand unused, sometimes in neglectful conditions. True, these horses are not always suffering physical pain, but the horse-human relationship is based on the horse's ability to perform, either in a natural or a trained state. When a horse can't perform, he becomes a problem for an owner who has limited space for animals but who may still be attached to the horse emotionally.

At the most pragmatic monetary level, the longer such conditions continue, the less valuable the animal. Our choices are limited and harsh, but there are choices.

EUTHANASIA

Euthanasia is a first consideration with aged or crippled animals. It's no kindness to leave an animal in severe pain for years when the one sure thing we know about life, human or animal, is that it isn't permanent. We have a duty to make the best decision we can about living in pain versus painless death.

Death is painless if done right. A properly placed bullet is cruder than a veterinarian's needle, but it can be just as humane. I once put down a yearling filly who had broken her back in an unsuccessful try at leaping out of a corral. Her screams were hideous, and her efforts to move her paralyzed rear legs were heartbreaking. I didn't enjoy pulling the trigger, but I didn't hesitate, either. Some of the spectators told me I was cruel. I've never understood their thinking. People impassively watch human murders by the dozen each week on TV, but recoil from the thought of an animal being shot. Most of us may never need to resolve that contradiction, but we should at least be mentally prepared to do so.

SLAUGHTER MARKETS

The most controversial way to get rid of horses is through the slaughter market, where they are eventually canned for consumption. It's so controversial that I've been dreading broaching the subject, fearful of the predictable backlash. Here goes.

The very fact that I try to address the subject in a neutral fashion may be misconstrued to mean I'm advocating the practice. Let me say this: there is a place for the slaughtering of horses, but that does not mean we should use the practice thoughtlessly, nor does it mean we couldn't get along without the practice—if we took other steps, which will be discussed.

Anyone involved in mass transport or slaughter of animals has to detach emotionally from those animals. Consequently, the stories of canner horses being mistreated have some basis in fact. For instance, a facility in Montana was cited for animal cruelty in 2004, when upwards of forty horses being held prior to shipment to slaughter were found dead in extremely muddy conditions following heavy rains.

But before we get too judgmental over abuses in that industry, let's keep in mind three things. First, animal abuse charges against individual owners are common, yet we would never try to outlaw private ownership of horses. Abuse is certainly not confined to the canner folks.

Second, most of us don't think twice about sending cattle, hogs, and chickens to slaughter, ending their lives early in useful service to mankind. From an objective standpoint, there are situations in which horses are livestock just like these other animals. Thus, if we can accept slaughter of one species, we are contradicting ourselves if we fight slaughter of other species.

Third, when there is no horse-slaughter market, as is the case as of this writing, we face the law of unintended consequences. Animal rights groups have successfully lobbied legislators to drop funding for federal inspection of facilities that slaughter for human consumption overseas. (Inspections are mandatory for any slaughtering for human consumption.) Slaughterhouse owners won't pick up the tab for inspection. Instead, they simply quit slaughtering horses.

Advocates appear to have won the battle, but life isn't that simple. The immediate result of having no canner market is that horse numbers are ballooning. Anonymous horses are showing up dead and dumped out of sight on federal lands. Live horses—blind, crippled, or diseased—are abandoned and hungry on open lands such as Kentucky's strip-mined hills. They're standing ill fed and ill cared for at "rescue" farms. Were there a viable canner market, these excess horses would end their lives early, but as something useful. And if we work to improve the canning industry rather than eradicate it, the horses would suffer less, too.

In an ideal world those unwanted horses would be put to pasture and fed until their natural death. Realistically, however, there is not enough food, space, or human energy to provide good care for all of them. We horse owners have to a large extent created this excess ourselves with our unwillingness to be objective and discriminating about breeding for more horses. We've become part of the animal overpopulation problem just as surely as puppy-mill dog breeders.

All that being said, the canner market is no place for a faithful horse or for the kids' pet of ten years, even if that market is your last chance for some economic return and keeping the horse means more years of expense. We don't can our friends, I hope. But if you wind up with an incorrigible kicker, and she remains violent even after you have taken steps to try to cure the problem, and your own safety and that of others is at risk, there is a place for that horse, and it isn't a breeding farm.

Here's what happens when a horse is sent to a canner. The horse is trucked from the sales barns to the slaughter facility. That may be a long haul, and a weak horse may suffer. It's partly because of these hauls that legislation has attempted to regulate the industry. Of course, one might ask why the horse was weak in the first place. Owner neglect? Was the horse so old that he should have been euthanized at home? In these cases, we shouldn't fault the transport folks.

During the haul and at the facility, care may be minimal but so is the time the horse spends there. There's an investment to be protected. Abusive care and weight loss mean money lost, so it's in the best interest of the canning company to get the job done fast.

On the appointed day, the horse is killed with a stun gun just as cattle and pigs are. His carcass is turned into useful products including pet food, meat for human consumption, and baseball coverings. Some carelessness is probably inevitable, but again that is no greater a problem than carelessness from owners. The whole thing isn't as neat as a veterinarian's needle and a backhoe, but needless brutalities serve no purpose for the canner and aren't the rule.

The canner market does the horse world a real service, one we often don't want to acknowledge. Without it, thousands of neglected or useless horses would still be mired in their miserable lives, taking up space and feed which could be used for others. I'm not advocating canning as an easy way out. I am arguing that canning is a necessary option, and that if we really can't abide the

Ol' Buck has roped a thousand calves, babysat the kids, packed hunting equipment, and provided mannerly company for many years. But his teeth are gone, his knees knobby with calcium, and on the best of pasture he can't eat enough to keep his ribs from showing. Winter wears him down to a skeleton. Ol' Buck is a horseman's ethical dilemma.

idea of slaughtering horses, we'd better be prepared to spend a lot more money and breed a lot fewer horses.

Retirement Farms

Retirement farms, generally speaking, are facilities that take in trained horses that can no longer do the jobs for which they were trained. These farms may be funded privately and run for the purposes the individual owner envisions, or they may be funded by a municipality that needs, for instance, a place for its aged police horses.

While retirement farms are an appealing possibility for backyard horses that need a different home, they are, unfortunately, more an ideal than a reality. Such facilities may not be readily available, since their number is limited, their resources may also be limited, and backyard horses might not meet the acceptance criteria of the local facili-

ties. Where they are an option, however, they are a good solution.

Sanctuary farms may take in animals that have been abused, or some that have been salvaged from slaughter auctions, but more generally they accept animals that, because of blindness, crippling, or advanced age, just need a special facility. Sanctuary farms are usually privately funded. Acceptance criteria may not be as stringent as at retirement farms. Of course, sanctuaries live with the same limitations as other facilities. There are always more horses, but there is not always more money or space to care for them.

Rescue facilities work more specifically trying to salvage animals from slaughter. They may be privately funded, but they may also earn some revenue from the resale of animals. PMU Rescue, for instance, is a widespread organization of farms that take in excess horses from the once-flourishing pregnant-mare-urine industry, which provides the basic chemicals for human female estrogen supplements. (Some PMU horses may be from well-bred bloodlines worth investigating for buyers.) Of course, in general, there is no place for excess backyard horses at operations whose purpose is strictly rescue.

While the intentions of these types of facilities are admirable, and while I'm sure in most cases the care they provide is adequate, cautions are still in order when backyard owners attempt to move animals to one of these farms. As the old saying goes, "The road to hell is paved with good intentions." The fact that a farm hangs out a sign saying "sanctuary" doesn't guarantee good care. You have to be very careful to ensure that your animal will receive adequate diet, shelter, hoof care, parasite control, space, sanitation, and, in some cases, protection from other animals. Since such care is expensive, you need to be prepared to foot the bill.

—PHOTO BY KELLY PRICE

CHAPTER 13

Rewards of Horsemanship

I approach the topic of rewards from the perspective of a noncompetitive horse owner, meaning that the greatest payoff from owning horses is not in the form of trophies, cash, or other prizes. Competition does have its rewards; in fact, competition is what hones the skills of horse and rider perhaps better than anything else. By avoiding competition, people like me limit our own progress. I've long ago made peace with that fact, but I'm not advocating the noncompetitive approach. I'm simply saying that the greatest rewards of horsemanship are subtle, intrinsic, and intangible. People who need more than these quiet personal satisfactions may never be truly happy with horses. On the other hand, my guess is that these same quiet satisfactions also come to competitive people once their trophies have been on the shelf for a while.

Just what can we expect to get from horses, and from the journey toward horsemanship? Let's say you take the plunge into horse ownership, and that you are honest along the way, looking at yourself with a critical eye and seeking knowledge wherever you can find it. Let's say you purchase quality equipment, plan and build an efficient and safe facility, and own a well-mannered horse or two, either purchased that way or trained under your care. Let's say you're even specializing to some extent—in jumping, for instance. Your horse is performing well at occasional shows and you win a couple of third-place novice ribbons. Your horse is healthy. You eliminate a few of your horse's quirks and learn how to live with those that won't go away. You learn to spot the most obvious disasters before they happen. Other jumpers begin to speak respectfully with you, without that little echo of condescension they use with obvious newbies. Just what exactly do you get out of all this?

One of the most obvious rewards is just plain fun. Fun is among the most elementary rewards, the aspect of ownership that beginners and kids often confuse with horsemanship itself, and that provides so many good memories. Although it is an elementary reward, it is the foundation for everything else. If there were no fun in it, horsemanship would die out.

Simply having fun, however, isn't enough reward to keep us going forever. And as we age, our definition of "fun" evolves. Fun ahorseback when I was eighteen meant a jousting contest with my brother, charging across hayfields, throwing crab apples instead of lances. Fun was jumping aboard a horse turned loose after a ride and hanging on without saddle or bridle while he thundered out to rejoin his herd. Fun was racing the last two miles home and looking back midgallop to see my brother's cinches, which I had loosened, waving in the air. Nowadays, fun means working cattle, bringing a young horse from blank-slate to well-broke, gentling a dozen wild yearlings, and fifteen miles of backcountry on a spring day.

A second fundamental reward is the emotional attachment to the horse. Despite what I've said throughout this book about the horse being a rather slow-witted beast capable of vast troublemaking, he is, after all, just what the misty-eyed romantics imagine: a pretty darned noble animal—at least when he's at his best. He appeals to our sense of beauty, evokes our admiration for his efforts to perform well, and gives us the opportunity to reach for communication far deeper than what we use in the superficial chatter of daily life. Perhaps we see in horses the best attributes of humanity.

Whatever the elements of this attachment, the horse rewards us by just being a horse. I like walking among my horses on a cold moonlit night, listening to them munch hay as their hooves crunch and squeak on snow-covered ground. I like watching them race ahead of a cold autumn breeze. I like thinking about how long horses have been doing what horses do. I even like talking to them, and I like hearing them talk to me, even though I know that the only audible "talking" they do means nothing more than "Hey, you! It's chow time!"

A third reward, personal growth, is more complex. In our efforts to improve our horsemanship, we identify our own limits, surpass them, see new possibilities, and succeed at these, too. Part of personal growth means taking pride in our facility, our equipment, and the condition of our horses. We begin to seek a particular quality of our existence. But any aspect of this fulfillment is easily perverted. It is easy to become boastful, easy to confuse a shelf of trophies with horsemanship itself. While owning the right gear and knowing the right moves are reasonable goals as well as rewards, mistaking these outward signs for the intangible essences of horsemanship may even diminish us in the eyes of other people. Who can blame them for their skepti-

cism if our costumes are perfect while our attitudes are overbearing and our values materialistic?

I doubt that true horsemanship really begins until this expansion of self emerges as part of what we are doing. I doubt that ownership alone can help us know ourselves, but horsemanship can.

A fourth reward is specific to kids: horses are good for kids. When the relationship between kids and horses succeeds, it benefits kids tremendously. With parents plugging along behind the scenes, horses contribute to a child's developing sense of responsibility, compassion, and self-confidence. When this happens, horses become a long-term reward for the whole family as well as for the child.

In my experience, one of the best ways to promote children's progress with horses is through participation in a 4-H horse program. Horse care, training, and showing are taught through a sequence starting when the child is eleven and offering eight or nine years of participation and competition. The program allows participants to use old campaigner horses, or to start from scratch with a young horse. Kids also get educated in

The visible reward for these 4-H competitors may be a colored ribbon.
The invisible rewards are far more profound.

The 4-H horse program provides children with goals, methods, activities, and rewards.

public speaking, record keeping, and grooming (their horse's and their own). I'm not aware of any other program so comprehensive, thoughtful, and widely available.

The fifth reward is a surprising one. Horses can bring you closer to people. As my own sons have noticed, if you have horses, you have friends. Kids who might normally ignore an adult are attracted by the horse and accept the adult as an extension of the horse. Passersby who ignore you when you're walking wave at you when you're on a horse. Mounted police note that people approach the horse and chat casually with the officer.

I've experienced this "friendliness side effect" many times. I was hiding out in the shade at a trailhead late one summer afternoon prior to packing into Montana's Bob Marshall Wilderness when a family stopped to pet my horses. While the dad went fishing, the children and their mother stayed, and the mom told me of the family's desire to move out of town, of their wish to have horses, of the need for kids to grow up with animals, and of

her own good times riding as a child. My horses broke down the natural reserve between strangers, provided the topic for conversation, and fueled that family's dream.

The sixth reward is the least tangible and probably the greatest reward: quality of life. It is subtle and complex, and therefore difficult to express. Some of the anecdotes I've related in this book have already touched on this quality. I'll add one more.

It was the end of a day of hunting with my son Jeff and my longtime horseback buddy Bob, and we were riding out of the woods in the dark. The first snows had melted and the second not yet fallen. The temperature was mild, the air damp, the sky black and clearing. I was comfortably warm, and Gus, my good red horse at the time, was hustling right along, heading for the trailer. I rode a heavy, utilitarian saddle, not as nice as custom made, but a quality saddle. I pulled an empty packhorse that would quietly carry anything I might ask. Jeff rode a little gray horse, whose short legs pumped fast enough to keep the bigger horses nodding to keep

Horses bring people together.

The author (standing), friend Bob, and Big M

up. Bob was right behind, comfortable on his roping saddle and big gelding named Big M.

We weren't rugged mountain men coming into winter camp. We were a teacher, his son, and a businessman riding a logging road in a second-growth forest a few safe miles from home. But that didn't matter. There was a feeling among us of good horses and good equipment and a good day passing. I felt peacefulness, or satisfaction, but those words don't quite capture it. It was a certain quality of experience, if we define quality as a feeling rather than a value, that came with the horses and was wrapped up in their presence and performance. I suspect that successful dressage riders, endurance riders, and many others sometimes get that same feeling. We see it in the arts, too, when the artist, in trying to capture a particular quality of life, becomes a part of that quality.

When horsemanship is no longer a matter of what we own or what we can do, but becomes part of what we are, it changes us. It is an internal force motivating our continued learning and growth. It is this quality of horsemanship that I've been driving at throughout this book. This is what will bring satisfaction with horses long after the initial excitement and romance have faded into reality.

This sixth reward depends a great deal more upon an individual's attitudes than it does upon this book, although I hope the book helps along the way. Here's to that lofty title "horseman," and to what it means for men, women, children, and their horses.

Happy trails

Glossary

barrel race. A competitive event consisting of timed runs around three upright barrels set in a cloverleaf pattern.

bars. (1) The portion of a horse's lower jaw naturally devoid of teeth. (2) The elongated parts of a saddle tree that sit directly on the horse's back.

bosal. A braided rawhide loop of Spanish origin used to direct a horse's turning, stopping, and backing, prior to doing the same with a bit in the mouth.

bridle. Formally, a headstall and bit; commonly, the headstall without a bit.

butt chain. Common in horse trailers, a smooth, heavy chain snapped behind the horse's rump from one side of the trailer stall to the other, to prevent the horse from backing.

campaign. To show or otherwise compete frequently and purposefully in one or more events over a year or more.

campaigner horse. A horse that has been extensively campaigned.

cantle. The raised rear portion of a saddle seat.

caveson. In English gear, a mild, bitless training loop placed on the horse's head to direct turning, stopping, and backing; similar in purpose to the Spanish bosal, but different in construction.

circle. A commonly used riding pattern for perfecting precise control of a horse's movements at speed, performed in training and in competition.

colic. Serious, debilitating equine gastrointestinal distress.

collect. Through subtle signals, bringing the horse to complete muscular control in readiness for fast or intricate maneuvers.

cowboy polo. A competitive event wherein teams of riders using long-handled mallets attempt to force a ball into a goal.

cross-country jumping. A competitive event using jumping courses set up over natural terrain rather than in man-made arenas.

croup. The horse's rump, from its highest point back to the base of the tail.

crupper. Smooth leather loop attached from the rear of a saddle directly under the horse's tail, to prevent the saddle from sliding forward.

curb bit. Any bit with shanks below the mouthpiece and operated with leverage.

curb strap. The strap or light chain that passes under the horse's chin from one side to the other of a curb bit.

cutter. A person or horse engaged in the cutting event.

cutting. A timed competitive Western event wherein the horse and rider attempt to remove a specific cow from a herd and keep it from returning to the herd.

dressage. A technical, competitive English event involving slow, intricate maneuvers; more generally, the foundational elements of a rider's mounted communication with the horse.

drill team. Mounted maneuvers by groups of riders, usually performed for demonstration and entertainment rather than for competition.

driving. Training or using a horse to pull wheeled vehicles.

endurance riding. Long-distance racing with condition inspections at mandatory rest breaks.

English saddle. Varying styles of saddles associated with English style riding or English events; generally, saddles which derived from European uses not associated with cattle work.

eventing. A three-day competitive event that involves stadium (arena) jumping, dressage, and cross-country jumping, all by the same horse and rider.

farrier. Horseshoer.

fetlock. Lower joint of a horse's leg, just above and attached to the pastern.

finished. Having reached the limits of training in one or more disciplines, and usually having also campaigned in such disciplines

flying lead change. A change in the leading foot performed at speed upon command.

founder. See **laminitis**.

free-longeing. Longeing without the aid of a line attached to the horse's halter.

frog. Bulbous rear portion of a horse's hoof.

gooseneck hitch. The livestock or utility trailer version of the "fifth wheel" hitch commonly used in the trucking industry. The connection point is set over the truck's rear axle rather than at the bumper

gullet. Raised, rounded opening at the front of a saddle.

hackamore. In the Spanish tradition, a bosal and the headstall used to secure it. A mechanical hackamore is a bitless nosepiece with metal shanks used to provide leverage.

headstall. A standardized set of straps attached to the horse's head to hold a bit, caveson, or bosal.

hide race. A competitive event, originating from American Indian combat maneuvers used to rescue fallen comrades, wherein a rider drags a cowhide from a long rope, and a second person rides the hide at high speed.

hock. The elbow-like joint halfway down a horse's rear legs (it does not actually correspond to the human elbow).

horn. (1) Protrusion from the cantle of Western saddles, the purpose of which is to attach a rope for dragging or holding cattle. (2) The outside covering of a horse's hoof.

hunter-jumper class. Competitive English events involving maneuvers related to mounted fox hunting.

hunt seat equitation. A competitive English event similar to hunter-jumper or other jumping events, but wherein the rider's performance is judged more heavily than is the horse's performance.

knee roll. Concealed pad in the flaps of English jumping saddles, the purpose of which is to provide security for the rider while jumping obstacles.

laminitis. An illness that affects a horse's feet, and that can be debilitating or even terminal; also called *founder*.

latigo. The strap connecting saddle to cinch on Western saddles; also, the oil-tanned leather of which the strap is commonly made.

lead. The leading foot as a horse canters (gallops). Turning left, he takes a left lead, turning right, a right lead. The lead lands farther ahead than the opposite foot.

leg aids. Signals from the rider to the horse via the rider's legs pressuring the horse's sides.

longeing. Working a horse in circles, generally in a small enclosure, on the end of approximately 30 feet of line for mild exercise, for training in voice commands, and for confidence over moderate obstacles.

martingale. (1) Any of a variety of devices used to position a horse's head during mounted maneuvers. (2) A decorative device attached around the base of a horse's neck.

navicular disease. A degenerative illness of the hoof.

neatsfoot oil. An animal-based oil used as a leather preservative.

pastern. The short, bony portion of the horse's lower leg, between the fetlock and hoof.

penning. Putting animals in pens or holding areas; in competition, a timed event wherein teams of riders place specified cattle into specified pens.

pleasure class. English or Western competitive events judging a horse's manners, willingness, and control while traveling at walk, trot, and canter (slow, collected gallop).

plug. A slang term for a worn-out or lazy horse.

pole bending. A competitive Western event wherein riders maneuver through a series of vertical poles at speed.

poll. The top of a horse's head immediately behind the ears.

ponying. Leading a second horse from the back of a ridden horse.

pulling. Like driving, but usually involving more weight; e.g., a horse is driven in a buggy or sleigh, but he pulls a load of hay on a wagon or bobsled.

reining. Turning, stopping, or backing a horse; in competition, an event judging the horse's level of mastery over high-speed turnarounds (spinning), circling, and stopping.

rollback. In reining events, a maneuver in which the horse travels at speed, slides to a halt, then turns (rolls back) 180 degrees and instantly moves out at speed again.

roping. Any competitive or noncompetitive maneuver wherein a mounted rider uses a long rope (lariat) to control actions of a cow or of another horse.

running martingale. A device that makes all the rider's reining signals touch the horse's mouth from the same angle, regardless of how the rider's hands are held. See also **martingale**.

schooling. Training. In the past the term *schooling* was reserved for technical training in English disciplines, but its uses have broadened in recent years.

shank. An extension below the mouthpiece of any bit, or below the nosepiece of a mechanical hackamore.

side pass. A maneuver wherein a horse walks sideways upon command.

sliding stop. A maneuver wherein a horse stops from high speed, appearing to sit down and slide in one continuous motion rather than bouncing to a halt.

snaffle bit. Any bit that operates without the leverage provided by shanks, and intended to produce a direct pull on portions of the horse's mouth.

sorting. In cattle work, sorting one class of cattle from another; in competition, the same work but done at speed.

spin. A maneuver in competitive reining wherein the horse performs multiple 360-degree turnarounds at high speed.

splint. A hard minor blemish of a horse's leg, usually not debilitating.

stadium jumping. Competitive jumping on prescribed courses set up within a stadium or other enclosed area.

starting. The initial training of a young horse. In the past it was synonymous with *breaking*, but more recently *starting* connotes quiet, natural methods, while *breaking* connotes harsher or more mechanical methods.

tie-down. A martingale directly positioning the horse's head.

tree. The solid foundation of any saddle, providing shape and security for the rider, but concealed by other parts.

unstarted. Said of a horse that has had no training, particularly no mounted training.

war bridle. Any of several styles of harsh, corrective headgear used for controlling recalcitrant horses. War bridles are made redundant by proper initial training.

Western. Style of events, methods, and gear associated generally with the American West, particularly with cattle work. Much of what is considered Western has evolved from Spanish and Mexican origins.

wind puffs. A soft minor blemish of a horse's leg, usually not debilitating.

withers. The point of a horse's shoulders at the base of the mane; the connecting point between shoulder blades and spinal column.

woolskin. The natural or synthetic sheepskin underside of a Western saddle.

Further Reading

Back, Joe. *Horses, Hitches, and Rocky Trails*. Boulder, Colo.: Johnson Books, 1994. First published 1959 by Sage Books. For campers and recreational packers, this book is less timely than Hoverson's, but is a fun read in older methods of horse packing. Ideally, read this book first, then Elser's, then Hoverson's.

Baskins, Don. *Well-Shod: A Horseshoeing Guide for Owners and Farriers*. Colorado Springs, Colo.: Western Horseman, 2004. A how-to book with professional photography and up-to-date information. Probably a best-buy for owners starting their own efforts at hoof care, especially if balanced with 'natural' hoof care information.

Dunning, Al. *Reining*. Second edition. Colorado Springs, Colo.: Western Horseman, 2002. Meticulous photography makes this book easy for the novice to understand.

Dutson, Judith. *Storey's Illustrated Guide to 96 Horse Breeds of North America*. North Adams, Mass.: Storey Publishing, 2005. Comprehensive histories, descriptions, and genetic information about common and obscure American breeds. Useful as a textbook on individual breeds, but also as an antidote to breed fanaticism when the reader realizes that most of the descriptions of ideal qualities (sound hooves, strong bone, sloping shoulders, etc.) are the same from breed to breed.

Elser, Smoke. *Packin' In on Mules and Horses*. Missoula, Mont.: Mountain Press Publishing, 1980. Possibly the most comprehensive book on the subject, written by an outfitter who understands the combination of packing, livestock, people, and backcountry use.

Freeman, Bill. *Cutting: Training the Horse and Rider*. Austin, Tex.: EquiMedia Corporation, 1994. This is A-to-Z information on the subject, technical enough that it makes slow reading for beginning horsemen but is an important work nonetheless.

Green, Ben K. *The Color of Horses: The Scientific and Authoritative Identification of the Color of the Horse*. Missoula, Mont.: Mountain Press Publishing Company, 2001. Detailed descriptions of horse colors, illustrated by reproductions of oil paintings by Western artist Darol Dickinson.

Hoverson, Bob. *The Packer's Field Manual*. Stevensville, Mont.: Stoneydale Press Publishing, 2005. Concise and practical, a how-and-why treatise from a master professional packer in a format easily transportable in a saddlebag.

Hunt, Ray. *Think Harmony With Horses: An In-Depth Study of Horse/Man Relationship*. Fresno, Calif.: Pioneer Publishing Company, 1987. One of the foundational works of soft horsemanship, written by the master horseman. Difficult but critical reading for those who want to be horsemen.

Hyland, Ann. *Training the Roman Cavalry: From Arrian's Ars Tactica*. Dover N.H.: Alan Sutton, 1993. A fascinating look at horsemanship methods and motives two thousand years ago.

Lyons, John. *Communicating with Cues: The Rider's Guide to Training and Problem Solving*, Part 1. Edited by Maureen Gallatin. Greenwich, Conn.: Belvoir Publications, 1998. This and all subsequent parts of the series are detailed and useful explanations of methods based in communication rather than in force.

Miller, Robert M., and Richard A. Lamb. *The Revolution in Horsemanship and What It Means for Mankind.* Guilford, Conn.: Lyons Press, 2005. Encyclopedic but very readable treatise tracing the roots of soft horsemanship as well as the most up-to-date practices and practitioners.

Miller, Robert W. *Western Horse Behavior and Training.* Garden City, N.Y.: Dolphin Books, 1974. Not specifically a soft-horsemanship book, this is nevertheless an important work applying known principles of equine behavior to training methods and situations.

Myler, Dale, Ron Myler, and Bob Myler. *A Whole Bit Better: Effective Communication through Proper Bitting and Relaxation.* Lake Oswego, Oreg.: Toklat Originals, 2000. Written to promote Myler-brand bits, but very useful nevertheless. Succinct but detailed descriptions of bit styles, horses' oral anatomy, and what happens when a particular bit contacts a particular mouth.

O'Connor, Sally. *The USCTA Book of Eventing: The Official Handbook of the United States Combined Training Association, Inc.* Reading, Mass.: Addison-Wesley Publishing, 1982. A complete and detailed overview of three-day eventing.

Parelli, Pat. *Natural Horse-man-ship.* Colorado Springs, Colo.: Western Horseman, 1993. As with other Western Horseman books, this one uses photography so comprehensively that the information is easy to apply for any reader. Parelli has made his fame internationally in the natural horsemanship movement at least partly by capitalizing on the fact that owners need as much training as do horses.

Phinney, Peter, and Jack Brainard. *Training the Reined Horse.* South Brunswick, N.J.: A. S. Barnes, 1977. A very wise early book on the subject of reining. Lacks comprehensive photos but is worthwhile nevertheless, an excellent starting place on the subject.

Ramey, Pete. *Making Natural Hoof Care Work for You.* Fayetteville, Ark.: Star Ridge Publishing, 2003. Open-minded readers with some experience in doing their own hoof care will find this book absolutely fascinating because it explains so well how the natural hoof works, and why humans may have been misusing it for a long time.

Richards, Lockie. *Dressage: Begin the Right Way.* North Pomfret, Vt.: David and Charles 1975. Concise and more comprehensible for novices than were some older books. Very informative and a good read.

Speed, John Gilmer. *The Horse in America: A Practical Treatise on the Various Types Common in the United States, with Something of Their History and Varying Characteristics.* New York: McClure, Phillips, and Co., 1905. Reprinted by Russell Lutes, 1982. Originally written when horses were the primary form of transportation and long before soft horsemanship became popular, this book is profoundly wise and forward looking on the subjects of breeds, breeding, care, and gentle use.

Wiseman, Robert F. *The Complete Horseshoeing Guide.* Norman, Okla.: University of Oklahoma Press, 1968. An older book, but readable and informative about tools, metalwork, horse handling, and shoeing techniques. Useful as a supplement to other books or as an owner's foundation for starting hoof care.

Note: While Internet sources are consulted and in some cases listed throughout *The Backyard Horseman*, the author believes such sources cannot replace the books listed above, or other similar books, simply because books from noted authors and established publishing houses undergo editorial scrutiny while Internet sources may not. Consequently, books are in general more reliable.

Index

ramps, 39; restraining within, 126; safety, 124, 127, 151; slant-load, 37, *38*; tires, 39; utility, 37

trail riding: and age of horse, 133; backcountry, 16; competitive, *64*, 144; etiquette, 16, 152; pleasures of, 163, 165, *165*

training, of horses: and age of horse, 29, 42, 67–68, 115, 120, 132–33; of chargers, 102–3; for competition, 83, *140*, 141, 144, 145–46; facilities, 49; and feed, 83, 87; fundamentals, 110–12; goals, 62; with hobbles, 117–19, *118*; importance of, 7, 61; in increments, 107, 110; limits, 151, 152; to load, 36–37, 122–27, *123*, *125*; longeing, 119–22; for loud noises, tolerance of, 120–21, *121*; mounting, 127–28; and natural horsemanship, 3, 95–97, *96*; of nervous horses, 102; by owners, 5, 6, 42, 109–10; pace of, 130, 132, 107, 110; packhorses, *129*; by professional trainers, 62, 77, 109–10, 132; psychological aspects of, 95, 98, 100, 105–6; for riding, 128–30; sequences, 107, 123, 142, 151; springtime regimen, 81; tire-packing, *122*; for tying, 112–17

training, of riders, *128*, 130–31, *140*

Training the Roman Cavalry (Hyland), 145

traits, dangerous, 76

traits, inherited, 66, 68

transportation, 35–40

treadmill, 46

trees, saddle, 19, *19*

trial period, 77

trotting, 141

trucks, 35–36

turnbuckles. *See* tighteners, fence

twine, 84

twist hobbles, 117, *118*

two-acre plot, *48*, 49

two-year-olds, characteristics of, 132

tying, 112–17; and age of horse, *115*, 116–17, 132; belly loop, 116, *116*; buddy system, 117; in backcountry, 149; techniques, *112–13*, *113*, *114*, *115*, 116, *116*; with tie rings, 116. *See also* tie-downs; tie stations

urbanization, *12*, 154

USCTA Book of Eventing, The (O'Connor), 141

use *vs.* abuse, 92–93

U.S. Forest Service, 137

utility trailers, 37

vaccinations, 91–92

vans, horse, 38

vaquero, 29

vehicles, 35–36, 38

veterinarians, 49, 74, 90, 91–92

vinyl fencing, 52, 53, 54, 56

walkers. *See* Tennessee walkers

walking speed, 75

walk-through gates, 60, *60*

watering, 42, 46, 81

weather, 43–44, 46, 151

weaving (stall vice), 75

weeds, 4, 13–15

weight, appropriate, 76, 79, *80*, 100–101

weight-bearing ability, 72–73

well-broke horses, 61, 67, *68*, 128–29, 132, 155

well-broke riders, 130–31

Well Shod (Baskins), 87

Western Horse Behavior and Training (Miller), 95

Western Horseman (magazine), 91

Western saddles, 19

Western seat, 22

West Nile virus, 91

"white horse disease," 76

white horses, 76

Whole Bit Better, A (Myler), 30

wild horses, 87, *97*

windbreaks, 79

winter: coat, 79; feed, 84, 85, 92; pasture, 49, 84, 92; riding, 42; shelter, 41, 43–44

wire fencing, 53, 54–55, *54*, *55*, 60, *148*

wire gates, 60

Wiseman, Robert F., 87

withers, 23, 73, 79

wolf tooth, 89

Women's Barrel Racing Association (WBRA), 143

wood: chewing, 75; floor, 45; gate latch, *59*; gates, *57*, *58*, *60*; fences, 51–52, *51*, 53–54; preservatives, 51, 53, 54

working condition, *80*, 80–81

World Team Roping Championship, 137

worms, 90–91

young horses: buying, 5–6, *6*, 61, 132–33; competitive reining with, 139; dangers of hobbling, 117; driving with, 122; injuries in, 5–6; light hand with, 130; limitations of, 67; loading, 124, *126*; longeing, 120; mental and physical maturation of, 132; raising, 6; training, 29, 42, *106*, *115*; tying techniques for, *115*

zoning regulations, 154

About the Author

Ron Rude's professional career was in public education, but horses have always held a fascination for him. After growing up with horses in a rural environment, he has kept a few horses on a few acres with a limited budget for nearly forty years. He is the author of *Waiting for Otto* and *Wild Horses Running* as well as a variety of articles in national education and equine publications. Ron rides extensively in backcountry, occasionally works cattle for neighborhood ranches, starts young horses, and reads widely on the subject of horsemanship. His wife, Karen, has tolerated his horse habit and him for over four decades. Together they have three grown sons and four grandchildren.